A WORLD ERASED

A WORLD ERASED

A Grandson's Search for
His Family's Holocaust Secrets

NOAH LEDERMAN

ROWMAN & LITTLEFIELD
Lanham • Boulder • New York • London

Published by Rowman & Littlefield
A wholly owned subsidiary of The Rowman & Littlefield Publishing Group, Inc.
4501 Forbes Boulevard, Suite 200, Lanham, Maryland 20706
www.rowman.com

Unit A, Whitacre Mews, 26-34 Stannary Street, London SE11 4AB,
United Kingdom

Distributed by NATIONAL BOOK NETWORK

Copyright © 2017 Rowman & Littlefield

British Library Cataloguing in Publication Information Available

Library of Congress Cataloging-in-Publication Data
Names: Lederman, Noah, 1981– author.
Title: A world erased : a grandson's search for his family's Holocaust secrets /
    Noah Lederman.
Description: Lanham, Maryland : Rowman & Littlefield, [2017] | © 2017
Identifiers: LCCN 2016008764 (print) | LCCN 2016009490 (ebook) | ISBN
    9781442267435 (hardcover : alk. paper) | ISBN 9781442267442 (electronic)
Subjects: LCSH: Lederman, Leon, –1999. | Lederman, Hadasa, –2010. | Jews—
    Poland—Biography. | Holocaust, Jewish (1939–1945)—Poland—Biography. |
    Grandparent and child—Biography. | Lederman, Noah, 1981– | Lederman
    family.
Classification: LCC DS134.72.L435 L43 2017 (print) | LCC DS134.72.L435
    (ebook) | DDC 940.53/180922438—dc23
LC record available at http://lccn.loc.gov/2016008764

Printed in the United States of America

For my grandparents,
Leon and Hadasa Lederman

CONTENTS

A WORLD ERASED

1

THE HOLOCAUST
THROUGH NIGHTMARES

"They murdered my mother," Grandma said, slamming her knuckles down on the dining room table. I stopped scribbling in my notepad and looked up. Her eyes were wet.

"How did they . . ." I began but couldn't complete the question. We sat quietly in her Brooklyn apartment. My mouth tasted like cotton. I put down the pen and picked up a spoon. Instead of eating, I just stirred at the soup, which Grandma had ordered from the diner. She hadn't cooked since Poppy died. She always made certain to remind me of both—her inability to cook anymore and Poppy's death, six years earlier, near the turn of the millennium.

"My mother's hand wouldn't let go of mine." Grandma clenched her hands together and lifted them from the table to show me how their fingers had locked. Her hands shook.

It hurt to swallow.

"I needed to run," she continued. "But my mother's grip . . . it was too tight. I don't know how it happened, but I got free. So I ran to the barn. Can you believe it?" Again, she struck the glass tabletop. Grandma pressed her lips together in an attempt to restrain the quiver. Then she uttered a few mournful Yiddish words. "Can you believe? I left my mother there."

I wanted to tell her that it wasn't her fault or that there was nothing she could have done, but it was hard to speak.

"In the barn there was a chicken," she said and then cut herself off.

"A chicken?" I asked, not following. The only chicken I saw were the bits sunk in the yellow broth, tangled in a web of noodles.

But the mention of the chicken had somehow lifted Grandma's spirits. The permanent frown she wore crinkled with a slight smile. "In the barn," she repeated. "This is where I find the chicken." The bird seemed like it was attached to fond memories of jumping rope on the streets of Poland, where she had spent her childhood.

"I didn't know what to do, so I pick up the chicken." She clutched the imaginary bird the way a child unskilled in running with a football might hold it: out in front, like an offering. "Then I hear a Ukraine soldier outside. He say, 'Look in the garbage. That's where the Jews hide.' Can you believe this? They were worse than the Germans. The Ukraines, they volunteered for this. *Oy.* No more with the stories. I can't. No more." Grandma grabbed her head with both hands and dragged them across her face so that she could whimper into her palms. The smile was gone.

The refrigerator buzzed.

"Let's stop then, Grandma." I stood up from the table, abandoning the notebook of fragmented sentences. I knew that when I left her to go home and create a timeline of her memories—to rebuild that family that had completely vanished one summer day, to rescue something from the carnage—it would be exciting, like watching a coveted image develop in a darkroom. But for Grandma, the pictures that we rekindled now would haunt her through the night.

I looked down on Brighton Beach. The sun glimmered off the ocean fifteen stories below. The beach and the boardwalk swarmed with people. Genocide was probably the last thing on any of their minds. But Grandma and I were continuing with her stories.

"Sorry that we're doing this, Grandma."

"A lot of pain, *tatehla.*"

I wanted to tell her that I understood. Though what could I really know if learning the stories tormented me only slightly, and the over-whelming feeling I experienced was the thrill of resurrecting something from the past? But I guess that's what happens to a grandchild when the stories have always been banned.

"I was in pain when the Ukraine soldier, the one who shot my mother, threw us down from . . ." Grandma held her hands above her short, gray hair like a pair of parentheses. Her hands shook, and the loose skin of her triceps was in full wiggle. "How you say it . . . this place above a barn?"

"A loft? An attic?"

"Yes, like this." She lowered her arms. "*Oy, oy, oy.*" Just moving her hands from her head back to the table had caused more suffering. "After I hide and take the bird and a shawl, like a head covering, I run. The Nazis and Ukraine shoot at me. One shouts, '*Panenka, steib laben! Panenka, steib laben!*' You know what this means, Noiach?"

"No. What does it mean?"

"*Panenka, steib laben.* He's saying to me to stand still, girl. So I stop. And I feel blood from my head. I think I am shot. But no. This is from when I fall. The blood does dripping down my face. I turn around and I say to the Ukraine, 'Jesus help me!'" Grandma's small eyes opened to twice their size. Her frown was now overwhelmed by an expression of shock.

I smiled at the cruel irony.

Her mother had been killed, men had threatened to murder her, more than ten thousand of her Jewish neighbors had been sent to the gas chambers of Treblinka or lined up above ditches in the woods and machine-gunned to death, and still Hadasa had stood in that forest—and sat at her kitchen table seven decades later—in disbelief, worried that she had offended the God who had allowed all of this to happen.

"I swear to you, Noiach, I never say these words ever before or ever again. I do not even know where these words come from. Can you believe I say this? *Oy.*" Grandma moaned as if this statement to save her life—this bit of cleverness, of acting, of instinct—would put her soul's future in jeopardy. "But then he say to me, the Ukraine, 'Go, child. Be careful for your chicken. There are Jews.' Can you believe it?"

I could believe it. And yet I couldn't believe any of this had happened, that humanity could sink to such turpitude. I had watched a documentary the previous evening about a survivor who made it her business to forgive her perpetrators; that I couldn't believe either. Who could be that evil? Who could forgive that sort of wickedness? All I knew was that I wanted to know more about my family's past.

Grandma's eyes fell from my face to the food before me. "Eat, Noiach, eat. The soup will get cold."

I looked into the bowl and pushed it toward the center of the table.

"You writing this?" Grandma asked.

I had stopped taking notes about the time she had found the chicken. The shock of the story, of receiving this news of 1942 for the first time in 2006, made me forget my intentions. I fumbled the pen and jotted down notes about her mother, the barn, and the chicken. About the Ukrainian and Jesus.

"There's more, Noiach. There's always more. *Oy.*"

I could see it in her eyes, but I knew the rest should wait. "Another time then, Grandma."

"I come to these people"—the time was now—"people from Otwock, *goyim*—you know *goyim*, non-Jews, the Poles. These are bad people, not all *goyim*, but the Polish *goyim*, terrible people. These are our neighbors.

You know what they did? They traded us in for sugar. Anyway, this is another story. I see them in a gathering. They want to buy the chicken from me. But I see they hold sacks. Outside of Jewish houses." Grandma tilted her head, welcoming my guess as to why the *goyim* were holding sacks outside of Jewish houses. I waited out the silence. "They hold sacks because they are stealing from the Jews. The Jews being gassed in Treblinka. *Oy gevalt*. So I tell to them, 'I will not sell you this chicken.' And I run to find my brothers in Karczew."

I smiled at that act of defiance, that last thread of innocence that seemed to remain in the world.

"We were only teenagers," Grandma added. "Younger than you. Okay, Noiach, enough. No more stories. *Oy oy oy oy oy*," she chanted as she struggled to lift herself from the chair. Grandma shuffled through the kitchen toward her pill vials, which stood on the counter like white-capped troops prepared for linear warfare.

"You have the story now?" She brought back to the table one of the translucent orange vials.

"I have it." I reached out for her arm and felt her cool skin, where the five green numbers remained, as if touching those digits allowed for the transfer of pain.

Grandma looked off into the living room like a solemn tribal chief gazing out upon a ransacked village, weighing the future of a destroyed people. She had a big nose, heavy earlobes, and cheeks that hung with gravity. Only her eyes were small. Little brown pearls formed with layers of sadness.

"I need a tranquilizer." She opened the vial and removed a horse-sized pill. She swallowed it without liquid and then, bobbing her head around hopelessly like a baby animal learning to feed, tried to catch the straw in her drink. Even that simple task had become difficult for her.

Grandma hadn't always been so forthcoming about her life during the Holocaust. When I was a kid back in the 1980s, my grandparents had kept their stories a secret. All I really knew back then was that Poppy had been the only person to survive from his family and Grandma and her cousin, Helen, were the only two to survive from theirs.

On the weekends that my parents dropped me off in Brooklyn to stay with my grandparents, I had one objective: snoop about their apartment and uncover some locked-away secret from their past. But Grandma's apartment was tidy—no loose ends—and it seemed like the best hiding spots were filled with neatly folded clothes, untouchable china, cleaning supplies, and kitchen items. It was empty of the artifacts that would tell the story of the 1930s and '40s.

"Can I use your binoculars?" I asked Poppy, who sat at the kitchen table calculating the returns from the Burger King franchises he owned.

"Anything you want, *tateh sheine*." He combed fingers through my crew cut, a haircut he and Grandma despised.

("Samela, you let the boys get a haircut like this?" Grandma had said to my father the first time my brother, Jake, and I had entered their apartment with shaved heads. "They look like they in Auschwitz.")

The high-powered aviation binoculars sat beneath the mothball-scented sweaters in the television room. After I had retrieved them, I perched myself on the cement terrace cradled above Brighton Beach. I pretended to home in on the half-naked beachgoers below and the old-timers who inhabited the boardwalk benches; but when Poppy was completely distracted with the numbers in his head, I turned the lenses on him.

Was that the face of a man who could beat up a Nazi and live to never tell about it? What did he do during the Warsaw Ghetto Uprising? How had he survived all of those camps? I had heard pieces of stories that warranted such questions, but whenever I asked about the camps, I was quickly silenced with a smile and a loving dismissal.

Watching Poppy through binoculars proved useless, so I joined Grandma back in the television room. She was, of course, tuned in to channel 6—the snowy image of the building's lobby that fed into all of the apartments via closed-circuit security camera. Though Grandma had only ever worked one day of her life in America, taking a shift at Barton's chocolate factory, she should have collected a steady paycheck from the building as a member of the unestablished security force. Channel 6 was the only station she ever watched. It was her reality television, way before Jonathan Murray and Mary-Ellis Bunim had ever conceived of *The Real World*.

"Grandma, is that someone who belongs in the building?" I'd ask, exercising her nerves.

She lunged forward in her seat, squinted at the person entering the lobby, and gasped. When the lobby door opened, she yelped. "*Oy. Oy.* Who buzzed them in, Noiach? Somebody didn't pay no attention and buzzed them in." She clutched the phone beside her; I wondered how many times she had called 911.

After a few minutes of watching lobby traffic and listening to Grandma's *oy*ing, I, too, somehow became convinced that the high-rise apartment building was no longer safe.

"Noiach, you want to bring the trash to the incinerator for Grandma?" she asked as another serial killer entered the lobby.

I shook my head.

Grandma squinted at the television, calling out all suspects when she recognized them. "This is Yadja. And there is Shmulich, that bastard. And this is the lady from the twelfth floor." It was always most peaceful when she could identify her neighbors and the "bastards" she had known from the camps.

As Grandma scanned the static lobby, I studied her. She leaned forward, not appreciating the arrival of the latest cast member of channel 6. "Who's this?" She lifted the phone to her chest, her fingers ready to dial. The man had a broom. "Oh, this is the man who do the sweeping."

Hadasa Lederman found comfort in anxiety.

When we completed our surveillance, Grandma returned to the kitchen to clump foods together—matzoh balls, gefilte fish patties, salmon croquette disks, the bulbous insides of stuffed cabbage. Poppy napped on the living room couch. Opposite him stood the wall unit. The mahogany fixture served primarily as a display shelf for holiday cards and housed Grandma's priceless, never-to-be-used china and silver platters. But only one drawer captured my interest: the smallest compartment, the one dedicated to Poppy's habits.

I pulled open that drawer, careful not to wake him, and lifted the gray electronic garage opener and the packs of blue-backed Bicycle playing cards until I found the red and white box.

I removed the pack of Marlboros and slinked out to the terrace. As a seven-year-old, I was too frightened to actually light a cigarette, but by placing it between my lips and pretending to inhale huge puffs of imaginary smoke, I hoped that in mimicking Poppy I would somehow approach his past. In between mouthfuls of air, I tried to re-create Poppy's thick Yiddish accent, the one he was convinced he did not have. "*Voos ee doos,*" I'd practice saying for the seagulls gliding by. "I'm from Auschwitz," I'd tell the birds, though Poppy wasn't actually from Auschwitz. He, like Grandma, had only been a slave there during the war. But what did I know? At seven, I just wanted to be in his shoes or at least understand where his footprints had originated.

Grandma always found me outside on the terrace with the Marlboros. "Feh, feh," she *kvetched*. "Why do you do this when you come here? This is not for a boy. Leon! Leo! Leo!"

He awoke, startled, and then saw Grandma with the cigarettes.

"See what Noiach does 'cause of you! Cut it out with the smoking!"

Poppy flapped his hand at his wife and lay back down, rolling over so that he could cover one ear with the couch cushion and the other with a pillow.

Grandma turned back to me. "This is no good, *tatehla. Oye broch. Oy gevalt.* Here. Come. We'll eat instead."

But the only thing I truly hungered for were the stories behind those faint, haphazard, vein-colored digits tattooed forever on Poppy's and Grandma's arms.

"Please, just tell me one story about the war," I begged Poppy as he and I waited for Grandma's chicken soup to warm on the stove.

His wrinkled dimples and quick smile let me know it was all right to ask, but informed me that I would never get an answer. Grandma served us. The number 47398 drooped on her wrinkled skin. Beneath the numbers, the Nazis had inked an upside-down triangle. Grandma said that it was half of the Star of David. To me it looked like a pyramid, a reminder to the Jews of their first stint as slaves. I wondered whether the Jewish slaves from Egypt, the ones who had marched, liberated, across the desert, had ever uttered "*Never again.*" We ate in silence. The number 128142 flexed on Poppy's forearm as he rotated his wrist, bringing the spoon to his mouth.

"You want more *lokshn*?" Grandma asked after I had devoured the noodles from the yellow broth.

"No thanks."

She ladled another giant spoonful into my bowl anyway.

"Grandma, can you tell me about the camps? What was it like in Auschwitz?"

She held the pot in one hand and her ladle in the other.

"There was this girl in my barracks who took my bowl—the bowl we ate and drank out of. Everything." This was Grandma's preferred PG-rated Holocaust story. The one she always told when she tired of telling me "Not now."

The first time I had heard the story, my world changed. I was filled with fear and excitement, like an underground explorer who had stumbled upon a stray piece of treasure and then found a key hanging outside the door of a vault. I imagined everything else inside that chamber. But when I inserted the key to access the rest of the vault's riches, it snapped; this was the only Holocaust story she would share. She had told it so many times that I knew it verbatim.

"And one night she took a *pishy* in my bowl. You know, like it was a bathroom. Why?" Grandma asked, avoiding the possibility of having to ignore another one of my questions or delving deeper into that crypt of Holocaust secrets.

"Because she didn't know what she was doing," I said at the same time as Grandma.

"They treated us so bad," Grandma continued. "What did I do? I had to eat from the bowl. Otherwise I would starve. Noiach, more soup?"

I looked at the yellow broth and shook my head. She walked back to the kitchen and placed something on a dish. "Here *tateh sheine*. Eat this then." Grandma handed me a large gray lump of gefilte fish that slid around the plate like a hockey puck or a child's organ.

"I'm full," I said.

Grandma smeared a fuzzy purple blob of horseradish on top.

"Eat. Eat. Eat."

"Grandma, what about—"

"Eat, *tatehla*. Eat."

I stuffed the fish down my throat and left the table for my grandparents' bedroom. Nailed up above the light switch was Grandma's family portrait. It hung like a page torn from an obituary. Thirty-something people—babies, adults, brothers—all murdered. Thirty-something stories that all ended the same way.

"Who are they?" I asked Grandma when she came to check on me. I wanted her to name each member of my late family.

"What do you want I should say? That's a cousin, an uncle, mine brother. Dead, dead, dead. There were more at the house that day, but they couldn't fit in the picture. They're all dead."

I studied the smiles of my exterminated relatives the way one reads the untimely dates etched into tombstones. In my seven-year-old mind, they would be forever gathered around that crammed Seder table in my great-great-grandfather's home. I didn't fully understand then that they would become human smoke or skeletons in mass graves within a few years or months or days of that Seder. But I knew that they were a family tree chopped down at the base. Grandma was the last little branch clinging to what was left of the stump. I examined her parents, David and Chana, who sat at the head of the table. Then my eyes traced over the exterminated relatives to her older brother, Shmuel. I knew him only as the well-dressed boy, the boy who had survived the entire war by hiding in an attic only to be gunned down by a Polish cop a few weeks before liberation. (Later in life, I would learn that Shmuel actually wrestled the gun away from the cop. But the anti-Semite had carried a second weapon in his boot.)

One less bullet (one less gun) and maybe I would have had a great-uncle, another channel into the past.

In the photograph, Grandma's pudgy arm popped out from a white-collared black dress. That arm clutched her youngest brother, Shama, a cute, disheveled child who appeared out of breath, as though he had just sprinted in from playing outside, making the picture at the last second.

"He kind of looks like my brother," I told her.

"*Oy, oy, oy,*" she chanted and left the room, as if a family resemblance between the living and the ones who hung from her wall would fore-shadow something tragic.

She was the only one in the picture to have survived.

My father picked me up at the end of the weekend, and we drove home via the Belt Parkway. "How was your visit with Grandma and Poppy?"

"What's the story about Poppy beating up a Nazi?"

"He beat up some Nazis."

"*Some?* Like more than one?"

My father rubbed his black beard and adjusted his glasses. "I don't remember the stories. I know Poppy was in the Warsaw ghetto and was a part of the uprising. And I know there were some Nazis before and after the camps that he beat up. I heard all of the stories when I was a kid, but I don't really remember them. I blocked them all out."

I found this inconceivable. Every second I spent at Grandma and Poppy's I had dedicated to trying to gather the stories. My father, on the other hand, had grown up with the stories, with full access to the details, and he had erased them all from memory.

"Why would you block them out?"

"When Grandma and Poppy came to America, what did they know about kids? When they were told to leave us with a sitter, I was lucky that they didn't leave me alone in the crib with a *siddur*." My father was king at transforming serious situations into jokes, and his latest pun—the hom-onymy between babysitter and holy book—made me wonder whether this was just a consequence of being a child of survivors. "They raised me and Aunt Anne on their stories from the concentration camps. Try going to bed with that on your mind. Every night we had nightmares."

"So," I said, "I have nightmares now and I don't even know any of the stories except for the one where some girl pees in Grandma's soup bowl. And that's never in my nightmares."

I couldn't picture my father having nightmares. He was tough.

"Growing up, every night, I had the same nightmare," Dad said, stepping on the brakes to idle in the congestion of the Belt. "Always in black and white. I would hear goose-stepping and it kept getting louder. There would be fog. Something in the fog would grab my legs and I wouldn't be able to move. And I could see the Nazis getting closer."

"What's goose-stepping?"

"Marching, the way the Nazis did it."

"Why did they call it goose-stepping?"

"I don't know. Do you want me to tell the story?" he asked. I stopped talking. "One night, Anne woke up and told Grandma that she was having that same nightmare. Grandma said that when she was in the barn"—all I knew then was that Grandma's mother had been killed in a barn. I was not yet privy to the full details of the story—"when they threw her from the top of the barn and when Grandma went to run, she couldn't move. My sister and I were having that nightmare probably because of that story." My father concentrated on the road but sensed that I was not satisfied with his reasons for letting the Holocaust slip away from memory. He continued.

"I kept a suitcase packed beneath my bed when I was your age because I was positive that the Nazis were coming to get me in Brooklyn. I can tell you stories about after the war. I just don't know too many about Grandma and Poppy during the war. Not anymore."

"Fine. Tell me a story from after the war."

"I ever tell you about my friend Nathan?"

"No." My mind raced with possibilities. Maybe Nathan had uncovered the Holocaust secrets. Maybe all I needed to do was find Nathan.

"Nathan was insane. You think Grandma's crazy now? You should have seen her around Nathan. One time, Grandma told him to take a seat. Nathan grabbed a chair and walked home with it." (Nathan would also go on to perform other stunts in the Lederman home, including faking a hanging with a noose around his neck, nearly giving Grandma a heart attack.)

Dad dropped me off at our apartment on Long Island and Mom came downstairs.

"We'll be back at eight o'clock," Mom told me, and I walked upstairs to find my brother and the sitter—not the *siddur*.

The three of us spent the evening playing cards. As it neared eight, I watched the clock. At 8:01 p.m., my parents were not home. So I began the task of killing them off in my head. Since my grandparents had lost everyone in their families, I figured this was the norm—whether by genocide or car accident, everyone, inevitably, will become orphaned. I prepared myself for the tragic news, for the cop who would come to the door and remove his cap or for the phone call at 8:07 p.m. When 8:07 came, I pushed the time out by fifteen minutes.

If Grandma and Poppy had spent their time in the camps mourning the murder of their families, they would have died in Majdanek, or Treblinka, or Auschwitz. So, as they would have done, I sat on the couch, breathed heavily a few times, choked down my sadness, and scrolled through all the possible macabre scenarios. I imagined the conversations I would be forced to have with the police officer, with my brother, with my grandparents. It would be my job to calm down the babysitter, too. I had to be strong like my grandparents. I looked through Mom's coupon collection to figure out what I could afford at the grocery store. One had to be prepared.

Then I heard the key in our door and felt like the rare survivor who would come to discover a brother or sister in a displaced persons camp. Life was happy again.

Later that night, while I lay awake in bed for my fourth hour of sleeplessness, I went through all of the scenarios and plotted out strategies in the event that the Jewish town I lived in were transformed into a ghetto by morning. I reached underneath my bed for the plastic prescription vial that I kept in a wooden toolbox. I opened up the tube and took inventory of its contents—matches, Band-Aids, miniature flashlight, miniature pocketknife, bandanna. Stowing the emergency kit back beneath my bed, I went over certain numbers in my head, trying to accurately determine the distance from my third-floor window to the second-story fire escape platform in case I had to make a quick escape. Outside of family, I counted through all of the people I could trust on one hand.

By the fifth hour of no sleep, I kicked the bunk-bed boards above me, which held my brother and his mattress. The boards, mattress, and sibling lifted.

"What?" Jake whined. "I was sleeping."

"Do you think you could jump from our bedroom window to Meri's fire escape without running? Do you think you'd make it or hit the ground?"

"Shut up."

He won't survive, I thought.

When I did fall asleep, it wasn't for long. I woke a few hours later from my recurring nightmare. Creatures, like those of Maurice Sendak's *Where the Wild Things Are*, chased my family and me uphill through a wooded trail. The only escape was a turbulent river, which always ran red by the end of the dream as the bears that waited for us tore everyone to pieces.

"You're just having a nightmare," Mom said, sitting beside me and rubbing my back.

I wondered whether perhaps the nightmare stemmed from some Holocaust story I had accidentally overheard and forgotten or one that had been discussed around me while I slept and had slipped into my subconscious. Then I thought about Grandma in the camps. She was a kid then. What did she do when she had nightmares in the camp? She didn't have a mother to rub her back. Maybe Grandma's mother was a part of her nightmare.

2

SUPER POPPY AND
THE *MESHUGGE* GRANDMA

In fall 2006, when I was in my midtwenties, the Jewish Museum in New York City had on display comic books that had been created by Jewish artists. Many of the works dated back to the 1930s and '40s. In one sketch, Captain America cracked Hitler in the face. In another, Nazi bullets ricocheted off of Captain America's shield. Superman bent Nazi cannons on the cover of the forty-fourth issue of *Action Comics*. On every wall of the museum, superheroes, from the Human Torch to Sub-Mariner, combated Nazis.

The artists had attempted to induce pride with these covers. I felt only anger at the world's indifference then. American Jewish comic book artists and writers fought Nazis with onomatopoeias and plotted out battles on gray-stained palettes. My family died because only the cartoons in America waged war on Hitler.

Overseas, in Europe, the superheroes looked like urchins, planning warfare in the Warsaw ghetto, stuffing cloth into gasoline-filled bottles, and slogging through the shit in the sewers beneath the city in an effort to smuggle in broken guns and rotten potatoes. I knew one of those men whose superpowers had evolved from the ashes of his people. A man who had kept the Holocaust inked in the tombs of memory, stories as cloaked as a superhero's secret identity.

"Make a muscle," I demanded of Poppy.

He rolled up his sleeve. I kneeled on the gray couch for leverage and attempted to crush his bicep with my ten-year-old's grip. On television, a phony superman bounded off the top turnbuckle and body slammed his opponent. We always watched the World Wrestling Federation matches together.

"Poppy's not weak, *tateh sheine*," he said after I had tired. Poppy was smaller than my father but stronger. "*Kine hora*," he said with affection. He rolled down the short sleeve of his white cotton V-neck shirt—at the site of the *V*, thin wisps of chest hair squiggled out. It was the early '90s, and I never would have imagined that he'd be dead by the end of that decade.

"Which wrestler do you like the best?" I asked.

"Who cares? Do they think about you?" Poppy waved an indifferent hand at the screen. Still, we always watched the matches as though he required the brutality on television in order to keep a sense of peace in his mind.

Poppy's face was handsome, but rough to the touch. Kisses felt like sandpaper. The etches that his dimples once made as a younger man were now engraved beneath his white bristle. His nose was a thick pyramid, and beneath it flowed a permanent smile. In fact, it was more like a smirk—the same dubious grin that stretches across the face of a lion.

I wrapped my fingers around his numbers, disappearing the bluish-green tattoo that matched his eyes. He had lived a life that seemed as if it had been placed upon a precipice in high winds. A life that could have ended at any moment during the Holocaust. And because of this past—that decade of confrontation with impermanence, with death, those untold years of fighting in the Warsaw ghetto and surviving the concentration camps—Poppy and his stories were most important to my life.

"Poppy, when did you fight Nazis?" Sometimes I felt one right question away from his past.

"They couldn't beat your Poppy." A non sequitur was the closest I would come to a relevant response.

"I heard my dad talking about you and a fight and a boat. What happened on the boat?"

Poppy didn't say anything; instead, he smiled and placed a kiss on the top of my head.

"I heard a sailor said something bad to you, you know, about being a Jew and stuff, and you nearly killed him. Is that true? Did you nearly kill someone?" I dug my fingers into the Auschwitz numbers, as if to squeeze out the answer.

"All you should know is that Poppy loves you, *sheine yingle*. No more questions, we're missing the match." One of the wrestlers got clotheslined into unconsciousness. "Ahh, he's *farkakt*."

Poppy frustrated me. *Who was this sailor and what did you do to him?* The wrestler kicked out from the pin, having found his scripted second wind.

Poppy leaned in as the underdog stood again. *I'm not the only one who's going to feel frustrated.*

I reached up for Poppy's combed-over white hair and flipped it off his head, revealing his bald spot. He reset the white flap to its unnatural position and prepared to scold me. But as soon as we made eye contact, he smiled. He forgave my every fault and action.

"Poppy?"

He looked up, his eyes permitting the question that I had yet to ask.

"Do you think you could ever forgive the Germans or Polish people?" I wondered.

Earlier that week, during a soccer match, I had been standing on the sideline beside one of my teammates. His cleats had flags on them: red, black, and yellow flags. I asked him about his soccer shoes. "The flags are German," he told me. "Germany? But you're Jewish. How could you wear the German flag? The Germans were the Nazis," I said. "It was a long time ago," he replied. "Get over it."

Poppy glared as if I had crossed a line. "Not in a million years." I had expected him to respond to this question with that same gentle dismissal he always gave for my Holocaust questions—*not now*—a response that spoke of the possibility of later. But *Not in a million years* meant, essentially, never. They were never to be forgiven. This was his *Never again.*

After my teammate had told me to *get over it*, I had considered the idea of forgiveness. But the thought of excusing Germany of its past now felt like a betrayal of Poppy. Could there be no forgiveness?

Poppy interrupted my newest troubles and reminded me, "Poppy loves you, *sheine yingle*. Come. Let's play cards."

We moved into the dining room. Poppy counted out the deck onto the plastic tablecloth. Fifty-two cards; a pair of jokers sat in the box. He shuffled the worn-out cards and then dealt.

I won the first game; Poppy winked. I announced my victory to Grandma, who stood over the cauldrons in the kitchen.

"You so smart, Noiach. You wanna take a break to eat?"

We played a few more hands before the soup was foisted upon us. My winning streak improved.

Casino was a game of algebra and card counting. My adding skills were sufficient, but as a preteen, I could not yet track the suits and numbers played in my head. Yet I somehow never lost to a man who could count through a dozen decks. Even though I didn't make the gifted program at school, I knew I had to be a genius because I could crush Poppy at cards. That was how cards with Poppy went for my first twelve years of life.

"Noiach, make five spots in your head," Poppy explained the year I got bar mitzvahed. "Aces, kings, queens, jacks, tens. You count them. One of something. Two of something. Up to four. You also should remember spades."

As I learned to count cards through trial and error and accents, I scratched at the slight facial hair that began to bud on my chin and wondered how—after acquiring strategy—my winning percentage could possibly plummet.

Still, I always won that last game.

At the end of our tournaments, Poppy would pull a wad of cash from his pocket and peel off twenties. "Noiach. Take. Get something nice, *sheine yingle*. Poppy loves you."

"Did they let you play cards in Auschwitz?" I wondered, trying to create bridges between his pleasure and pain.

"Poppy loves you."

He was skilled at avoiding conversation, too. Our phone calls always consisted of "How are you, *tatehla*?" followed by a response. Then one offering of "You know Poppy loves you."

"Of course. How have you—"

"Noiach," Grandma would interrupt, having been handed the phone before I could inquire about his life. "What's mommy cooking for dinner?"

Most trips to my grandparents' apartment included the entire family, which was still less than one-third the size of Grandma's murdered family hanging above the light switch. My parents, brother, Aunt Anne, and her two daughters sat with Poppy at the table, while Grandma made it sound as though she were butchering livestock before some helpless, faint-hearted old lady. Yet it was she who produced the dying bleats of the animals, the grunts of the butcher, and the *oy*s of the old woman.

We sat at the table during the kitchen ritual, where the conversation usually turned toward personal finances as my father championed tax-deferred annuity programs to his nieces, who had just become teachers.

I leaned toward Poppy and whispered, "Did it hurt when they put the numbers on your arm?"

Poppy smiled and winked.

"*Oy*." Grandma delivered the second platter of kreplach for the soup. "*Meshugge*," she yelled at the oak table, under which my brother, Jake, who was four years my junior, scurried. He spent most meals crawling along the ocean of blue carpet, pulling at legs and shoes, forever avoiding the Jewish feast. "*Tateh sheine*, you're too old for this *meshugas*. Sit like a *mensch.* Grandma cooks all this delicious food for you and none of you eat."

The rest of us had mouths stuffed with food, unable to argue back. We looked around and wondered how it came to be that we shared in the consequences of Jake's poor table manners.

In my grandparents' apartment, the Holocaust felt global—it hung from the walls in the form of Holocaust survivor convention posters and stood furled on the china cabinet as a recent newspaper clipping that featured a photograph of Grandma and her tattoo at a remembrance event. But at the same time, the Holocaust was nowhere to be found.

Grandma returned to her one-woman factory. I followed her to retrieve the seltzer. She manned the stove in her floral-print housedress, the loose skin of her arms wobbling like a rooster's wattle as she stirred, mixed, and flipped, creating an ensemble out of her pots and pans. Somehow, her carefully permed hair would hold strong against the humidity in the kitchen. *What were her stories?*

"Mom, sit down and eat," Aunt Anne begged.

"She's not gonna eat," someone else yelled.

When I returned, Dad forked out a pile of brisket onto his plate. "She'll feed friend or foe, but she won't eat. I once found Grandma serving brisket to a cabdriver."

"He was nice enough to drive me home," Grandma barked.

"Mom, that's what cabdrivers do. They're paid to drive you home. You don't have to feed them."

"He was hungry," she yelled. "He should starve?"

So long as food was a part of the equation, Grandma felt safe. Food meant that the world was in order. When my father was a boy and lived with his parents, his Japanese friend, Saki, stayed with the family. Saki was polite and kind. He was also the first gentile to ever spend the night at the Ledermans' home. Grandma served him kugel and kasha and kreplach. She was happy and comfortable; but then night fell, and the eating stopped. The next morning my father found her at the dining room table. She was watching Saki as he slept on the couch.

"Mom, what are you doing?" Dad asked.

"I've been up all night," she explained. "I had to make sure he shouldn't murder us in our sleep."

The absence of food meant the absence of trust.

Grandma brought us the next course and then snuck another bowl of the gefilte fish starter onto the table. The food induced gas and nostalgia. My father pointed at the fish.

"When I was six, I came home and saw a carp swimming in the bathtub. My new pet, I thought. I'd never been so excited in all my life. I got into my bathing suit, ran back into the bathroom, but the fish was gone. Where could a fish have gone to? So I walk into the kitchen to ask Grandma about the missing fish. I find her clubbing my new pet to death." Dad cut through his patty of gefilte fish, which he had draped with a mane of horseradish, and popped the deliciously mournful piece into his mouth. Deliciously mournful. It was officially a Jewish feast.

"You should have seen your father as a boy," Aunt Anne said. "He was Grandma's pride and joy because he was such a good eater. I hated to eat when I was a girl." It was posttraumatic stress disorder once removed. "Whenever Grandma would return to the kitchen to bring us more food, I would slide my meal onto your father's plate."

"I was a fatso because of you," Dad said to his sister. "Grandma took me to Ripley's, the clothing store on Pitkin Avenue, and asked the employees—mind you, she asked ecstatically—'Where's the chubby department?' And when I cried because she referred to me as chubby, she would say, '*Tatehla*, don't cry. Eat a cupcake.'"

"You laugh from Grandma?" Grandma accused when she returned to the dining room.

My laughter turned into a cough, and her castigation transformed into flagellation.

"Up, up, up," Grandma instructed and paddled my back with her hand until the coughing fit stopped. (I preferred the cough remedy to her panacea for sneezing. A sneeze was as painful as the Heimlich maneuver, and if Grandma had her way, every restaurant would have her instructions posted on its wall: "Pull your ear," Grandma would shout first, before hollering the mandatory series of Yiddish incantations. "*Oye vecht. Oye broch.*")

Grandma banished herself to the kitchen to clean, but was tuned to the scrapes of a fork against an empty plate. The noise would signal her return with a cauldron of kreplach or a tray of matzoh balls. And when we were stuffed, Grandma would confuse us with paradoxical language. "Are you full? Eat."

Knight of the kitchen, she wielded a *shmate* and swooped in when something spilled. Drip. "*Oy.*" Drip. "*Oy.*"

But she never joined us at the dining room table. Not once. Auschwitz and Majdanek, it seemed, had trained her to never break from her routine.

("That's every Jewish grandmother," my friend once insisted. "They all adopted that role." But the difference was that Jewish grandmas worked all night, watched their families eat, and felt things like pride and joy at the end of having fed their broods. A grandma of the Holocaust stood by the table with fear in her eyes, as if she suspected that the Nazis would arrive before dessert.)

When the meal was over, Grandma made oversized doggie bags, which you could not refuse, for refusal was worse. Aunt Anne had once declined such a farewell gift, drove the fifteen minutes home, heard rustling at her door later in the evening, spotted an old woman in a housedress scurrying down the hallway, and found a bag of leftovers swaying from the doorknob.

"I had to take a car service so you should eat?" Grandma had complained.

While Grandma packed away our week's rations, Poppy sat at the head of the table and reached for my hand. He always reached for the grandchild who sat closest, who occupied that coveted seat.

His sisters had been murdered. His mother had been murdered. His father murdered. Cousins. Aunts. Uncles. Grandparents. Friends. Neighbors. Murdered six million times. But he seemed to find peace during these dinners, surrounded by the small family he had re-created.

When the pandemonium simmered down, he retired to the cozy television room to watch wrestling, that world in between comfort and brutality, reality and fantasy. I always joined him.

3

THE HOSPITAL

During finals week of my first semester in college, I received a phone call from my father.

"Poppy's in the hospital. He's going to be fine. When you finish your tests, you'll visit him. I just wanted you to know. But really, there's nothing to worry about."

I wasn't worried. Poppy was the toughest person I knew.

Exams ended, and I boarded the Greyhound to New York. Dad picked me up outside of the Port Authority and we drove across the city to Beth Israel Hospital. I expected to find Poppy with his engraved smile, flexing a solid bicep across his chest to ensure that all was well. But when we pulled back the curtain, it had been like revealing the disappointing Wizard of Oz. He was lying on the hospital bed, his arms lifeless alongside his body. The green numbers appeared faded. Tubes had curled around his arms, and others burrowed into different orifices as little lights and beeps brought a male nurse into the room.

"How do you feel, Poppy?" I asked, finding it hard to speak, to make sense of the scene.

"Fine, *sheine yingle*. This is my grandson," he said to the nurse who assessed the machinery. "He's in college at Maryland." The way he said the name of the university made it seem like the happiest place on earth— *Merry Land*. "You did good in the school, Noiach?"

"I did okay," I said, touching the tattoo. His skin was as loose as Grandma's. It had always been taut to his muscles. Now, he looked like the photographs of concentration-camp *musselmen*, those whom disease and starvation had united to death.

"Good, good, good. Poppy will be fine." He could move only the upper half of his body.

"Can I get you something from downstairs? Maybe a magazine?" As soon as I had proposed the offer, I realized how pathetic it sounded. Whenever I visited him, he'd hand me five twenty-dollar bills just for showing up. And here I was suggesting a tabloid, the adumbration of afterthought purchased by grocery-store shoppers with nothing better to do while waiting in line.

"You're too good to your Poppy." He smiled. "I have a newspaper."

My father leafed through the *Times*. "You see this article on Elie Wiesel?" he said to Poppy.

"Yeah," Poppy said, unimpressed. "He was in Auschwitz for eight months and doesn't stop complaining about it. I was there two years; what do you hear from me?"

My father smiled and put down the newspaper.

"Noiach," Poppy said. "When I get home, I give you money for doing well."

"You don't have to—"

"Shh, *sheine yingle*. Poppy wants to."

I leaned over his bed and kissed his cheek, which hosted more bristle than ever before. He was too weak to shave. The hospital sheet over his body was a straitjacket. Poppy required machine-pumped oxygen to breathe. Cotton and tape held an IV needle in his vein.

"Go, Noiach. You see Poppy when I get home."

I went up to the Berkshires for a weekend of skiing with my mother and brother; Dad stayed in New York. Everyone said that Poppy would be fine.

On the second-to-last day of the millennium, Dad drove to the hospital to bring his father back to Brighton Beach.

We arrived home from our vacation that same day, sometime in the evening. As post-trip tradition would have it, I entered my parents' bedroom, where the incessant red light of the answering machine flashed through the darkness.

Fourteen was illuminated on the screen. The number of messages was no aberration. Grandma usually left at least ten, which always played out like a humorous monologue: "Sem? Noiach? Where are you guys?" "End of message. Next message." "Sem? Semela? Jakela, it's Grandma. Where are you? Come home already. What you need to run around for?" Then there would be a few messages in only Yiddish. The angriest Yiddish ever spoken. It was as if an entire language had been created just for invectives. "Message nine." "Hello? Hello? Give me a call when you get home." "Message ten." "Where are you? Give me a call, goddamn it."

But on December 30, 1999, none of the fourteen messages came from Grandma.

The first message was my father's voice. "Please call me back."

"Message two."

"I just don't know . . ." My father's voice trailed off.

"Message three."

I could hear the background and then his breathing.

"He died. Poppy died. I'm sorry."

The recordings continued, but I stopped hearing the words. I stood by the answering machine with no tears. Everything felt slow and fictional.

Poppy had said that he would see me when he left the hospital. That had to be true. The mechanical voice announced that the messages were complete. The red light stopped blinking. I exited my parents' bedroom.

"What happened?" my mother asked. There was something knowing and nervous in her voice, even though she had only heard the last of the fourteen messages, which still captured the unspecifics and panic of loss. "What happened?"

I heard Dad's footsteps in the stairwell. He entered the apartment; Mom had her answer. Tears were instant and unanimous. Even with a bad heart, Poppy—we had all been certain—would outlive Grandma. But he didn't, and we were now facing that truth.

That night, I sat at my desk and tried to begin Poppy's eulogy. I wanted to pay tribute to the loving grandfather and to the heroic survivor, but I couldn't figure out how to write about a man who had devoted most of his life to keeping that second persona a secret.

I had never had trouble creating eulogies before. I was well versed in crafting encomiums to the dead, despite having never delivered one to a congregation. If the Holocaust had taught me anything, it was that unexpected loss was guaranteed, and in order to overcome, one had to cope quickly. Better yet, beforehand. So I had always practiced eulogizing the living, preparing for the inevitable, making loss easier to handle. However, in all of my rehearsals, I realized that I had never once thought up words for my Marlboro-smoking, Holocaust-surviving, overstressed, ill-hearted, seventy-four-year-old Poppy. It wasn't that I had avoided his eulogy because I couldn't handle his loss. I had simply accepted all of the case studies that pointed to a simple conclusion: I had been given a grandfather who could claw his way back from death time and time again. I was even witness to his revival back in 1989.

It was one of those typical weekend mornings when the responsibilities of elementary school were put on pause. Usually I enjoyed the theatrics of professional wrestling, flicking between the two stations on the thirty-nine-channel cable box that was connected to our television by a short black wire. But when I entered the living room, I found Dad pacing, gripping the telephone, fueling the veins in his hand with stress and anger.

"What's wrong?" I asked.

"Not now," my father responded as if he were Poppy and I had asked about Auschwitz.

Jake shrugged and commandeered the cable box, a newfound victory.

But I was suddenly indifferent to the television. I listened to the one-sided conversation and tried to piece together the facts.

"What do you mean Dad's not home?" my father asked. "Atlantic City . . . Last night . . . Why didn't you call me then, Mom?"

I imagined Grandma's rebuttal: *You don't think to call me when the boys get a good grade on a test. Why should I call you when you father goes missing?*

Additional conversation revealed that Poppy had gone to Atlantic City with a ninety-year-old man. The nonagenarian driver and Poppy hadn't made it home the night before. Grandma was calling for the first time this morning.

Rowdy Roddy Piper body slammed *a nobody*, Poppy's term for the wrestlers who had signed up to be the punching bags for the more popular athletes. Jake cheered. My heart raced as the news grew more dire.

For the next few hours, Dad continued to pace the apartment, keys nearby just in case he had to drive to Jersey to identify the body, which would have been a simple task. Not many people were branded with 128142.

The phone rang. These were the days before caller ID. It rang again.

Dad placed his hand on the phone, but allowed his father to live for one more ring. And then, after the third chime, he lifted the phone from its cradle.

"Hello," my father said. "Where were you . . . ? What . . . ? How do you run out of gas . . . ? You walked . . . ? In the dark?"

"Let me speak to Poppy . . . let me speak to Poppy," I kept insisting, and when it was finally my turn to receive proof of life, to question him, to inquire about something un-Holocaust related, I received his customary denial.

"Poppy's okay, *sheine yingle*. I had to walk a few miles for gasoline. Nothing to worry for," he said like some rare breed of modest fisherman reducing a shark to a tuna, reducing a trek down a dark stretch of highway to a walk in the park. "Go, *tateh*. Poppy loves you."

"But—"

"Noiach," Grandma said, having been handed the phone. "I was so nervous. You don't call Grandma to see if I should have a heart attack?"

The morning of New Year's Eve 1999, a black limo pulled up in front of Grandma's building. Now it was *only* Grandma's building. Brighton Beach looked like a ghost town. Plastic bags rolled like tumbleweeds. Seagulls stood on the edge of the boardwalk, compressing their necks to keep their heads near the heat of their bodies. Grandma finally came downstairs in mourner's black. She shouted "Leo" down the empty streets. Without her husband, she would forever be a different person. Grandma, who *kvetched* and worried and criticized, had never mourned for her dead family except on Yom Kippur, when she sat before the *yarzheit* candle and honored her murdered mother. But with Poppy gone, she stopped *kvetching* and worrying and criticizing. The tears that began on the street that morning would continue for half a decade more.

"Sorry for your loss," everyone told me. That made everything worse.

When did you get the news? I pictured them asking.

After I returned from my ski vacation, I would have to admit or at least remember.

Poppy had endured the camps and ghettos without family. And on the final day of his life, the family he had created went downhill skiing.

At the cemetery, I grabbed the shovel and poured dirt into his grave. We passed the shovel around and took turns holding onto Grandma, who struggled to break free and throw herself into the hole, atop her husband's casket.

Afterward, when Poppy was buried and Grandma was no longer at risk, I placed a rock above his earth, where the tombstone would eventually stand. A knot slid into my throat as if someone had tightened a noose.

A maze of Jews surrounded us. Something like six million graves. With the congregation, I said a prayer that I did not believe and studied the fresh soil that we had placed atop Poppy. He was gone and buried. And Poppy's Holocaust stories, which I had always wanted as a way to preserve my hero, were in that hole, too.

4

KEYS TO THE HOLOCAUST VAULT

During the *shivah*, Grandma's living room saw a procession of survivors. They consoled her as she shouted her late husband's name up to the heavens, by way of the sixteenth and seventeenth floors.

"Maybe we could move them in together," my father said to cousin Alice, pointing at Grandma and Alice's mother, Helen, who sat beside Grandma on the blue felt couch, stroking her cousin's arm.

Aunt Anne nodded in approval.

"Don't be ridiculous," Alice said with big hand gestures and a furious shake of her graying brown mane. "Your mother is depressed, but she'll get over it. My mother is gone. Did I tell you that the cops found her again, wandering the streets at midnight in her nightgown?"

The survivors were dying, while their children, the keepers of the stories, were getting old, too. Above the aged cousins hung my father's bar mitzvah portrait, when he still had hair and could have passed for a studious, frightened Torahphile. Next to him hung my aunt. She wore short brown hair, a thin frame, and what could have fooled anyone as self-assurance. At the dining room table, thirty-five years removed from their former selves, Grandma's children had becomes opposites of those timeless profiles. My balding father had no interest in religion. Aunt Anne's hands shook as much as Grandma's. Worse, the Holocaust stories that my father had known in the year he had become a man had been intentionally abandoned, lost like Poppy.

After my bar mitzvah, Grandma, who had probably tired of the retelling of the soup bowl story so many times, had decided to reveal a PG-13 Holocaust story to me. It was the bar mitzvah gift that had trumped all of the cash. The story was her account of how she and Helen had been reunited in Auschwitz. Helen's family—the Jurishes—had a different version.

27

But on account of Helen's Alzheimer's and decayed memories, Grandma's telling was now the story of record.

"We was in Auschwitz-Birkenau," Grandma had said. "Helen, in the nighttime, had left her barrack to use the toilet. It was dark in the camp and when she came back to the bed, she entered into the wrong barrack. The next morning, at roll call, they called Hela Zylberberg to step forward. This was a name that both of us used because it sounded more German than Hadasa. You see, Noiach?"

"I thought they called you by your numbers," I said.

"This time they didn't. What should I tell you? Listen, so the guards saw you Grandma step forward. But I see another girl step forward, too. They beat me with a whip." *Vit a vip*, she said. "Then we go to work. We go into the field to pick the poison ivy for the soup."

"You could eat poison ivy."

"Noiach, what should I tell you? This is what we ate sometime. We should know from food? Listen, the whole time I'm in the field I think to myself, who was that girl? The one who stepped forward? We all looked alike. Shaved heads, no meat on us. But later that evening, I go up to her. You know, she was so shy. If I wouldn't go to her, she wouldn't have never come to me. And we were cousins and we didn't even know it because we looked like this." She held up a shaking fist and an extended pinkie to highlight the emaciation. "Can you imagine?" Just thinking about starvation made her push the bowl of gefilte fish toward me. "Eat, *sheine keit.*"

"Can you tell me more stories like that?" I had asked, severing off a chunk of fish patty to humor her. I shivered with excitement.

"Just that one," Grandma said.

Five years later and she had kept her word. There had not been another story. A bowl of piss and the discovery of a cousin; that was it.

Now, at the *shivah*, I watched Alice, Dad, and Aunt Anne conference at the dining room table, attempting to figure out what to do with the survivors who had become their responsibility after disease and death made them dependents.

"They were always so close, Alice," Aunt Anne said, watching the two cousins mourn in embrace. "I remember the two of them waited on the line on Eastern Parkway with all the Lubavitch to visit with Rabbi Schneerson because they wanted to see if you would be coming home." Alice, like my father and aunt, was but another damaged child of survivors. One day, Alice had decided to leave home to live in California with a cult. After having been missing for years, the two survivors went down to receive some soothsaying from Rabbi Schneerson. Anne continued: "Mommy kept saying,

'Don't worry. Alice will come back. The rabbi will tell you. You'll see.' Hours later, when they finally had the chance to speak with Schneerson, to ask him if you would come back, you know what he said?"

"It's time to go on with your life," Alice answered. "I remember this story."

"And Mom," Dad said, taking over the story, "stood up and shouted at the rabbi, 'You don't know what you're talking about.' This, by the way, is the man that she keeps a magnet of on her fridge and she has—pardon my expression—the balls to tell Schneerson that he doesn't know shit. You were supposed to leave Schneerson a dollar for his fortune-telling. Grandma threw the buck at him and dragged Helen out of there." My father slapped his forehead. "Nobody spoke to Schneerson like that. Except . for that nutso."

We all turned our attention to the woman who had thrown a bill at Schneerson's face, as if the revered rabbi were no more pious than a stripper on a pole.

"My husband," Grandma wailed to the ceiling.

When the Brighton Beach rabbi came to pay his respects later that day, Grandma added another page to her temple record. "I give to *tzedakah* all the time," she screamed at the rabbi, lifting the five-pound can weighted with change. "And *He* takes my husband?"

Grandma wanted answers.

"I understand." The rabbi lifted his hands up from his lap as if to comfort the old survivor, though possibly he had heard of her reputation to throw currency at unhelpful holy men and had instead raised his hands in defense.

"What do you understand?" she reproached and then waved off any future words of consolation.

I walked into the kitchen for some seltzer and found Schneerson still holding his position on Grandma's refrigerator magnet. She had such deference for the rabbis and such anger toward them, too. How could she hold onto those tenuous strings connected to the God who continued to fail her? Regardless, Grandma loved Hashem; Poppy, however, had always seemed more torn, less dedicated, more unforgiving.

When I returned to the table, Shmulich had arrived at the *shivah*. The old survivor had pancake-flat cheeks that sagged from his face. His Yiddish accent was even thicker than Poppy's had been. Shmulich fancied himself a clever man, inclined to joke at any opportunity. But like my father, who had taken a respite from laughing, Shmulich had also been humbled by this unexpected death.

"Semmy," Shmulich said to my father. His cheeks flapped when he spoke in the way that Grandma's triceps wobbled when she cooked. "I'm very sorry for your loss."

Normally, when the survivors came to the apartment, they spoke in their coded Yiddish, an easy way to return to Europe and deceive the grandchildren. My father spoke Yiddish, too. But for whatever reason, Shmulich went with English on this day of mourning, and his condolences eventually shifted to a memorial.

"We didn't know nothing, me and you father. You know you father and I were married on the same day with Hadasa and Yadja?"

My father permitted the impreciseness of Shmulich's sentence to pass without a joke—*You married my father?*

Grandma looked over at Shmulich and waved her hand at him, discounting every future word that would come out of his mouth. "Ech," she added before returning to her dedicated tears.

The two couples had shared February 17, 1946, as their wedding day. They were married in the former concentration camp Bergen-Belsen, which, in the previous year, had also served as the place of Grandma and Yadja's liberation, and it was the couples' first home in the four years after the Holocaust had ended.

"I take photograph with you Poppy," Shmulich said, turning to me. "And Yadja take a photograph with Hadasa. Who should know to take a photograph together?" His lips made the *who knew* noise of flatulence. "But you Poppy had a knack for acquiring things. A *fency* suit for himself. A blue dress for you grandmother. He got us an umbrella for the wedding and hid the *traif* from the Russian rabbi—delicious sandwiches." Shmulich kissed the tips of his pinched-together fingers, the unkosher sandwiches fresh in his mind. "We have no money for rings, so he give you grandmother a candelabrum."

"The one Grandma lights every Shabbos," my father added.

Grandma held her face in her hands now, as if in prayer, rocking back and forth on the couch for Poppy.

Shmulich's simple story had been powerful, like the first rains of spring. His reminiscing had watered the dormant seeds of memory planted for decades in my father's mind. We spent that day in the past, as if stepping into the DeLorean of *Back to the Future*. But the vehicle into the past was an Oldsmobile 78.

"I must have been twenty-seven—nine years older than you," Dad said. "Poppy just got this brand new Oldsmobile. A top-of-the-line car. It was weeks old."

I had heard the story about the Oldsmobile countless times, but I wanted to see where the car would transport us.

"Grandma asked me to bring over a bucket of paint to Helen's house." He began to smile and shake his head, wishing he could somehow prevent the story's inevitable resolution. "When I took a left turn, I picked my right hand up and it was completely covered in white, oil-based paint. Poppy tried to clean it up with turpentine." He paused. "I remember it was a cold winter that year. Since Poppy smoked so much, he had to spend the winter driving with the windows open because he was afraid the car would ignite from all the turpentine. But Poppy never yelled at me."

The story was a pit stop—a fuel-up before accelerating into a family history concealed. My father went on to explain how he had driven the Oldsmobile through a deep slush puddle a few months later, killing the engine. Then, as winter became spring— after the turpentine dried out and the engine had been replaced—he got caught breaking into Poppy's car.

"Why were you breaking into Poppy's car?" My fingers had actually punctured Grandma's fabric-backed plastic tablecloth.

"I wasn't. He let me borrow it. I just happened to lock the keys inside with the engine running. So I tried to break in. It just so happened that I was doing this in front of a few cops."

"Poppy must have been pretty patient with you."

"The Poppy I knew was different. He was a great man, but he didn't have the same patience that he has . . . had with you and your brother." We both paused at the correction of tense. I swallowed down the knot. My father picked up his story. "I remember when I first started school, I was so nervous, and Poppy had to take the day off from work to show me where to get off the school bus. I kept asking him over and over again, 'Where do I get off the bus?' He kept explaining, 'You get off at the drugstore.' Naturally I asked him, 'What happens if the drugstore should burn down?' He said, 'So you get off at the burned down drugstore.'"

The next story had probably come to fruition by tales about school or Grandma's near assault on the rabbi.

"There was this rabbi at *yeshiva* who hit me real hard. Hard enough that my teeth loosened. It still hurts," Dad said, smiling and rubbing the skin beneath his beard. "When Poppy found out, he came to the *yeshiva* and I'll tell you what, no rabbi ever put his hands on me again."

We went on like this for hours. The memories filled the *shivah*, while Grandma wailed in the background. The innocent stories told felt like an attempt to fill the void Poppy's death had created. But the harmless anecdotes ran out by the end of day one. The rest of his life, it seemed, had to have been Holocaust and hard times, because by day two of the *shivah*, the same stories repeated and the talk diminished.

But seven days is a long time to not remember the things we bury.

"Can I have this?" one of my cousins asked Grandma, holding up one of Poppy's jackets. It had been time to empty the closets of Poppy's material past.

"Take. Take. What can Poppy use? He's dead," Grandma reminded us just four days after burying him.

My brother, two cousins, and I started tearing through the house like the Poles who had looted the Jewish homes in my grandparents' neighborhood after all the inhabitants had been sent to Treblinka. But I wasn't searching for gold; I wanted only the stories, and I attempted to find those objects that would link me to the camps.

I pulled out a white sailor's cap. The accessory rekindled some fragments of memory. I recalled the unconnected bones of a story—one of the few—that I had once overheard. It had included Poppy and a boat and an anti-Semite. As a kid, I had titled that incomplete account the Boat Story. For many years the story had occupied a chunk of my mind's real estate and I thought about it often, like some treasure in a distant, unmarked cave to which I had a nearly unreadable map. As the memories aged, the map became even less readable, and after many more years passed, it went overboard, unremembered. The sailor's cap, however, brought it all back.

I returned to the mourners in the living room. "Did Poppy ever work on a boat?" I showed everyone the cap. I received a few odd stares. But, in my mind, it was not such a ridiculous question since my other grandfather was, in fact, a boat captain.

"He looked so nice in that hat," Grandma said. "I bought him the nicest things. The nicest clothes. He was so handsome. My husband." The last two words returned her to tears.

Dad was at the table going through papers.

"Dad, wasn't there a story about Poppy and a boat? Something to do with an anti-Semitic guy?"

"There was. When Poppy and Grandma were on their way to America, Poppy got a job as a policeman on the ship. And there was this Polish sailor that said to him—"

"A German," Grandma interrupted, pausing from her sadness to set the record straight. "Ah, what's the difference? They all anti-Semites. Poles. Germans." She waved off both nations as if swiping at the air could dislodge both countries from their continent and send them adrift.

Dad continued with the story. "The sailor—the Pole or German—said 'You fucking Jew bastard. You're still living. It's a pity you should live and see the world.'" My father stopped to let those words sink in, though maybe he just needed a minute for himself, a moment to quell that inherent rage, a condition of a passed-down Holocaust.

"What did Poppy do?" I asked, nearly crushing the cap in my hands.

"He smashed him across the face." My father smiled. "When Poppy and this anti-Semite were brought to the ship's officer, the officer laughed at the sailor and pointed at Poppy—who was what, five-six, five-seven on a good day? He said to the sailor, 'This little Jew did this to you?' And that was Poppy. A real badass."

It was a story from their post-Holocaust years, yet still I felt the excitement of a sailor glimpsing land after weeks of watery horizon. With the Boat Story complete, I felt as if we were ferrying closer to Europe, over a divide that would bring us from PG-13 to R. Despite the sadness of the week, I found a way to smile.

"And they sent him to the jail," Grandma shouted, again finding words between the depression that had burrowed into her like a parasite. "I was a nervous wreck. I didn't know if I'd ever see him again." Her words reminded her that now she really would never see Poppy again. This made her hysterical. Aunt Anne rubbed Grandma's back.

"I thought you knew these stories," Dad said.

I shook my head. "So that's the Boat Story?"

"Do you know the Barn Story?"

"The Barn Story," I repeated. Could every structure and vehicle link us to another story from Poppy's past? The Tenement Story. The Sewer Story. The Tank Story. The Northrop Grumman Stealth Bomber Story.

I know that Grandma's mother had been killed in a barn, but I didn't know the details. I wondered how Poppy was connected and asked Dad to tell it. I leaned forward as he began.

"Poppy and a friend had been hiding in a barn in Otwock, their hometown. This was just after the Nazis had sent the Jews from Otwock to be murdered in Treblinka. Well, Poppy and this friend had been searching for food in this barn when an SS soldier walked in on them."

This was a different Barn Story. My vertebrae were stacking.

"The SS man saw that Poppy had these great boots and ordered him to give them up. Poppy said no, so the Nazi raised his pistol. Poppy told his friend to shut the lights."

Dad stopped the story suddenly, as if he had planned to tell the second part after the *shivah*.

"Why are you stopping? And what do you mean lights? Like a light switch or lantern or torch?"

"Lights. I don't know." Dad took a sip of seltzer. "Anyway, while the lights were out, Poppy grabbed a pitchfork and then shoved it right through that Nazi's throat."

"He killed a Nazi?" My eyes were wide, and the sailor's hat was now crushed in my hands. We were where I had always wanted to be: sitting in my grandparents' apartment, lifting the lid off of the Holocaust. But it was bittersweet because . . .

"Poppy's gone," Grandma shouted.

In death, Poppy had transformed from Warsaw ghetto upriser into Nazi killer. The tattoo, 128142, didn't seem like a branding anymore; it was an emblem. Larger than Batman's bat symbol. Bigger than the *S* on Superman's chest. It was six digits that could be printed on T-shirts and sold to those who wanted real-life heroes.

"He was younger than you are now when that happened," Dad said. "Sixteen years old maybe. Can you believe it?"

I nodded.

"Well," my father continued, "when I first heard that story, I didn't believe it."

"What do you mean?" I panicked, fearing that this was nothing more than a tale. The story had to be true.

"But Helen always told me that Poppy wasn't the same man she knew in Europe. *Vild*," my father said, mimicking that Yiddish tendency to turn *w*'s into *v*'s. "That's what she always said about Poppy. Wild. Helen told me he did things that I would never believe. But you knew Poppy. So who could believe that he could kill a man in a barn? I couldn't."

"Do you believe it now?" My posture was perfect and tense.

"I'll never forget it for as long as I live. We were down to Miami visiting your grandparents. Poppy had introduced me to this man, a man named David Handwold. This was a *landsman*, you know, a guy from their country. And David Handwold looks at me, tilting his head and shrugging as if I'm supposed to recognize him. He said, 'Didn't Leo ever tell you how we know each other? Didn't he tell you about what happened in the barn in Otwock? I was there. Your father, he's a tough one. I was the one who shut the light.'" Dad stopped and nodded. "I believe it."

Confirmation allowed me to slouch with relief, to sink into the comfort of the story, the desired horrors of the Holocaust.

But the relief was hard to enjoy, for it was Poppy's death that had cut the key to the Holocaust vault.

5

ADRIFT

W hy don't we go for a stroll on the boardwalk, Grandma?"

"Noiach, I should walk? Poppy can't walk. He's in the ground and I should walk?"

It had been more than three years since his death and still Grandma found a way to remind me each and every visit that Poppy was dead. She no longer got her hair done and hardly ever left the apartment, opting instead to sit all day in her muumuus. Her only activity was wiping at her tears. Around her neck she wore a gold plate tattooed with an image of her deceased husband. His white hair wrapped around his head like a halo. Poppy's blue eyes were set like precious stones. He swung there, laser-printed to metal, like some Jewish saint.

The vault door that had opened at the *shivah* had only been budged ajar for the briefest of moments, enough for a few stories to spill out. The rest of the stories—the darkness of the camps and the tales of the "sewer rats," that glamorous title given to boys of the Warsaw ghetto, like Poppy, who had traveled through shit and piss and then the murderous Polish streets to fetch supplies for the uprising—remained trapped inside.

Dad shared a few other memories besides the Boat Story and the Barn Story, but insisted he knew nothing more; Grandma spent her time welcoming death. But her stubborn, concentration camp–trained body would not allow her an easy exit from this world.

Anything I said to her, Grandma found a way to link to her beloved husband and then cried over his absence. To ask about the Holocaust was the easiest way to break the dam. But she wasn't crying for all the dead people who hung above the light switch; she cried for the dead husband who hung from her neck. The best strategy was to keep silent during the visits. My father limited trips to Grandma's to forty-five minutes because any longer was maddening. Three quarters of an hour was enough time to pay her bills, write out checks, hold her shaky hand and pen in place as the point kissed the paper above the signature line, and confirm that she was still committed to her only goal: to wither away at the dining room table where Poppy and I had once played cards.

I walked over to the china cabinet to inspect that one drawer. But the Bicycle playing cards and Marlboro cigarettes were gone. There was nothing left from those fond years of adolescence. The possibility of getting to that coveted past, I had come to accept, was over.

My heart sank. I read my father's cue and kissed Grandma goodbye.

"Noah and I are going to get food," Dad said, the easiest way to convince her that it was time to leave. Grandma would never deny her son and grandson food.

"I'm sorry, but Grandma can't cook no more," she reminded us.

"You don't need to cook," I told her and wrapped my arm around her.

"Why should I cook?" she replied, as though I had made the opposite statement. "Why should I cook when you Poppy's dead?"

My grandparents had had a rather stereotypical relationship for two elderly eastern European Jews who had immigrated to America—she cooked, he worked, she cleaned, he watched television. They had spent most of their time separate from each other except when they occupied the bed and the car. When they crossed paths in the apartment, she'd reproach and he'd defend.

"Leo, I fall into the closet and call you to come get me, and what do you say?"

"I was coming to get you," Poppy shouted back, winking at me, feigning sincerity.

"But you stay at work even later. This is a husband?"

"You got out from the closet," Poppy said.

"And what if I didn't?"

"So I would get you out after work. You wasn't going no place."

Grandma waved him off. Poppy and I returned to our card game, the ones that he allowed me to win because, at the time, I wasn't quite thirteen. Grandma went back to cleaning, stalking out specks of bread that had found their way into the thick blue carpet. She moved like a tracker—back bent, eyes on the floor, fingers picking at the clues that would lead to bigger crumbs lurking within the threads. Grandma was Gretel, if the girl had been Jewish (or at least not German), and obsessive-compulsive.

"Time to eat, *tatehla*," Grandma announced after the crumb hunt had concluded. She carried a bowl of soup toward me, concentrating on not spilling the liquid that she had filled to the brim.

"I'm not hungry," I said.

"Eat," she argued.

"*Nisht hungerik*," Poppy shouted, coming to my rescue.

"Noiach?" She appeared shocked, as if I had been the one to raise my voice. But what I had done was worse: claiming to be full when at least seven more meals were scheduled to precede dinner. "Eat something. You need to eat something, *tateh sheine*. You mother doesn't feed you."

"*Gey a vec*," Poppy yelled, fending her off. "*Meshuggana*, you Grandma."

"Hitler made me crazy," Grandma shouted back.

Poppy waved her off. "Please, I knew you before the war. You were crazy then. Don't blame Hitler for everything."

Grandma launched Yiddish invectives.

"You crazy. They should give me a medal to deal with you," Poppy proclaimed.

"I'm crazy. You drive like a madman. A big shot. Noiach, we go around a band in the car."

"What do you mean, a band?" I asked.

"In the country. A band in the road."

"A bend," I corrected.

"*Oy! Oy!* I was this nervous." She held her hands two feet apart. "Poppy gonna crash the car. Like a madman he drive on a band."

"I gonna crash the car cause you stop on my brake. This why I make you Grandma sit in the backseat."

"Cause you a big shot," Grandma shouted.

"Tell her *reyd tsu di vant*. Say this to Grandma: *reyd tsu di vant*," Poppy instructed me.

"*Red suit of aunt*." My Yiddish sounded Italian.

Grandma stopped screaming. "*Tatehla*, you speak good Yiddish. This makes Grandma proud." Of course her huge smile was brief, and she quickly followed compliment with criticism. "You can't speak it more often?" Then she turned to her husband. "Leo, this is what you teach him? To say this to Grandma?"

"Tell her again." He threw his arm in her direction as if conducting a firing squad to drop some unyielding beast.

"*Red suit of aunt*."

Grandma smiled and scolded again.

"Again," Poppy instructed.

"*Red suit of aunt.* What am I even saying?"

"Talking to her is like talking to a wall." Poppy smiled. "Go ahead *sheine keit*, deal the cards."

Grandma was livid and then she wasn't. "My husband." She smiled and cupped his face in her doughy mitt. "Eat, Noiach."

"You can't win with that one," Poppy said when she returned to the kitchen. He threw down the good ten atop two aces and an eight, sweeping up four points and a few spades, forgetting in the chaos that I was supposed to win.

But Poppy had always relied on Grandma intensely. While the camps could not exterminate Leon Lederman, if the cards had been reversed, if Grandma had died first, everyone in my family was convinced that Poppy would have soon followed. He could not survive without her stifling love.

Grandma, on the other hand, fueled herself on this newest misery.

"Grandma, this is the last time I'll see you for at least a year. You'll take good care of yourself?"

She shrugged. Grandma couldn't care less.

It was May 2003. I had graduated college and my plan was to spend the next year or so in search of the best waves in Central America, New Zealand, Australia, and Europe.

It had been nearly three and a half years since the funeral—the death that served as the impetus for Grandma's new religion. Leoism. Its most devout follower remained at the dining room table, praying for his timely return or her own quick demise. The photograph of Poppy that was incarcerated in gold shone on her chest. Grandma looked fragile. She had been freshly sprung from the hospital, overcoming another bout with congestive heart failure or pneumonia or whatever it was that she most likely considered a collaborator rather than a killer. I felt sadness and relief knowing that I might never see her again. I loved her, but she appeared more miserable now than I could ever imagine her to be when she was in Auschwitz. Was it even a life worth living?

I considered how her death would play out. My parents would probably send an e-mail a few days after the funeral, their attempt to save me from the compunction of having to race home for an abbreviated *shivah*; or, if I were in an Internet-free fishing village, I might not receive the message for weeks.

"You want to come surf the world with me, Grandma?" Ridiculous questions had become a fact of conversation with Grandma, a tool to break through the girth of her depression.

"Noiach, what you need to see around the world? You have a family here. You have a college degree. What you need to run around the world for? Look at the life Poppy created for you here. *Oy*, you Poppy. He's gone. Three and a half years he's gone." She said all of this through those relentless tears.

"I know." What more could I say? How else could I attempt to comfort her? The clock in the kitchen ticked off the minutes. Then I touched the numbers on Grandma's arm and kissed her goodbye. Never would I touch those numbers again. I was resigned to the fact that my grandparents' Holocaust stories—the thousands of memories logged away as incommunicable events—would be lost forever.

As I traveled, there was little to do in between waves. I watched life in the fishing villages unfold and waited for travelers to leave their food behind on the hostels' free-food shelves, a detail that would have led Grandma to suicide—*Eating from the garbage?* It's not the garbage. *It's the rubbish.* I also spent a lot of time writing and making the acquaintance of fishermen and surfers, discussing things like wind speed and swell direction, the contours of the ocean floor and the way waves wrapped around points. In that year of studying the agnostic seas, my connection to the Holocaust—which had always been my strongest link to Judaism—eroded.

This absence of the Holocaust at the forefront of my being was at first unsettling. After all, I had lived a childhood paying attention to details that most would never think to consider. I had always counted the Jews in my presence the way a congressional whip might forever tally votes: *Jew, Jew, Christian, Jew, Christian, Christian, Hindu or Buddhist or something from the East, not sure, Jew*. Something in me, something grim and innate and guarded, had always wanted to know who would crouch beside me on a ghetto rooftop if the Nazis ever returned. But in these surfing villages, the illusion of the Nazis faded from my reality; the necessity of a paranoia inculcated by survivors lifted from me like the fog from the morning surf.

Questions about Auschwitz turned into queries of *las olas*—the waves—as I sought the swells of Central America. Hanukah passed and the only eight-night miracle I recognized was that my flashlight had had enough juice for that week and a day I camped out on New Zealand's Great Barrier Island, where I was the only surfer with a tent pitched before this perfect, empty wave. And sometime just after the Passover celebration, the holiday had eluded me as I waited for the Basque country's famed wave at Mundaka to leaven. It did so on day six of my stay. The wave sucked up so much water into its face that the ocean floor was almost revealed. Moses would have marveled at Mundaka's ability to part without his staff.

Only twice during that first year of travel did my Jewishness ever register. Days before I had arrived in Mundaka, I had been attempting to bus from northern Portugal to Bilbao in Spain. But when I had arrived in Santiago de Compostela, a connecting city, the final bus for that day had already departed. Without a ride until the following morning, I walked the cobblestone streets of town in search of a room.

Santiago felt like *Guernica* if Picasso had painted a sequel—dead, empty, blue. Yet every establishment that rented rooms had no vacancy. I climbed staircase after staircase, lugging my board and thirty-pound pack up and down flights of stairs to no avail. Everything was booked, but it made no sense. Santiago was lifeless. The hotels were as quiet as libraries. My footfalls on the old staircases and the creak of the pension doors were the only sounds. It wasn't until I ascended to my eighth hotel of the evening did I find the last room available for rent. Relieved and confused, I took it, showered, and readied for bed.

But as I attempted sleep, a metallic thunder erupted outside. The beat was steady and piercing and grew in volume. I dressed and walked downstairs to investigate. The once empty streets had filled with the town's population. Between the throngs of locals, hooded men marched. Their pointed cloaks would befit members of the Ku Klux Klan. On a platform, the Spanish Klan carried a crucified Jesus, who cast his betrayed and pained expression down on the people; his chest and appendage wounds leaked; his crown of thorns pierced his forehead. For a moment—a fearfully long and inquisitive moment—I knew the fears of my grandparents. I understood why my father had always kept a suitcase packed beneath his bed.

This is what it's like when they come for the Jews.

"¿Que estos?" I asked in my limited Spanish to a woman beside me.

"Santa Semana," she said.

"Week of the saints," I translated aloud and briefly wondered whether that was a euphemism for "lynch the blacks" or "gas the Jews."

Despite the Klan outfits and Christ's gaze of censure, I soon learned that the elated faces and lack of violence signaled a celebration. (Later, I would read that the pointed hoods belonged to a Roman Catholic tradition that predated the symbolic dress worn by America's bigots.) I spent that night roaming the festive warrens, eating tapas, and listening to street music. After that initial trepidation, it did not occur to me again that I was different from these Spaniards.

The only other instance to remind me of my Jewishness occurred a few months earlier while I was sleeping on my friend's futon in Sydney.

"But you're Jewish and I'm Catholic. How will we even raise our kids?" said Gabriela, at that time my Chilean, suddenly *über*-Catholic girlfriend. The question lingered in the phone as I remained speechless. When we had been together at university, our disparate religions never once came up. Now that we were on a break and separated by multiple oceans—she completing her senior year of college in Maryland before meeting me in Europe for the summer—the faith of our hypothetical children had engendered serious doubt.

"I don't think we need to worry about children right now," I said. "We're not even married and—"

"Yes, but if I come to Europe and we travel for three months, things progress. And the question will come up: How are we going to raise our kids?" She couldn't stop impregnating herself with this idea of marriage and kids. "I mean, I'm devoutly Catholic and you're not. I love my religion and you don't really seem to follow anything. I mean, are you going to come to church with us? With the children?"

Grandma had always said, "If you fall in love, you fall in love." *You can't choose love; love chooses you.* But she remembered to add her most important point. "But never fall in love with a *shiksah*."

"Why?" I had asked.

"Because if you marry a *shiksah* then the baby is not a Jew. And then what did we survive for? To make more gentiles? *Ptoy.*"

"I don't go to synagogue; why would I go to church?" I asked my *shiksah*.

"That's what families do, baby. What do I tell the children when Daddy doesn't come to church?"

We left it at that: she brooding over how to inculcate our nonexistent brood, I heading off to check the surf.

But after a few months of reconsiderations and other less controversial conversations, Gabriela met me in Europe and daddy went to church. Every town had several and Gabriela stood beneath the gold and glass and myriad representations of her God in a bath of glory. She made no attempts to splash me with holy water or babble incantations that would influence me to take communion, but whenever she read our *Europe on a Shoestring* guidebook, she'd make it a point to tell me about the churches.

"Oh wow," she'd say, hoping to get a response.

"What did you read?" I'd ask, as one does.

"Nothing. It's just . . . never mind."

"What? Tell me."

"It's just that there's another church in this town that we're not to miss. It's different from the last one."

While I remained unbothered by our daily church visits and Gabriela's speciously adorable attempt to culture me on baroque, Renaissance, and Gothic architecture—but only if the buildings were built for God—I couldn't help but feel that I was being tooled around like the protagonist's fool in a low-budget Christian soap opera. While she marveled at the interiors of each building, I started to recall a secondary function of many of these houses of worship. They had served as bully pulpits. These were the buildings where my people had been pronounced Christ killers.

Now that surfing had been abandoned for travels with Gabriela on the continent where nearly all of my family was extinguished, I started to remember my identity. The first year of my trip had changed me. It was the year that I had learned to trust. I had hitchhiked with anyone who would stop and slept among strangers in crowded hostel rooms without ever thinking that they might slit my throat the way Grandma had felt when my father had brought Saki to stay with the family.

But as I stood in these churches, I was reminded more and more about being a Jew in Europe. My newfound trust dissolved like a fragile pillar of salt in the waves.

"What do you think?" Gabriela would ask as we stood in the shadow of Christ.

What she meant, I had no idea. *Is the building nice? Does bloody Jesus in that stained-glass scene speak more to you than the sallow-eyed acromegalic Jesus towering above us? Are you ready to convert for me and our unborn gentiles? Could the Holocaust happen again? Here?*

"There's quite a lot of gold," I told her.

"What else, baby?"

I wrapped my arms around her and she nudged me off.

"I want another gelato," I decided. "That's what I think."

Neither of us would be willing to change the things fundamental to our identities. She waited until we were outside the church to kiss me. I kissed her back and knew that our love was finite. We would be lucky to last through Europe.

Despite Gabriela's numerous church visits and silent prayers, once we reached Italy's Amalfi Coast, we discovered that her bank account had been hacked when the ATM conjured up only one zero. *No funds.* If we wanted to sustain globetrotting for another two months, we realized we would need to head to the more affordable east.

"Where do you want to go?" Gabriela asked, unfolding a map of the continent.

"I'll go anywhere except Poland and Germany."

This had nothing to do with logic. It was principle. I grew up in a family where Volkswagen and BMW sightings stirred the equivalence of road rage. To the question *Where are your grandparents from?* my answer had always been "Europe." *Yes, but where in Europe?* "Eastern Europe." *What country?* "Between the Atlantic Ocean and Russia." Maybe the young Poles and Germans were not to blame. Maybe they had been changed by history. Maybe they felt guilt for the crimes of their families. But maybe they had no guilt and would love to see me fly like smoke through a chimney.

I studied the map a bit longer. "I guess we can head to Slovenia and figure it out from there."

Up until that point, it was only the church visits and the Christ statues stricken with gigantism that reminded me that I was a Jew. But after Slovenia we left for Budapest, and Judaism found me the way lightning locates a skyscraper.

On the train to Hungary, the sun rose and cast its illumination on a bucolic Austria. We passed forests and farms and red barns that could have inspired a European musical. The only thing I knew about Austria was that it had reared Hitler. If it takes a village, as they say, then the responsible village could have easily been one that appeared as a picturesque vista outside the windows of our train. As we clanked into the next station, something innate switched on inside me, like antibodies awakened when bacteria invade.

My grandparents had always used the word "gentile" like an inoculation. They introduced me to the word, decorating it with distrust and rancor, tones that were more noticeable than their accents. If it happened that the gentile in question was affiliated with Austria, Germany, or Poland—the triad of culpable nations—Grandma or Poppy would tag the word with an even more dire and miasmic warning.

I watched as the Austrians boarded the train. Something whispered from my subconscious, as if the familiar voices of my id and superego had both departed, and filling in were the dead relatives above Grandma's light switch. *Why would you come back here?*

If Germany had been the brain of the Nazi machine and Poland had been the feckless appendages that participated in the bloodshed, giving up my grandparents and the rest of the Jews to the Nazis, then Austria was the womb.

I was once again wary of my surroundings, the way a tourist might feel after wandering into a warren of dark alleys. This alley had no exits. Everyone was a suspect again.

The conductor entered our cabin and asked us to move our bags off the opposite seats.

"Why does he want us to move our bags?" Gabriela asked.

"We have to share the cabin with them."

Behind the conductor stood a large Austrian man. He looked stunningly like Arnold Schwarzenegger. Arnold had to duck in order to enter our compartment. A woman followed who looked just like Arnold, too, though more aged and wigged, with a doughy face and fertile chin replete with curly hairs.

The pair of giants—mother and son, it appeared—sat on the bench across from us and took up most of the space between the two benches with their legs.

Gabriela went back to sleep. I stayed up.

Arnold smiled dumbly out the window. After a while he got up to use the restroom.

Arnold's presence and our setting reminded me of one other story my father had told at Poppy's *shivah*: the Train Story.

After the war, my grandparents had been traveling through Germany by train. Helen and a family friend, Raymond, accompanied them. They entered their assigned cabin and in it they found a German soldier sprawled out on one bench, asleep. Grandma and Helen sat across from the man, while Poppy and Raymond stood. When the soldier awoke, he looked at Grandma and Helen and began to laugh. He called the women "Fucking Jewish sluts."

Poppy split his face open like a melon.

I would be foolish to think that attitudes like that hadn't been passed down and implanted in the next generation. It felt not unreasonable to assume that we were shuttling through Europe with Nazis in wait. I looked over at Gabriela and wondered what I would do if Arnold returned and offered up a similar insult. The absurd affront—one made more impossible by Gabriela's Catholicism—still metastasized in my mind. For the duration of Arnold's absence I kept thinking of the ways, if need be, to physically cripple him. I decided that I would go for his throat. Maybe I would gag him with his swastika armband. I started to feel incredibly ready and guilty and confused.

After the Holocaust, Poppy had never allowed anti-Semitism expressed in his presence to go unpunished. The Train Story and the Boat Story confirmed this.

I had seen the swastika on a person twice, both times as homemade ink jobs in a country with a name that sounded similar to Austria, though instead of killing Jews, they had a notorious history of hunting their Aborigines. Both times I had done nothing.

While I had traveled halfway around the world to witness such an insult and acknowledge my own inaction, my younger brother, Jake, only had to cross a bridge into the Bronx to face a similar provocation at his college.

Because he had turned the space between his shoulder blades into an identity map—inking a blue arachnid posing inside a Star of David—whenever he walked to the showers in the dorms and rugby locker rooms with his tattoos exposed, he became a target. (But he had his reason for getting the tattoo, which he once explained to my parents: "I'm a Scorpio and a Jew. These are two things that nobody can change about me." "You're also an idiot," my father replied. "I don't see that word tattooed to your back.")

While our high school, which was only ten miles away from this Bronx institution, had a majority of Jews, his college, from my brother's stories at least, sounded like an enclave where 1930's German philosophy was preached.

"You sure you're not overreacting? It's the fucking Bronx," I said to Jake when he told me about the anti-Semites he lived with. After all, I had played water polo at the University of Maryland, where, as the only Jew on my team, I dealt with comments about my Judaism from one or two players. But I never felt a need to retaliate. The way my brother told it, however, he experienced pure hatred. And when he defended himself against the slurs, he got in trouble while the bigots were pardoned.

It got so bad for Jake that he actually threw one anti-Semitic classmate through a window.

On a rainy weekend night in 2002, Jake called me while I was down at Maryland. We rarely spoke on the phone, so the call had caught me off guard. I figured there had to have been a bad accident. A death to come home for. I went through that process of killing off my loved ones quickly, preparing myself for the news.

"I think I did something bad." He slurred his words. "I really hurt this guy tonight."

"You got into a fight?" I asked. "Who cares? It's a fight."

"No. Worse. I kept hitting this guy. His friend came at me and I knocked him out. But this other guy, I just kept hitting him."

"Where was this?"

"At a bar near school."

"What did they do to you?" I asked, assuming that my brother was just another drunken college kid in the wrong.

"They told me to go burn in the ovens like my family. Maybe . . . maybe I should go back and see if the guy's alright."

"You don't have to," I told him. "Go to sleep. Poppy would have done the same thing."

I worried that I couldn't.

The blond-haired and blue-eyed Austrian giant returned to the cabin and sat back down across from Gabriela and me. Arnold dug through his luggage. What was he looking for? A celebratory bottle of champagne to pop open for when our train passed concentration-camp row?

Why did people ever talk about forgiveness?

His hand emerged with a plastic bag filled with a half-dozen pastries. Arnold dove his hand into the pastry bag and then extended the dessert toward Gabriela. "Here. Eat. Eat." Then he said the same to me. "Eat. Eat." He had borrowed Grandma's vernacular for when she had brought chicken soup to the table. Gabriela hesitated but took the dessert. Arnold patted a sugarcoated hand upon his giant chest and introduced himself. "Karl."

Karl, or Arnold, gave us his train-seat tour of the Austrian countryside. When we crossed the border into Hungary, when he no longer knew about the geography or the nation's history, he told us he was training to become a mime. "You want to see me do robot?"

Gabriela and I looked at each other to make certain that we had heard correctly—the Terminator proposing to move like Michael.

"Yes. We would love to see you do the robot," we both said.

Karl dropped his chin to his chest and held his hands in front of his body like a confused mannequin. The train hit a few seams in the track, but Karl remained motionless. Then, suddenly, he powered himself to life, raising his head mechanically. His arms took turns chopping through the air with robotic stutters. His face remained serious. He moved and halted. Moved and halted.

Meanwhile, the woman, who was in fact his mother, applauded his performance. She kept repeating, "*Schön, schön, schön.*" (Afterward, Karl explained that his mother was saying "beautiful.")

"You do a *schön* robot." I felt awful that I had envisioned ripping out his windpipe earlier.

Our time in Budapest was filled with walks through the hills of Buda and down the boulevards of Pest. The realization that I was a Jew in the land of the dead, in the land of the millions of people who had been just like me—born into something that wasn't physical or genetic, born into a faith that may not have even been believed—was ever-present. It was strange to return to those familiar thoughts, ones that had been supplanted in the past year by waves. Maybe the train ride through Austria or perhaps the myriad uncircumcised penises that flopped about in the communal baths in Budapest helped these feelings to resurface. Or maybe it was Gabriela's push toward Prague—a move closer to Poland.

"I hear it's what Paris was like before Paris became Paris." She showed me the map of Europe. Prague, on the map, was a star in the Czech Republic, a nation that dangled like a cling-on to the anus that ran between the ass cheeks that were Germany and Poland.

"We can catch a train tomorrow evening," she said.

"We have to fly from Amsterdam," I told her. "It's out of the way."

"Yeah, but that's in like five weeks," she said, not understanding my logic.

I studied the map. How would we get from Prague to Amsterdam without flying? The straightest line was not a possibility.

"This is not rational thinking," people have told me over the years. "The Germans. The Poles. They have changed their views."

But people and places are like earthquakes. Even if the tremors had moved from Germany to Cambodia, to Bosnia, to Rwanda, to Darfur, the fault lines never change locations. Some may shrug off today's Nazi salutes and graffitied swastikas in Europe as harmless. But to me these were only decades away from being acceptable again. They were waiting with the patience of S waves . . . with the patience of SS waves.

And anyway, what is rational when one grows up with his murdered family staring down at him from above a light switch?

"Never again" was an optimistic fantasy that blinded people to my reality: *Again, certainly, so be ready.*

Gabriela and I hadn't slept together since Slovenia. Something about accidentally procreating a non-Jew in these once culpable countries had turned me off. But I held her hand wherever we went. I felt a pressing need to protect her. Everyone would be a suspect, and it would be irrational to think otherwise. But Gabriela wasn't for constantly holding hands.

"It's too hot," she'd say and pull away.

"Sorry."

"Stop grabbing my hand, baby."

"My fault."

During one of our long walks through Pest, however, I was the one to drop her hand.

"Baby?" She looked nervous.

I must have appeared as though I were staring up at a ghost. The two words written on the side of a building did, however, appear out of nowhere like an apparition.

HOLOCAUST MUSEUM the wall read, magnified by the blankness of the rest of the stone edifice.

I hadn't seen the word *Holocaust* for more than a year. Not printed in a book; not scribbled in a journal; not in a novel; and certainly not chiseled into stone as it was now in Budapest. The chance encounter with the museum was like running into a cousin while overseas. It was so familiar, so comforting, so much like home.

"Let's go in," I said.

"Yeah, of course," she said.

We entered the museum and stopped at the security checkpoint.

"We are open only for private tours," said the guard.

Ahead of us, standing in the lobby, stood a group of silver-haired visitors surrounding a docent. The docent pointed up, and the silver-haired heads swept to explore the space.

"We're with them," I told the guard, who looked skeptical but waved us through.

"It was March of '44 when the Germans entered Budapest and forced the Jews into the ghettos," the tour guide said to the twenty elders. "By May, the Nazis had organized the largest and fastest deportation, removing a half-million Jews out of Budapest in less than two months. Most were murdered in Auschwitz-Birkenau."

The well-dressed group shook their heads at the horrors.

We moved with them through the museum, but with my sun-bleached hair, our unwashed clothes, and Gabriela's dark skin, youth, and beauty, we were politely outed for tour crashing.

"Where are you from?" a grizzled man asked. His accent clearly connected him to the States.

"New York. She's from Maryland."

"Sorry for jumping on your tour," Gabriela said. "We just wanted to learn about what happened here."

"Well, we're happy to have you," the man's wife said. It turned out that most of the people from the group were my neighbors back home, living in the towns to my immediate west and east.

"What brings you to Hungary?" I asked. We hadn't run into many Americans on our travels, let alone neighbors.

"We're a think tank out of Washington," the grizzled man explained. He introduced himself as Joseph. "The Jewish Institute for National Security Affairs. Maybe you've heard of us. JINSA." We told him that we hadn't. "Anyway, Hungary abstained from a vote for us and this is a trip to return the favor."

"A vote?" Gabriela asked as we moved to another room with more sad artifacts.

Nobody answered her. I shrugged. Clearly, this was a group of powerful Jews.

"How did you manage to get in here?" the man's wife asked as we all stopped in front of the Auschwitz Album.

"Uh," Gabriela began.

The older woman sensed Gabriela's hesitation and kindly added, "It's just that we had scheduled a private showing and the museum isn't yet open to the public."

"His grandparents are Holocaust survivors," Gabriela said, looking at the couple to see how this non sequitur would play inside this space.

"My parents are survivors, too." Joseph appeared excited over our connection through murders and oppression. "Where are your grandparents from?"

"Poland," I said.

Joseph revealed his family's tragic genealogy as we wandered the museum, ignoring much of what was on display and instead delving into the private collection of his memories.

When the tour ended and the JINSA seniors boarded their bus, Joseph handed me a business card. "This is the hotel we're staying at," he said, pointing to the card. "This evening we're taking a dinner cruise on the Danube, departing from our hotel in one hour's time. We'd love it if you joined us."

"Thank you," I said, looking at the card and Gabriela. "I don't think we'll fit in exactly. I don't even own a pair of pants or jeans."

"And I don't have a dress," Gabriela said to Joseph. "Or makeup."

"Nonsense. Meet us outside our hotel." Joseph tapped the card and boarded the coach bus that was parked out front.

We hopped a street trolley back to our hostel and jumped in the shower. I lifted Gabriela off the shower floor after her wipeout and she pressed toilet paper to clot a razor wound, which I had inflicted to her tricep in my failed attempt to catch her. Somehow, however, we left the hostel, sans ambulance, dodged traffic, and sprinted for the hotel named on the card. We arrived just as the JINSA group boarded the bus parked in front of its palatial residence.

"Ah, you made it," Joseph declared. He bowed slightly and extended his arm to usher us up the stairs. "After you."

"Duck, sir," the waiter announced later that evening, serving the entrée portion of the five-course meal. Another white-gloved man filled my half-empty champagne flute and then poured for the gentleman across from me, who happened to be a former admiral in the United States Navy and past Supreme Allied Commander of NATO.

"So where are you lovebirds off to next?" asked the former commander.

Gabriela looked at me. Her smile crinkled to see whether I was on board with her desire to visit the dingleberry hanging from the crack between Poland and Germany.

"Prague," I said.

"I hear it's beautiful," said the former commander.

"It sounds so romantic," Gabriela said, squeezing my hand with gratitude and adding, "in the same way that Paris was romantic before Paris became Paris."

After the meal, Gabriela and I stood on the bow and watched the moon shed its light on the Danube.

"This is incredible," she said.

I nodded, but I wasn't thinking about the tranquil river and the constellations of city lights. Instead, I wondered about the river in my grandparents' city of Otwock. The museum and the JINSA folks had returned me to the Holocaust.

"I can't wait to kiss you all over when we get back to our room," Gabriela said. To her, the boat had set the mood and managed to transform the dorm room that awaited us, with its two steel-framed twin beds, into a luxurious hotel.

But I couldn't shake the river in Otwock—the one stained with my people's blood. I wondered whether it ran into this Danube.

The morning after the boat ride, Gabriela asked me whether there was anything else I wanted to do in Budapest before leaving for Prague.

"I want to take you to synagogue."

She smiled. I smiled. But I wasn't kidding.

We trekked across the city to Europe's largest temple. We weren't there for worship—I hadn't been to temple since my bar mitzvah—and we weren't there to witness the synagogue's majesty and photograph its architectural survival, like most. We were visiting for the dead Jews.

I stood in the courtyard beside a silver memorial tree, dragging my fingers gently across the silver leaves imprinted with the names of the murdered.

"Are you okay, baby?"

I hugged Gabriela into me as if it were the last time I would ever feel her skin. "Of course."

"What are you thinking about?" she whispered into my ear.

I watched the silver leaves glint in the sun. "Nothing."

But I thought about the leaves. The names of the murdered Hungarian Jews that hung just like the photograph above Grandma's light switch. How many stories on the tree could have been another *Night* or *The Diary of a Young Girl*?

We arrived in Prague, where we had work lined up at a hostel just outside the city. But after commuting to that hostel, which smelled of cat urine, we learned that in exchange for our labor we would be holed up in shared, lofted sleeping quarters with six other employees. The single room looked like it had once been built to stow away Jews and the owner was just slow at reconverting the loft back into something more livable. We decided to head back to the city for less creepy accommodations that would also be more proximal to the attractions.

Eight hours later, however, we were still walking the city's twisted streets, entering and exiting hotels with disappointment. Everything was either without vacancy or out of our price range.

Gabriela collapsed and cried against the cobblestone road. "I can't do this anymore. Maybe we should just go home. Back to the United States."

"If you didn't give up after your bank account got hacked, we're not giving up because we're having trouble finding a room. Plus, this is like Paris . . . before Paris was Paris."

Gabriela did not return my smile but resigned herself to stand.

"It's all right. We'll find a room," I said, and helped balance her and the thirty-pound pack.

Just before dark, after we had crossed the Vltava River for a third time, passing the painters who were relieving their posts to the nighttime musicians, we traveled to the far edge of the city and found a former gymnasium that had been converted into an eighty-person dormitory.

The gymnasium was terrible. The moth-eaten blankets were also cigarette-singed, the lights stayed on for all twenty-four hours of the day, and each of our roommates had gathered around boom boxes blasting electronica, passing around pills before heading off to the nightclubs, their sole motivation for staying in Prague. But for six dollars apiece, we were given beds and a key to lock our valuables in a cubby. I stood my pack against the bunk and placed my passport and cash in the cubby. Inside the locked box, I also placed my shoes.

"Why are you putting your shoes in there?" Gabriela wondered, watching me from the top bunk.

"I don't know," I said. But I didn't take them out. I locked the cubby and climbed up to the top bunk. After lying down beneath the globes of fluorescence, I remembered what Grandma had once said—a Holocaust fact that she had revealed accidentally and that I ignored as inconsequential, I guess because it had been about shoes—*I would never fall asleep in the camps without protecting my shoes. Shoes were life.*

That night I dreamed of running toward the river, attempting to escape those creatures that looked like Sendak's wild things, that familiar nightmare from my elementary school days. I woke at six in the morning and wondered whether that body of water flowing through my subconscious could have been the same river in Otwock.

Gabriela was up, too, packed and pacing.

We left the gymnasium hostel and splurged on a much nicer room near the famous clock tower, where herds of tourists waited hourly for the bells to chime and for the statuettes behind the clock's face to reveal themselves in a lackluster rotation.

We spent the morning enjoying coffees and bagels down the street from our hotel. Gabriela marveled at every cobblestone—"It does remind me of Paris," she said—as if seeing Prague for the very first time, as if yesterday's eight-hour search for accommodations had been done blindfolded, as though we had not already passed eastern Europe's reply to the Eiffel Tower, its answer to the Seine, its Gothic counter to Notre Dame, fifty times the day before.

"What do you want to do today?" she asked.

I looked in the guidebook to see what Prague had to offer. We—or at least I—had seen most of the attractions during yesterday's search. The one thing that we hadn't done was follow Prague's trail of death. I suddenly had that urge.

6

DEATH IN THE CZECH REPUBLIC

An entire human body dangled above our heads as if it had exploded, causing all the organs and epidermis to disintegrate, leaving behind only a beautiful bouquet of bones that hung as a chandelier. They called this place in Kutná Hora the bone church. Besides assembling the corporeal light fixture above, a grim woodcarver had also piled thousands of femurs and skulls into four pyramids, which occupied each corner of the room. He had transformed the endless remains of those who had died from the Black Death or war into art. Garlands of skulls hung from the vaults, and the dead eyes of men offered hollow stares from their perches on the stems of candelabra.

"This is incredible," Gabriela said. "But it gives me the creeps."

"Do you want to leave?" I asked.

"No way. I didn't think I would be able to stomach thousands of dead bodies," she said, staring at one of the skulls mounted to a candelabrum. "But somehow I can."

Later, when we took the bus back to the city, passing endless fields of sunflowers, the yellow petals getting clipped by raindrops, I wasn't sure how I felt about the dead displayed in Kutná Hora. I wondered how many hundreds of churches it would take to house the murdered Jews of the Holocaust, even if most of those bones had been turned to ash. Instead of hoisting up the king of the Jews to remind people of their sins, what would the world be like if these same churches displayed man's sins—the bones and ashes of all genocide—as evidence?

Back in the city, the rain ceased. I pulled out our map and folded it down to the one square I needed: the Josefov. But on the map, the words were printed in English: *Jewish Ghetto*.

During the war, a Jewish doctor named Augustin Stein had somehow convinced the Germans that the ghetto in Prague should be preserved to show future generations why it was necessary to destroy the Jews. Stein's cunning had helped to save a vast collection of Judaic art, literature, and artifacts, as well as half a dozen beatific synagogues.

I didn't care to visit each of the synagogues, nor did we have the money to spend on exploring the interiors. Witnessing the existence of these architectural survivors was enough. We spent the remainder of the afternoon wandering the Josefov.

"I can't believe anyone would attempt to wipe out a people," Gabriela said.

"Believe it," I told her.

She was taken aback. Not the response she had expected. "Your grandmother doesn't talk about it?"

"When I was younger I always asked her to tell me her stories, but she never did."

"What about now? Now that you're older?"

"You met her. She only does one thing."

"She's so sweet and sad. All she does is mourn for her husband. That's so sad and so beautiful," said Gabriela.

"That's not a life."

Gabriela grabbed my hand, and we sat down on a bench outside one of the surviving temples. She rested her head on my shoulder.

"Is this making you want to convert to Judaism?" I joked.

She slapped my arm softly. I didn't need her to be Jewish. But Grandma's warning—*If you fall in love, you fall in love. But don't fall in love with a shiksah*—made her the Augustin Stein of the Lederman family. Grandma had found the words to preserve Judaism in her nonreligious grandson.

It was strange to be so committed to a belief system that I did not follow, based on stories that were as literal to me as *The Tortoise and the Hare*. Yet this thing, this religion, this divisive identifier mattered more to me than the girl I loved. My grandparents had given up everything to survive as Jews. I kissed Gabriela and then looked at her the way a kid might look at his favorite pet before the veterinarian administers that lethal injection. It was only a matter of time.

We walked to the end of the Josefov and stopped to admire the red-roofed Pinkas Synagogue.

"You sure you don't want to go into any of them?" Gabriela asked.

"We are closing," the man at the ticket booth said, overhearing her question.

"Maybe tomorrow," I said.

"But tomorrow, we're going to the camp, and then the next day we're heading to Český Krumlov. This might be the only chance we have to see this," Gabriela said, pointing to the Pinkas Synagogue.

"It's not a big deal."

"Sorry," said the man in the booth, apologizing for the inconvenience.

Once more, Gabriela looked at me with a pained expression. She pulled out her best argument: "Sir, can we please go through? His grandparents are Holocaust survivors."

"I . . ." the man began, but stopped. He glanced both ways as if crossing a dangerous street and then pulled back the rope. "Come. Come."

"Look at you saving the day," I said as we walked toward the entrance.

"You don't say things sometime," Gabriela said, almost angry. "But I can tell what you're thinking."

I kissed her head. "You have *chutzpah*."

"What's that?"

Maybe Grandma would amend her philosophy.

Let it not come unto you, all ye that pass by! Behold and see if there be any pain like unto my pain . . . I read off the gray wall before entering the temple.

Stepping over the threshold to the Pinkas Synagogue was like walking into a cement heart that suddenly arrested. I stood motionless in one of three chambers that had been scarred with eighty thousand names. The names belonged to the murdered Jews of Moravia and Bohemia. The pink columns extended onto the vaulted ceiling like arterial branches.

In my family, the number six million had been ubiquitous. Grandma would use it as a non sequitur. When my father was growing up and claimed to be bored, Grandma would say, "Bored? When I was your age we had no food. Your family is dead. Six million Jews dead and you're bored?" When I refused a fourth bowl of chicken soup, she pulled out the number as well: "Six million Jews die in the Holocaust and you're not hungry." Six million was printed on a poster that hung on their living room wall, greeting guests with that integer twisted up in a barbed wire Star of David.

Still, I had always found that enormous figure too difficult to grasp. What was six million? One six followed by a string of zeros. How did you feel something as flat as a number? The number was spoken and written so often that it grew into something emotionless and digestible, a textbook statistic served up like one historical corpse. We hardly even glanced at death tolls from the Crusades and the Inquisition. What would happen when the liberation of the camps reached its century anniversary? How would future generations react to six million and the Holocaust?

But here, inside the Pinkas Synagogue, the eighty thousand names looked like an entire phonebook had been copied onto the walls. The magnitude of eighty thousand—a number little more than one percent of that gross sum associated with the Holocaust; approximately the number of corpses inside of Kutná Hora's church—was finally palpable in the Pinkas Synagogue. I wondered how many of these victims had become the air that my grandparents breathed in Auschwitz.

Upstairs, we entered a small gallery, where the paintings of the dead children of Theresienstadt hung. In their art, I could see all that they yearned for: family, jump rope, Seders, childhood. The knot that had climbed into my throat at Poppy's funeral had returned.

"Do you know how hard it is for a kid that age"—Gabriela pointed to a sign that showed that the artist was five—"to overlap objects in a painting? I read somewhere that if a five-year-old could overlap and create perspective in art, he was a genius."

"They murdered geniuses, too," I said, squeezing the words past that hitch.

A tear rolled down her cheek.

Each child sought normalcy with paint, even though the new normal had become bodies huddled in attics, incoming transports, and the listlessness of concentration camp life, which they had depicted in their art, too.

So many things with wings flew across each illustration; butterflies were tattooed to the canvas, frozen in flight.

"I can't stay in here anymore," Gabriela said. She had been in no rush to leave the pile of bodies in Kutná Hora. There, the tens of thousands of dead were simply incredible to her. But here, the couple dozen artists chased her out into the cluttered graveyard behind the Pinkas Synagogue. Tombstones stood like barbs scattered over the hilly plot.

The most prominent gravestone in the cemetery, which had been packed with paper prayers like the Western Wall in Jerusalem, belonged to Rabbi Loew ben Bezalel, the creator of the mythical golem, a mud creature that had risen to protect the Jews of Prague.

Everyone marched through the cemetery somberly, but regained hope before the rabbi. Tourists with crosses dangling from their necks shoved their notes into the gaps as if this rabbi could transcend the grave and would then choose to overlook religion, blessing these gentiles when he had done nothing for his own.

"The most failed superhero in the world," I said, wondering why the rabbi who had created a false hero was still celebrated.

The skies opened again, and everyone ran for the exit. I smiled at the image of Grandma hurling a dollar at Schneerson or the five-pound-tzedakah bank at the head of the rabbi visiting during the *shivah* if he had stuck around for a moment longer. I wondered what she would have hit Bezalel with if he had tried to convince her to believe in the disappointing mud creature of Prague.

The next morning, we were on the bus to Theresienstadt. I had never entered a concentration camp before, yet it all felt familiar.

Theresienstadt (or Terezin, as it is commonly known) was a propaganda camp. When the Red Cross came to inspect it to determine whether or not the Nazis were committing human rights violations, the Germans ushered a naïve group of surveyors through Terezin, showing them how the interned Jews performed plays and worked on the crafts that were now on display in the museum. The Red Cross approved of the treatment. By war's end, of the more than 100,000 Jews passing through Terezin, only 3,600 had survived. Most had been sent to and murdered in Auschwitz.

After walking through the museum, I sat in the park just outside. Theresienstadt had gone back to being a town. The locals had reinstalled restaurants and shops where barracks and Nazi offices once stood. I watched three children play around the fountain. They laughed, plucking at the dessicated pink and red flowers that grew at awkward angles. The sun beat down on the yellowed lawn. I thought about the incinerated kids whose art hung in the Pinkas Synagogue. I didn't want to hate anyone, but I despised the people who now lived in Terezin.

"Were your grandparents here?" Gabriela asked.

"I don't think so," I said. "I really doubt it." I couldn't believe that even this simple fact—a timeline with locations—was information that I did not possess.

"Who would know for sure?"

"Maybe my father."

"He has to have the information written somewhere."

"My dad chose to forget."

"How could people choose to forget?" Gabriela asked.

"That's how the children of survivors survived," I told her. "They either forgot or were consumed by it."

"But the grandchildren don't forget. You don't forget."

"I have nothing to forget. My father and aunt heard these stories growing up. I didn't have that . . ."—the only word that came to mind was "luxury," though it was so far from the right word. The untold stories, though, were priceless.

"Maybe he could ask your grandmother."

"She's done speaking about all of this. She stopped many years ago and now, even if she wanted to, it would just remind her of Poppy and she would break down."

"That's sad."

Gabriela and I crossed the river, where the Small Fortress stood. AR-BEIT MACHT FREI was painted above the yellow-walled, arched entrance. I had grown up reading these infamous words scrawled above the gates at Auschwitz. Even then I had understood the mendacity of the German phrase: "Work sets you free."

I moved through the camp in a daze. The dark rooms—the isolation areas and the hospital—smelled moldy. It began to rain outside, and the air grew danker. The execution site was alive with vegetation. Bullet holes nested in the crumbling brick.

I wondered whether Grandma would last for one more month. Would I have the opportunity to ask the millions of questions that had built up since stumbling upon the Hungarian Holocaust museum? Even if Grandma rejected the questions, Gabriela made me realize that I had to ask. I had to try one more time.

A few days before Terezin, I had e-mailed my father and inquired about her health. He replied with his intentionally brief and lowercase correspondence, the consequences of one-finger typing. He wrote, *grandma is grandma.*

It was the euphemistic way to say that she still mourned. She still waited to die. But her body had been programmed to survive.

A mirror hung on the wall of the camp's dark washroom, which the prisoners had once used. I looked past the brown patches that had grown like brown moss in the reflective surface and wondered what I would have looked like in this place sixty years earlier.

Nothing would allow me to ever understand what had happened here.

Before catching the bus back to Prague, we crossed the river once more and found the railroad tracks hidden by the untrimmed lawn. The twisting steel led us into a Jewish gravesite. In the field stood a building. Inside were the furnaces.

I can still recall the stench. It didn't reek of burned bodies—but then again, how would I know what that smelled like? The room stank like a damp, forgotten attic. One with a chimney that had leaked its exhaust into the chamber.

I remember thinking about the eighty thousand names scrawled onto the walls of the Pinkas Synagogue, the holiest words in that temple. These places in and around Prague were primers for the things that would follow.

7

THE E-MAIL

Gabriela and I spent the next few days in the small city of Český Krum-lov, where terra cotta roofs sloped toward the Vltava River, where cobblestone paths led to castles, where bears paced in the moat below the castle, where Gypsy music spilled from bars. It was a world removed from the Holocaust and the camps. The Middle Ages—those lovely times blemished only by pogroms and the small-scale mass murder of Jews, easy enough to ignore—was preserved in the present day.

That evening, I sent my father an e-mail: *Where did Poppy and Grandma live when they were younger? What camps and ghettos were they prisoners in?*

He wrote back the next day: *grandma lived at 15 berka joselewicza. poppy at 12 podmiejska. grandma's father owned three houses. both started in the otwock ghetto, then moved to karczew, then to warsaw. poppy and grandma were in majdanek, then auschwitz. grandma went to bergen-belsen. liberated there. poppy went to dora and ravensbruck. liberated from ludveissles in klein, berlin. all the info i know. be safe. grandma's still a real joy*

"Where should we go next?" Gabriela asked as we studied the map of Europe for a long while.

At present, we were in the turd beneath that alimentary canal that traveled between those two shitty countries. Pressing my finger against Český Krumlov, the map seemed to slide beneath my finger like a Ouija board. That e-mail that my father had sent supplanted logic. The new addresses and camp names left me whimsical.

"Are you sure?" Gabriela asked, looking at where my finger tapped.

It felt like a mistake. But there was no turning back.

My finger had floated into Poland.

8

OTWOCK

Grandma had always pronounced the name of her city in Poland with two tongues. When she referenced the Jewish life that had once filled the streets, and described the little city as a destination where Jews came from across Europe to sip in the clean airs that lifted off the Swider River, Otwock sounded as though she were saying *Oat Vox*. It was as if her home had once been part of the Roman Empire and poetically dubbed the *Voice in the Grains*. But when she spoke of her Polish neighbors, the ones who had turned her family and friends in to the Nazis for a sack of potatoes, she pronounced it *Utt Vocks*, a name that caused her to choke and retch.

"What are we going to do once we arrive?" Gabriela asked while I paced the train platform, a cement slab situated between Warsaw and Otwock. We were waiting for our connecting train.

I removed the piece of paper from my pocket, where I had written down the names of the camps and ghettos where my grandparents had been enslaved. Below that were the two addresses in Otwock. "I'm not really sure."

What was I hoping to find? The house? Some artifact buried in one of their backyards? A neighbor with memories? An apology that I could take back to Brooklyn? A way to forgive?

I studied the street names. I wanted to remember Berka Joselewicza and Podmiejska so that I wouldn't have to glance at the page once we arrived. I didn't trust the Poles enough to take my eyes off them. The night before, Gabriela had played a song by Phish called "Farmhouse."

Woke this morning to the stinging lash / Every man rise from the ash / Each betrayal begins with trust / Every man returns to dust.

I couldn't get that stanza out of my head. The first line felt like life in the camps. The second line read like a lie. The third line was a warning that would guide me through Otwock. And the fourth line was what had happened to most of the fourteen thousand Jews from my grandparents' city when they arrived in Treblinka.

As loving as my grandparents were, they had raised me to understand the necessity of their hatred. The Germans had been culpable and nefarious, but Poppy and Grandma faulted no one more than the Poles. These were their neighbors, and they had turned in their Jewish countrymen for baking ingredients, tubers, or mediocre schnapps. Anne Frank's claim that people were good at heart had its counterbalance in my grandparents' warning.

Was it rational to judge the kin of those who had helped send my family to Treblinka? I thought about the man who had murdered Grandma's brother somewhere near the place where Gabriela and I waited for the train. This Pole had killed him days before the end of the war. It would be preposterous to exact my revenge on his son. His grandson. But it also felt wrong to feel anything less than hate for that whole family line.

I felt anxious and worried and sick. Conflicted, I continued to pace.

The sky above the tracks was a dull gray and heavy with clouds.

"It seems to rain every time you and I go to one of these places," Gabriela observed, maybe to presage something or maybe just to observe something humorous about the world since I hadn't smiled in the twenty-four hours that we had been in Poland.

The train pulled up two hours late. We boarded. It poured.

I thought about the tenets that my grandparents and Anne Frank had preached. The major difference was that my grandparents survived and Anne Frank didn't. Maybe Anne would have revised her journal had she been liberated. I pulled Gabriela into a seat far from the other commuters and hummed the Phish song.

Each betrayal begins with trust.

The white terminal building with the burnt-auburn roof and tower launching from the symmetrical edifice looked like the entrance I had seen in pictures of Birkenau. Even the black letters—OTWOCK—stood over the archway like the Polish version of ARBEIT MACHT FREI. The station was quiet.

I thought of the faces that had gathered for the photograph around the Seder table decades ago in this town. Now they were preserved above the light switch near the entrance to Grandma's bedroom. *Dead, dead, dead.* Grandma's words, which had always sealed each biography, repeated in my head like the drops of rain against the steel train.

How many seats could we have filled on each Passover had none of this happened? How many doors could my extended family have opened for Eliyahu had Hitler lost power in 1940 or '41? But instead, my relatives went by train to Treblinka and were shoved into ovens.

I wondered whether they had resisted. Had any of them been gunned down instead? Died heroically? Foolishly? How many of them had been sent to their deaths by train? Down these tracks?

I looked down the empty rail line as if Treblinka stood, working, in the distance. A black cloud sat as if in a transparent urn in the sky, one that had been stuffed with the human smoke of lost generations.

Families are supposed to grow.

How could one forgive?

I grabbed Gabriela's hand much too tightly. We walked toward the town center, which consisted of two small streets lined with empty shops. Otwock, still, was larger than I had imagined; the village sprawled in all directions. The likelihood of finding Podmiejska or Berka Joselewicza without a map would have been difficult, especially since I wanted to avoid conversation as much as possible.

Berka Joselewicza, sure, you just head past the unmarked mass grave of the exterminated kikes and then hug a left down the path that we constructed with the bricks from the synagogue we tore down. You can't miss it beside the still-burning Torahs.

We entered the post office.

"Do you have a town map?" I asked the woman behind the counter.

She offered a queer glance and moved to the back office, out of sight. She returned with a postmaster, or maybe she was in charge but only he could speak English. His tiny-framed glasses pinched at his nose. The lenses weren't much bigger than his eyes.

"Ehh. Ehh," he began, warming up to speak a language that was rarely used outside of Warsaw and Krakow. "You will find . . . ehh . . . not many people speak the English here . . . ehh . . . What do you look for?" He adjusted his glasses.

"Do you have a map of the town? Or maybe some sort of brochure?"

"This is small town . . . Not much to see. Really. Warsaw more to see."

I blanked on the street names and had to remove the piece of paper from my pocket. "Where is Berka Joselewicza Street?"

"That street is not in Otwock," he said without pause.

"My grandmother used to live on that street, here, in Otwock." I wouldn't allow him to deny her that.

He waved for the paper. I hesitated before handing it over. He scrunched his face to better study the scrap, which also held the names of infamous camps and ghettos. He stopped reading and looked up to consider something. "This was before war then, yes?"

I didn't respond. I scanned the glass to find the reflection of the Poles behind me. I expected an uprising. Or at least the gangs that had long ago waited outside of my grandparents' homes with sacks, eager to lay claim to the left-behind valuables while the Jews were marched to the square and shipped to the chimneys of Treblinka or raced into the forests to be gunned down into mass graves.

In the glass, I spotted a mother rocking her newborn.

Still, my heart raced. The postmaster awaited my answer.

"Yes," I said. "Before the war. She lived on that street before the war."

We stared at each other, not unlike the face-offs that Poppy would initiate with another survivor in the Miami card rooms when three clubs sat open on the table and the pot was rich with crumpled bills and rolls of quarters.

There was a long pause. He was hard to read.

"Well . . . ehh . . . this I am sorry for, but many streets in Otwock changed names after war."

The word "sorry" hit me like a quick jab. Just to hear that word from his lips floored me, even if he were apologizing only for the town's amendments to street names. I cleared my throat. "How about Podmiejska street? Does that still exist?"

"Katrina," he yelled. A mail clerk shuffling through letters at a back counter looked up. "Ulica Podmiejska?"

She shrugged.

The young mother leaned over me and spoke to the postman, seemingly perturbed that she had to wait this long for stamps with a baby in her arms.

Jewish infants didn't have to wait, I considered explaining to her. *They were tossed into the air and used as target practice. Your baby should enjoy the gift of waiting. The gift of time.*

"This woman says that you must go a few blocks down that way," the postman said. The woman with the crying baby smiled at me. "Take a left . . . and then you see Podmiejska on the right. Good luck."

I was chagrined. I left the post office, folding my paper and tucking it into my pocket.

"What did you find out?" Gabriela asked.

"That the postmen in Otwock don't know the location of any of the streets."

We opened our one umbrella and walked down the paved road, which brought us to a dirt path. The street sign for Podmiejska was hidden beneath an overgrown tree.

"This was his street. Poppy's street." I was stunned that I was actually standing at the mouth of Podmiejska. For a good ten seconds, I could only stare down the dirt road and watch the puddles jump with rain. Poppy had played soccer as a kid, and I pictured him dribbling his way around each of the puddles as his Polish neighbors chased after him, hurling insults and rocks.

Gabriela wrapped her arm around my hip and we tucked beneath the umbrella as we traversed Podmiejska.

The first few houses looked war-torn—abandoned and leaning. But as we continued down the muddy path, the homes grew more lavish, with flowering gardens that led up to antebellum porches. It felt like a Polish Savannah or an anti-Semitic Charleston.

Otwock had been 75 percent Jewish just before the war. Then fourteen thousand Jews had been removed like a tattoo, which at first appears everlasting, but can actually be reduced to an unwanted memory.

Podmiejska 12 stood behind a fence.

"Is this it?" Gabriela asked.

"Poppy lived in a small, two-bedroom house." I wasn't sure how I knew that. But I knew it, and the detail about that dwelling was clear to me. The home before us stood two stories high. The lot for Podmiejska 10 was empty. Two elderly women in straw hats and raincoats pruned the hedges at number fourteen. They looked old enough to have memories of the 1930s.

"Excuse me," I said through the fence. One of the women retreated to the porch. *Do I look familiar to you?*

Her sister, her friend, her co-conspirator hesitated before approaching the gate.

"Can you tell me—?"

She interrupted me with a thrust of her hedge clippers, pointing the tool toward a house across the street, where two men worked on the siding of a house. One hammered at the façade from the eighth step of a ladder; the second kept it balanced and shouted up instructions.

"I'm looking for—"

But again she cut me off, stabbing at the air with her clippers. She appeared sad and uncertain, dubious and concerned. Maybe even scared. Should I even be sorry for that?

The old woman backed away from the fence, the clippers against her body and stationed between us.

I crossed the street and addressed the man at the base of the ladder. "Do you speak English?"

"Yes, of course," he said. "Are you from America?"

I nodded.

"How are you today? My name is Teddy." He spoke as though he had expected us. Teddy extended a hand.

I hesitated, but took his hand.

He removed his glasses, dried the lenses on his wet shirt, and raked fingers through his spiky black hair. "What brings you to Otwock?"

I looked back toward Podmiejska 12. The women at number 14 still studied us from their porch.

"My grandparents are from Otwock."

"Where do they live?" Teddy asked.

"My grandfather used to live on this street. At number 12."

"Number 12 is just there," Teddy said, smiling as if he had just solved all of our problems. But the grin receded within seconds, understanding that I was unsatisfied with that number 12. "You must understand, however, that the homes were much more spread out then. You see, I must assume that they lived here many years ago or else maybe I would know them and know of their American grandchildren. This is a very small city. We talk. And I don't think the people at number 12 have American relatives. Yes?"

I nodded.

"You see," he continued, "when new homes were added to Otwock they redistributed the numbers. So your grandfather's number 12 might be where, say, number 20 or 22 is now. You see? Where was your grandmother's street?"

"She lived at 15 Berka Joselewicza. But the man in the post office said that the street no longer exists."

"Please wait here," Teddy said. "I will check with my wife and grandmother to see if they know anything about Berka Joselewicza."

Teddy ran into the house. I looked up at the man on the ladder. He nodded and attempted a smile. Only half of his mouth cooperated, and the effort to be gregarious caused him to grunt. The rain intensified. Teddy was being so kind that I became immediately suspicious. I had heard stories about Jews returning to Poland after the war to reclaim their homes. The Poles had murdered these Jews to keep what they had stolen. Maybe Teddy had heard those stories, too.

After a few minutes had passed, I whispered to Gabriela, "We should go." I hadn't meant to put her in this position. I grabbed for her hand and then the screen door crashed open. I jumped. Teddy looked like he was carrying papers to fuel a bonfire. In his forearms, he held maps, brochures, and magazines.

"I woke up grandmother and she said that Berka Joselewicza was a Jewish area of the town."

We were outed. I had taught Gabriela enough about my grandparents' pasts and what life had been like for the Jews in Poland. She knew to squeeze tight.

"But you must understand," Teddy began, seemingly unfazed or too far removed to make the connection. "After the Nazis sent the Jews out from Otwock, the street names changed. Especially many of the streets in the Jewish area of town. I'm sorry. That is why it is not familiar to me." He tucked the papers under one arm like a haphazard scientist who would always lose much of his data to disorganization, and then Teddy attempted to unfold a map by shaking it open like a fan. "Here, you may take this map," he said after failing to whip it open.

I unfolded it and studied Otwock beneath the umbrella. The first thing I saw was the thin black train line.

"We are here." Teddy positioned a wet finger on Podmiejska and then planned our route, a wet little path that he had dragged across the paper. "I think here they can give you further information. Maybe you can check this place. We call it the Jewish Center."

The Jewish Center? Were there still Jews in Otwock? Or would we encounter pyramids of Jewish skulls and Semitic femurs like the structures built at Kutná Hora's bone church?

After each recommendation, Teddy would consult the man on the ladder. Each time, the man shrugged and smiled gutturally.

"If you would like, I can ask grandmother questions about your grandfather. But she must come downstairs first. Now I cannot because she is getting some rest. Can you describe him for me?"

I thought about Poppy and almost began by describing the old man, the one who had outlived his entire family by nearly sixty years. Then I realized that I needed to describe him as a boy, the way an old Polish woman may have remembered him. But I knew little of that child. "He had four sisters," I began, "and he was the only boy in his family. His name was Leon Lederman. His father, Samuel, worked as a *shochet*—that's a kosher butcher. His mother's name was Shindel. They're all dead. Only he survived."

"They were a Jewish family?" Teddy asked.

I thought Teddy had understood that when he pronounced Berka Joselewicza a Jewish street and when I had said "kosher butcher." But now he was asking for confirmation. Gabriela held the umbrella so that I couldn't see the man on the ladder. There was no hammering and no grunt. I swallowed and prepared.

"They were a Jewish family," I said, my body tense.

Silence. I didn't know what to expect.

"Grandmother is old now. Eighty-six. When she comes downstairs I will ask her what she knows." Hammering recommenced. "Hopefully she remembers something of this family. Maybe you come back later and we can see if she knows of them. Good luck in your search. Please see what they can tell you in the town hall."

Teddy pointed it out on the map. We walked to the town hall first.

"Teddy seemed nice," Gabriela said.

"I know." Even I could sense the confusion in my voice. Regardless, I walked around Otwock with one rule in place: Everyone was an anti-Semite until they weren't. This distrust felt like home, like chicken soup and kreplach. Now that I was in my grandparents' Poland, it was uncanny to think that I had spent the previous year free of leeriness.

The town hall was a mansion set back from a simple garden. The former bedrooms had been transformed into offices crammed with filing cabinets and poorly positioned desks, the latter of which had been inundated with papers that would most likely never see the insides of those filing cabinets.

"My family used to live here," I said to one of the town hall employees, pointing to Podmiejska on the map. "Number 12, and my grandmother lived at 15 Berka Joselewicza. Their names were Lederman and Zylberberg."

The woman lifted her eyes from the map and signaled to me with pursed lips that she would not be able to assist in this task. I explained my story three more times and each Polish secretary made their countenance tighter. Their English was poor; my Polish was nonexistent.

The dead Ledermans and Zylberbergs, the lost homes, the missing streets, and the wet Americans had turned into actual water-cooler conversation, which Gabriela and I could observe through the window. The women filled their mugs and either laughed or pointed or shook their heads as if the windows in this town hall were transparent on only our side and the women had always thought they had the privacy of walls. Gabriela sat beneath a rattling air-conditioner unit and clutched her arms, which were wrapped in her soaked turquoise sweatshirt.

"I'll get you to the beach again," I told Gabriela, which was where we had been traveling in the weeks before eastern Europe.

"Don't worry." She shivered. "We just spent two months doing beaches. I don't mind. I want you to find something. I just don't want you to be so mad."

"I'm not mad," I said.

"Baby. I can see it. Poland makes you furious."

I pulled at my face as if it were that easy to loosen the anger and then leaned in to kiss her.

Two of the women who had the misfortune of being assigned to my query returned to the hallway. They explained things in tag-team broken English, but spent most of the time arguing and pointing over each other's shoulders as if the requested files were simply in the cabinets behind them, perfectly labeled, waiting for the third generation to reclaim this lost history. Twenty minutes of debate, which transformed into a pure Slavic shouting match, petered out when a third employee entered the cramped corridor. One of the original two ladies took this new arrival's presence as a cue to leave. This third woman delivered a paper and then marched off.

"There is no much we can do," said the last of the Polish secretaries, who tugged nervously on the crucifix hanging from her neck. "We no have many records. The street you . . . you . . . desire, Berka Joselewicza, no exist."

"There must be some records that explain what happened to the street. Maybe one that explains what it became."

"We have war," she reminded me, as though it had been her people who had suffered most.

"Are there records of the people who lived in Otwock before the war?"

"No. None."

Town hall had no records of the town. The post office needed help from the locals to locate streets. Otwock was a shitstorm.

Outside, the rainstorm increased as we traveled away from the little city center, toward the Jewish Center, a place on the map that now bubbled up from Teddy's wet fingerprint. Tall pines lined the barren road and railway tracks.

An old man walked toward us and into a puddle. He reminded me of cousin Helen, wandering Brooklyn in her nightgown when the Alzheimer's had worsened. Innocent and lost. But then he also fit the description of the Christian boys who, decades ago, had shouted at Poppy, "Dirty fucking Jew!" One of the old boys who had thrown rocks at my grandparents as they walked home from *yeshiva*. The boys who had accused my family of the bloodletting of Christians for the preparation of matzos.

Who had this man been all those years ago?

"Do you know the Jewish Center?" I asked him as he stumbled past.

The old man ignored me. I repeated the question. He moved slightly quicker. Maybe his mind was gone. Or deaf. Or perhaps he always suspected that the grandchildren would return.

"Do you know Leon Lederman?" I asked as he shambled off, speaking more to the rain than to this witness who would forever be fleeing the scene. "Hadasa Zylberberg?" It came out as a whisper. Nobody cared.

Gabriela tugged at my sleeve. "Maybe you *should* take me to the beach."

I watched him vanish into the forest. We continued through the storm.

"Is that the Jewish Center?" Gabriela pointed to a fenced-in building. We studied the soaked map and moved toward what looked like a haunted mansion.

"I'm looking for any information about the Jews who lived in Otwock before the war," I said to an attendant in the lobby of the building. The floorboards creaked.

He led me over to a small plaque that paid tribute to an American who had helped the Jews during the war. After we had read the small sign, the attendant asked me to follow him into the living room.

Three disheveled couches sat in a semicircle in the middle of the large space. Four infirm residents occupying the cushions stared up, perhaps at the cloud of dust overhead.

Our presence attracted more of the elderly who had been camped out in the adjacent activity room. In they came: the scuffing walker wheels, the rickety wheelchairs, the clinking canes. I repeated my grandparents' surnames and the streets they had lived on to each of the new arrivals. I provided biographies. But there was nothing.

"Are any of you Jewish?" I asked, hoping that I had stumbled upon a colony of survivors. But the dozen or so residents shook their heads or appeared uncertain about the question, as if memories of the Jews had been the first part of their minds to go.

"I think this is more like an old-age home," Gabriela decided. "I don't know why Teddy called it the Jewish Center."

Over the next half hour, I discovered that the only thing Jewish about the Jewish Center was the little plaque's mention of the religion, and that was it. The Jews were like a mythical race of people that had roamed the land with the earliest Homo sapiens.

"What is it you are doing here?" asked a new entrant into the circle. She wore a long floral housedress beneath a white sweater and had a chain of fake pearls draped around her neck. "Do you have grandparents here?"

"They used to live here. Leon Lederman and Hadasa Zylberberg." I thought about what else I could remember about my lightning-struck family tree. "My grandmother's father was called David Havala even though he was born David Zylberberg." His mother's surname, Havala, had carried more weight. "He sold to the fishmongers in the Otwock market. My grandmother's grandfather was Meyer Szlama Kaufman. They owned a lot of property."

"Speak louder. We can't hear you," the old woman in the pearls said.

Everyone nodded or shrugged or smiled. We thanked them for their time and walked back toward the train.

"You always said you didn't know much about your grandparents. I think you know a lot more about your grandparents than you thought," Gabriela said.

"My father sent me a second e-mail with a few names and occupations. But I wish I knew more."

Our umbrella flipped inside out, the metal frame bending and snapping with the strength of the wind. The rain intensified, and we took shelter in a cemetery. Every stone had a cross and a Polish name.

When we left the cemetery, we walked a few blocks and stopped at Ulica John Lennon.

"That's funny," I said.

"What is?" asked Gabriela.

"Otwock chose to name a street after a man who sang about peace, love, and karma."

"Do you believe in karma?"

"I wish it were that easy."

We sang a few Beatles songs to make the hike back less cold and wet and terrible.

"You know, my father's favorite band was the Beatles when he was growing up," I said after we finished a hit from Abbey Road. "He and his friends had been driving around when 'Hey Jude' came on the radio for the first time. Their jaws dropped. They had misheard the lyrics and thought that even the Beatles were anti-Semitic. That's what it was like to have parents who survived the Holocaust, I guess. The children were always in fear that the Jew-haters were everywhere. And the grandchildren were always asking for the stories."

"Well, walking through the past and searching for answers is *not* what most grandchildren of survivors would do," Gabriela said. "I'm proud of you, baby." She kissed me.

I accepted the kiss, but figured that she was wrong.

Before we reached the station, we happened upon Podmiejska again. "Let's walk it one more time," I said.

This time the puddles were deeper, the gardening ladies had vanished, and Teddy's ladder was packed away.

I stood before Podmiejska 12 and knew that it had no connection to Poppy's family. Not this new house. Not this plot of land.

"Hey," someone shouted. Teddy stood beneath the trellised entrance to his home and waved for us to navigate the moat that divided the street. "Come for tea."

We ran for the shelter that he had offered, enticed by the thought of something warm. It all happened very quickly before it hit me: I was standing in a Polish home on the street where Poppy had been the target. Or maybe it was a Jewish home that Teddy's family had occupied after the liquidation of 1942.

"You are soaked." Teddy laughed as our wetness painted his foyer's orange tiles a deep red. "How did your search go? Was the map useful?"

Gabriela waited for me to answer, but when I didn't, she said, "We didn't find much."

Teddy seemed disappointed, puckering his lips and pulling at his chin.

I was confounded. Here was a man who had provided us with books and maps, smiles and reassurances, and now shelter and tea. Yet he had also sent us to town halls without records and Jewish centers without Jews.* I couldn't decide whether he was genuine or not. Maybe he was Otwock's diverter, some esteemed position that had been held ever since the Holocaust to flummox returning Jews.

"Hmm." Teddy continued to rub his chin, nonplussed. "Come take off these wet sweaters and join me and my wife in the kitchen."

In the kitchen, Teddy's wife nodded and smiled from the stove. Behind her legs hid their daughter, who peeked through the space between her mother's thighs.

---

* While there was no Jewish Center, there was a small museum on the outskirts of town with a modest section dedicated to the Jews who had once lived in Otwock. I only learned about the museum years later as I researched the town. Interestingly, in the 1990s, a few years before my visit, the museum had been housed in the town hall, though clearly none of the women working there in 2004 remembered it. And none of the locals on the streets seemed to know about the museum either.

"Here. Please," the woman finally said.

"She does not speak English well," Teddy said. "Sorry."

"We don't speak Polish well," Gabriela replied.

Teddy's wife knew enough English to smile at the comment. She poured us tea. A plate of cookies sat in the center of the table. Teddy disappeared upstairs.

"How old is your daughter?" Gabriela asked.

"She is three."

The little girl gave her age in Polish and held up the appropriate number of fingers, but kept herself shielded with her mother's legs.

We ate the cookies and clutched the mugs. Gabriela continued to make headway with Teddy's wife. I wondered whether there had even been a point to this day. Was it to prove to myself that my grandparents and their people had been erased from the land? Was I looking for a Teddy—someone to pin my hopes to—a Pole who could assuage my anger and confusion?

"This is Grandmother," Teddy said, returning to the kitchen with a woman who was bent so far forward that she must have worked the fields for the majority of her life. Teddy held his hands out in case she fell. She batted him away, determined to reach the kitchen table on her own. "She wanted to come down and meet you."

The grandmother kept her gaze to the floor, seemingly eyeing us with the bald spot in the center of her white crown. She took a deep breath and jumped right into her story. Teddy bent closer to hear her faint voice, one as emotionless as a court reporter reading back pages of a transcript.

"Okay, Grandma. Okay." Teddy wanted her to slow down so that he could listen and translate. But the grandmother would not pause. So Teddy translated quickly. "She says that this house here, which she was born in, is now Podmiejska twenty-one, but it used to be Podmiejska nine." He stopped to listen. "She thinks that Podmiejska number twelve was the one up the road, which I will take you to shortly." More listening. "She also says that she remembers a man, a butcher, who lived there. She says the family had many children and there were animals in the yard."

I stood up; so did my eyebrows. "They had German shepherds and sometimes there were animals brought to the house to be butchered. He was the kosher slaughterer."

"Grandmother says that the last person who lived there has died. Sometime last year. The house has been empty since."

The grandmother stopped speaking, and Teddy placed his hand on her trembling shoulder. He whispered into her ear, but she shoved him softly and continued.

"Grandmother also wants me to tell you that she feels very bad about what happened here. She wants you to know that she feels very terrible for the past."

I had always wondered how I would feel if a Pole apologized to me, specifically for the treatment of the Jews. But what does one do with an apology? If I took it back to Brooklyn, I could only imagine Grandma swatting at the words, as if they flew at her like malarial mosquitoes. It wasn't my place to accept apologies, not for the dead and not for the survivors who lived with the dead and the memories. Maybe if Teddy's Polish family had been our neighbors in the States, we would have grown to become good friends. But not here. Never here. I looked at the grandmother; I couldn't tell what was genuine. Her words could have belonged to a guilty soul. Anger stood its ground as a safeguard. Blame was a reminder.

Still, I smiled at the old woman, appreciatively.

All was quiet. Then the grandmother lifted her head, revealing her eyes for the first time: blue rings blurried by tears and cataracts. She spoke again.

"Grandmother says that she and grandfather used to sneak food to the Jews in the ghetto. She wants you to know this."

I wanted to believe her. But if I were an old Pole and a Jew came back to Otwock and sat in my kitchen, searching for answers, I'd say that as well.

"Please, give me your contact information." Teddy handed me his e-mail address. "This is mine. I have a friend who is a historian of Otwock, and maybe he can help you in your search. So you contact me upon your return home and I will e-mail him."

Meanwhile, the grandmother had shuffled out from the room. Teddy signaled for us to follow. Beside the foyer, as she readied herself for the ascent to the second floor, the old woman whispered something into Teddy's ear.

"She wants you to have this," Teddy said. The little woman handed us an umbrella. She smiled at the giving of such odd reparations, turned to go upstairs, took a half-step, but withdrew her foot, returning it to the tiled floor. Enervated by the past, I guessed, the old woman returned to the kitchen instead.

"I want to take you first to a Jewish cemetery, the one that I know of in Karczew," Teddy explained. "Then we will come back to where I believe your grandfather's house once stood."

We got into Teddy's sedan and drove a few blocks, but the road to Karczew had flooded. Though I never visited Karczew, a gentleman I had conversed with on JewishGen—one of the websites I had used to conduct my search for family and facts—sent me photographs of the cemetery a few years after I had returned from Poland. Broken and ransacked tombstones stood among a sea of litter.

We returned to Podmiejska, and Teddy pulled up alongside a fence.

"This is the property where grandmother says your grandfather's house was."

A squat home of brick and yellowed concrete stood at the corner of Podmiejska and a second dirt road. All of its windows were boarded up.

"May I?"

"Please. Take as long as you would like. Nobody lives there so you may go onto the property. I will wait here," Teddy said.

"I'll wait, too," said Gabriela.

I opened the car door and stepped into the downpour. Gripping the fence, I hopped over it and stood in the small yard. The property, fifty by twenty-five feet, had a bulwark of pine trees to one side and two small apple trees between the house and the evergreens. The apple trees had littered the lawn with rotten fruit. I tried the door, but it was locked. I thought about kicking it in so that I could explore inside. But this was Poland, and I was a Jew, and I imagined tomorrow's headlines in the local Polish news: *Jew Ransacks Home of Deceased Polish Woman.* So I just stood in the middle of the wet lawn, beside the apple tree, and then bent down, plunging my fingers into the soil. I plucked up a black stone and let the rain chip away at the mud concealing it. Part of the rock crumbled in my grasp, as though it had been eroding in this mound of soil for eons. It was a stone that Poppy could have used to defend himself against his neighbors, the ones who had hurled rocks at him.

I looked out at Podmiejska and imagined him as a boy, running in the rain, which fell now like rocks from an army of gentiles. I saw Poppy station himself beneath the apple tree and dig up stones while his four sisters stood in the doorway, berating and admiring their only brother. A mother at work over the stove for what could have been the last cholent, the last Shabbat. A father who had taught his boy how to hold the *hallaf*, the *shochet's* blade. Who knew that one day this would become a tool in the boy's profession, work that would allow him to make a life in America, work that would allow his family to grow and to return to Poland? To stand on his property under an apple tree, where it all began?

But for what? Why was I even here? Poppy was dead. And Grandma begged Death to remove her from this life, pulling the Holocaust into the tomb with her. What would I even gain from this moment? From Teddy's kindness? From his grandmother's words?

I placed the brittle stone in my pocket, spent a few more weeks visiting concentration camps and ghettos, took Gabriela to the shores of Poland, as promised, and then left Europe so that I could stand with my father in a Queens cemetery in front of Poppy's tombstone.

9

FROM NIGHT TO DAWN

"This is really from Poppy's yard?" Dad kept asking, amazed by the stone that he rolled in his palm, inspecting it, wondering whether it were even rock because it had cleaved again. Beneath his graying beard, Dad's lips curled into a sad smile. He placed one of the stone halves into his pocket and the other atop Poppy's grave. He spoke to the tombstone. "From Otwock, Dad."

I picked up another rock, this one from Queens, from the grass beside Poppy's burial site and placed it next to the soft stone from Otwock. My fingers read the biography carved into the headstone and followed the lines that made up the Star of David. The star encapsulated the words HOLO-CAUST SURVIVOR. I dragged my hand from Poppy's epitaph to the smooth half of the gravestone left blank for Grandma.

"She still cries nonstop," Dad said.

The only thing she looked forward to was having her date and name and little Jewish Star with those survivor credentials etched onto the gray rock beside Poppy's details. It was September 2004, nearly four years after his death, and Death had postponed her requested appointment.

"What were the people like in Otwock?" Dad asked.

I thought for a long moment as to how I would answer that question. On the way home from Poland, I had decided that they were mostly good. After all, Teddy had been nothing but helpful, and none of the others—albeit few—who discovered that I was Jewish caused me any problems. I felt foolish to have judged a people because of the things my grandparents had taught me, even though I couldn't blame Poppy or Grandma for their animosity.

But when I returned home, I visited the Otwock website. Entire paragraphs had been devoted to the city's beauty and advancements: the railway lines that opened Otwock to greater Poland, the appeal of the sanatoriums, and the apple orchards. But there was no mention of the railway lines that sent eight thousand Jewish residents to Treblinka. The Holocaust, which completed the anti-Semitic gentrification of Otwock, had been boiled down to one sentence on the site: *The years of the Second World War brought the extermination of the Jews, who in 1939 made up 75% of the population in Otwock, and a good percentage of the inhabitants in the surrounding areas.*

Words of the diverter.

I had circled the mouse over Otwock's coat of arms—some chimerical pure white eagle merged with a spinning snake in a silver goblet. It was an odd choice for a symbol. What did it imply: that it was a city of crafty citizens who benefited from a purified Otwock and looted fortunes?

I wondered whether Teddy and his grandmother were just trying to sell me on a lie. Anyway, how was I to exonerate a people when only a few residents knew that I was Jewish? Maybe the pitchfork shed had been locked that day. Or there was just too much rain to light the torches. Or perhaps the arrival of the lone Jew to Otwock was now regarded as some momentous event, in the way that the return of the pesky cicada excites more than only naturalists every seventeen years. Maybe the residents who had missed my visit bought their 2021 calendars in advance, so as not to miss the next visit.

I wanted to be wrong about the Polish people. Travel was meant to make people better. And that better part of me—the one who had just seen the world—knew that blaming Poles for the errors of their forefathers was wrong. But in the cemetery, as I stood before the words HOLOCAUST SURVIVOR, there was no *better part of me*. I was much more like the person my grandparents had taught me to be. And that was better than being dead.

"The people in Otwock," I began. "They were Poles."

My father looked around at the enormity of the cemetery and then studied his father's gravestone. "After I was born, Poppy left the butcher shop and went into real estate." Dad's voice was distant. I could tell that something reminded him of a story. "He was putting up new properties all over Brooklyn, and they were doing well for a while. We even bought a nice house, one that his company built, in East Flatbush. But there was war in Asia and the housing market went bad. His partners went behind his back and declared bankruptcy. Poppy lost everything. He had a lot of bad luck in business. I remember he used to joke that he could start a funeral home and everyone would stop dying."

I looked around at all the dead Jews.

"Every time we speak about Poppy, you seem to come up with another story. I thought you didn't have any more."

"I didn't," Dad replied. "But you went to Poland and I started remembering things."

Poland. The word was new to our vocabulary. Mentioning it would have made Poppy's blood boil. But now it was a conduit into memory.

"What else did Poland unearth for you?"

"We used to live on Rutland Road, in a Lefrak building—he's a Jew, by the way, Lef-rack, even though everyone pronounces his name like he's some French gentile, Le Fraq. I used to complain to Grandma that I was bored. She would tell me, 'You're bored? I didn't eat. And you're bored. Everyone's dead and you're bored. Go play outside.' So I went out to this communal patio in the back of our building and rode my bike, played handball, things a kid would do. But we had this piece-of-shit neighbor on the third floor. His window overlooked the patio, and one day he shouts down to me, 'The Germans should have finished the job they started.'" My father smirked at the affront.

"What did you do?"

"What did I do? I was a kid. I ran in and told Poppy." Dad pointed to his father's grave as if I could have forgotten the story's protagonist. "Ooh, he was pissed. He went outside and started yelling up to the guy. 'Come down and say it to my face.' But the neighbor wasn't that stupid and just taunted Poppy from his window." Dad stopped and grinned. "But, a few days later, Poppy walked into our apartment smiling. He had run into that neighbor in the elevator."

Shivahs and cemeteries brought Poppy to life. Or at least the Poppy I had always wanted to know.

"We should go," Dad said, looking at his watch. "Grandma's excited to see you."

The ride down the Belt Parkway was endless traffic, but the trip through Brooklyn was a journey into Dad's childhood. Into the extinct Brooklyn butcheries that Poppy returned to after his real estate business busted. Remembering, the old smell of blood and knives rekindled new stories. He opened up stores in Brownsville and then another one on Lincoln and Flatbush—A&L Butchers—named for the two survivors who went into business together. Archie and Leon.

"One of my favorite Poppy stories," Dad began, "took place at A&L. This guy walks into his shop and pulls a knife on Poppy. He tells him, 'Give me the money from the register.' Poppy says to him, 'You should have come in with a gun,' and then pulls out a cleaver, jumps the counter, and chases the guy down Flatbush Avenue."

I let the scene play out. Poppy: bloody apron, blade high over his head, a lion's smirk. The man with the knife: a doppelganger of the Poles who had sold out his family and delivered them to the ovens of Treblinka for a few potatoes.

10

PEERING INTO THE VAULT

The first Passover after burying Poppy, Grandma had reserved an empty place setting for him at the head of the table. His supposed presence overshadowed Eliyahu from the beginning; we didn't even bother to open the door that year. When the meal arrived, Grandma set Poppy's photograph before the soup, and when she had to use the bathroom, she dragged the image of her dead husband along for the ride.

"Mom," my father begged, "Daddy doesn't want to see you go to the bathroom."

"Sha! Quiet. He does what I want," she hollered.

"At least now it's without objection," Dad told the rest of us.

After that Seder, Grandma stopped cooking completely.

"Who should I cook for? Poppy's dead."

We grandchildren were all slightly offended.

That was four years earlier, when the depression occupied her heart like an open wound. While it had been evident that each of us thought we were Poppy's favorite grandchild, most would happily concede that I was Grandma's. The other grandchildren got annoyed with her noodging; I never tired of it and instead found that the *kvetching* was a source of both humor and love. When Grandma had cooked, I was also the last to say that I was full. That earned me points as well. Certainly, I thought, my return after fifteen months overseas would have some positive effect on Grandma's mood.

I buzzed 15K and rode the elevator to her floor. Grandma met me at the door. She poked her head out into the hallway, opening the door just enough to hug me and kiss me and allow me to enter. It was as if she were trying to contain Poppy's spirit.

"*Oy* Noiach, I missed you. You had time to visit Poppy." Saying "Poppy" had brought tears to her eyes and cracked her voice with conspicuous sadness. She collapsed into the melancholy that I had left behind more than a year before. Nothing had changed.

Grandma looped her arm through mine, and I led her back to the kitchen table, where Poppy stood in his frame. He also still dangled in the gold around her neck. His blue eyes and lion's smirk shone.

"Where's your father?" Grandma asked.

"He's parking the car," I said.

She shrugged as if she knew his plan: delaying arrival by parking far and taking the long route down the boardwalk.

"Grandma has no food for you," she reminded me. The faithful pot of chicken soup simmering on the stove and the purple jar of horseradish that stood guard beside the pool of gefilte fish had long vanished from her apartment.

"Don't worry, Grandma. I just wanted to see you. I missed you."

"You still should eat."

My father arrived. Within ten minutes, he had opened all the mail and written the two checks for both bills, guiding Grandma's hand so that the pen rattled along the signature line.

"Look how I shake, Noiach. Ever since Poppy . . ." The name Poppy caused her to blare. It cut short the rest of her sentence.

"Your hands always shook, Mom." Dad began pacing the apartment, already preparing to leave.

"Look," she said, holding up her trembling hands like evidence at a trial.

"They shook when dad was alive, too."

"*Oyyyyyyyy*. Now the shaking is worse. Noiach, I swear."

"I believe you," I told her.

My father looked at his wristwatch. "I can't do this for an hour." He walked out onto the terrace.

While Grandma regained her composure, I went into her bedroom and revisited the familiar faces of my murdered family above the light switch. I could not imagine living Grandma's life. Death after death after death . . . a spell of happiness . . . and familiar death once more. And then she herself, the woman who willed her own demise, could not die.

"Can I tell you about my trip?" I asked Grandma when I returned to the table.

"Forty-nine minutes," my dad shouted from the terrace, counting down that which remained of our visit.

"Were you safe?" she asked.

"I was safe."

"Did you eat well?"

"Not as well as I eat here." I poked her in the arm a few times and gave her my favorite-grandchild smile.

"Grandma don't cook anymore. You Poppy's dead," she reminded me.

"I know, Grandma. Not as good as I *once ate* here."

"Do you remember Poppy?"

"Of course I remember Poppy."

"He's dead." She let out another whimper.

My father came back inside and flipped through the bills just in case he had missed anything. He could think of nothing worse than returning outside of a scheduled visit because of an overlooked bill. But after Grandma let out a fifth "*Oy*," Dad slapped his side and banished himself to the terrace for the remainder of our stay. Grandma looked up at me like a helpless animal dying in a trap, shrugged, and then pointed at the picture frame.

There was no more finding humor in her neuroses. This was pure misery. Even I couldn't listen to her grieve for an hour. Not four and a half years after Poppy's death.

I pulled my notebook from my pocket, one that I had filled with questions after visiting the camps and ghettos. The questions, I assumed, would go unanswered. But I wrote them down while in Europe because it was better than allowing them to swim around my mind. I tapped the book's cover.

Would reminding her of a pain so distant be fair, especially now when her entire life was filled with hurt? But then again, how much worse could a life be than the one Grandma was forced to maintain?

"Grandma, did I tell you that I visited Poland? I went to Otwock, Warsaw, and Auschwitz."

Her face stiffened up.

"You went to Otwock?" It was the first time during the whole visit that I had heard her speak without self-pity. She said the name of her former town using that Latin pronunciation with postcard-like flair: *Oat Vox, where the air is pure and serves as a lovely destination for those who need to inhale the freshness of the Swider River.* "Did you see the Umschlagplatz?" Her eyes lit up like a child's who had just inquired about the details of a trip to Disneyland.

"I . . . I saw the Umschlagplatz. You mean the one in Warsaw, right?"

"Of course the one in Warsaw. The Umschlagplatz."

Of all the things she could have wondered about, I had no idea why she chose that site in the Warsaw ghetto, where the Jews had been rounded up for transports and sent to the concentration camps. I had no idea why this place of death had brought a sparkle to her eye.

Grandma smiled. "I can't believe you saw the Umschlagplatz. You know, *tatehla*, this is where I was." She had made this antechamber to the camps seem like the happiest place on earth. And the Umschlagplatz, which gave her pause from mourning Poppy, did, for one brief moment, feel like the grounds of jubilation.

"What do you remember about the Umschlagplatz?" My arms tensed, my fingers gripped the pen. I was ready to write every word.

Her smile faded immediately and she settled her grave eyes upon me. "Many things, Noiach, many things."

I had almost skipped over visiting the site of the Umschlagplatz. It hadn't been on my Warsaw map and on first pass, from across the street, I figured that the white and gray walls of the memorial set like a roofless cattle car was some sort of incomplete strangely designed store. On my second pass, since the sites in the city dedicated to the Jews were few and I was slightly curious about the structure, I crossed the busy road and inspected what turned out to be the memorial.

"Grandma, do you mind if I ask you a few questions?"

"What's to ask?" she said, as if she had grown up during the twentieth century's most uneventful decades.

The Umschlagplatz of Warsaw appeared as if it would serve as our depot into the Holocaust.

After our day in Otwock, Gabriela and I woke the next morning in Warsaw. Gabriela was sick and spent the day in bed. I searched the city for any traces of its annihilated Judaism. But as I had expected, most of Warsaw's Jewish past had been ripped up like uninvited weeds. The ghetto wall, the one that had kept the Jewish population imprisoned in a dismal wasteland, had been dismantled except for one section that stood in the courtyard of an apartment complex like an eroded handball court. More attention, however, was paid to the drying of laundry on the terraces above.

Farther along, I found the large Jewish cemetery. But it was locked. After another twenty minutes of walking, I came across Mila 18, the famous bunker where fighters like Mordechai Anielewicz and some of my grandparents' friends had planned their uprising. All that remained to mark that place of Jewish resistance was a mound of dirt, as if the bodies of those

Jewish rebels had not stopped swelling in the ground. To me it was a miniature Polish Masada.

Despite this proud lump in the earth, I couldn't believe what had been erased. Present-day Warsaw felt similar to what would happen if a church congregation took over a building that once housed a temple. The congregation would whitewash the walls of Semitic symbolism and change out the stained glass for scenes with Christ. Maybe they would overlook a doorframe, unintentionally leaving behind the grimy outline of where a mezuzah once hung. The section of ghetto wall and mound of dirt were those oversights.

There were, however, a few intentionally constructed memorials. Down the block, a cenotaph of Warsaw ghetto fighters stood in a park, where one Pole walked his dog. He stopped beside me as I stared up at the sculpture of men prepared to die. One fighter clutched a homemade bomb; others displayed the countenances of those offering a silent battle cry.*

"Where you from?" the Polish man asked me as his dog sniffed the steps that led up toward the sculpture.

I told him.

"America, heh? You must pay a visit the Stare Miasto tonight. It is the sixtieth anniversary of the Warsaw Uprising. Very proud moment in Warsaw. Very proud."

"Did you say the anniversary of the uprising in Warsaw?" I was stunned.

"Yes, tonight. Very big event in our city." He pulled the beagle's leash, but the dog pulled back. He waited so that the animal could urinate on the monument's steps.

But I pardoned this man's affront to the dead Jews. His tone and the news of the celebration were more important than addressing the disregard he and his dog had for the frozen uprisers.

"They celebrate the Warsaw Ghetto Uprising," I said aloud, shocked that the Jews were not completely forgotten.

Polish couples pushed strollers through the park. I was thrilled that these babies would grow up in a Poland that honored the Jews of the Warsaw ghetto. In the communist gray of the city, I saw sunshine. I felt the fool for having doubted the Poles to such extremes.

---

* It should be noted that in 2013 Warsaw opened an important museum to remember Jewish life in Poland, the anti-Semitism that existed in the country long before the Nazi invasion, and the genocide that took place in Poland and throughout Europe during the Holocaust. The museum stands in the same square as the memorial to the ghetto fighters.

By evening, I arrived at the crowded Stare Miasto. Gabriela stayed back; her cold had worsened.

I stood stunned by the celebration held for the Jews. These people didn't hate the Jews, I realized. Look how they celebrated and remembered what the Warsaw ghetto Jews had tried to accomplish. I swallowed an amalgam of relief, pride, and chagrin.

Families shuttled their children around the statue-filled promenade, explaining the stories connected to the bronze people. Kids in scout uniforms marched with pride. If I had owned a Jewish Star necklace, I would have worn it on the outside of my shirt instead of trying to conceal my identity in Poland.

A mother pointed her little girl's hand toward a statue of a boy wearing a bronze helmet too big for his head. He held a machine gun in his little hands.

"Who is this boy?" I asked the woman, already proud of the story that I had planned to exchange with the child and her mother about the uprisers whom I knew.

"Tell him, sweetie," the Polish mother said to her daughter, having prepared her daughter to pay homage to the Jews.

"That's a boy who was killed for singing songs," the little girl said shyly and then pulled herself into her mother.

I thought up all the songs I had learned in Hebrew school. Had he been singing "Dreidel, Dreidel, Dreidel"? Or maybe a few choruses of "Dayenu"?

"He was killed singing patriotic songs while fighting for Poland in 1944," the girl's mother amended.

1944? I thought. I traveled back along the Holocaust timeline that I had committed to memory. Jews had been removed from Warsaw by April of 1943. By the following year, they were nearly an extinct people in this city, especially by August 1, the date of this Warsawian celebration.

"What exactly are you celebrating today?" I asked.

"Today is the anniversary of when the Poles fought back against the Nazis and pushed them out of the city for good."

All of this—the streamers, the noise, the pride—had nothing to do with the Jews. It was a celebration of a people who had, prior to 1944 and forever after, been indifferent to the fate of the Jews. My heart dropped. That mixture of pride and chagrin and relief had lost its potency and spoiled into a fuel of confusion and hurt and anger.

The mother ushered her little girl on to the next statue.

I never realized that the Poles, who had waited for the Jews to vacate their homes, to leave behind their heirlooms, to bleed out in the ghetto, had finally fought back.

How foolish of me; I had nearly exonerated them in an afternoon. I wanted to go back in time and curse the man for allowing his dog to piss on the statue dedicated to the Jews.

The scouts paraded down the avenue. Candles, flowers, ribbons adorned buildings and fortresses. I exited the Stare Miasto and stopped when I had reached a gate. A garden of red candles had their flames lean with the wind.

A man in his early fifties bent down to light another wick. Grandma had always lit a white *yahrzeit* candle on Yom Kippur for her mother, who had been murdered only miles from this celebration.

"Who did you light the candle for?" I asked as though I were giving one more chance for someone to refute my anger.

"My mother." The man spoke with an American accent. "I come back every year to celebrate this Independence Day. The Nazis imprisoned my mother because she fought for Poland. And you? Any connection to all this?"

I noted my exits and the direction in which the youthful Polish storm troopers marched. The roar of the festivities traveled away from the candles.

"My grandparents fought in the Warsaw *Ghetto* Uprising."

He cleared his throat. "My mother was very fond of Jews. She never saw them as an alien nation. To her they were Polish."

It seemed like the modern thing to say.

How could it have been that every Pole, from Teddy's grandmother to this man's mother, loved the Jews, yet my people were shipped so easily to the gas chambers? Why was it that each time Poppy snuck out of the ghetto and scurried around the streets of Warsaw in search of extra rations, some Pole shouted, "Jew"? How was it that the Polish revolution, honored by the flames we stood before, was delayed until the human smoke of my people became ubiquitous? I didn't repay his words with the same kindness. I couldn't.

Grandma once told me, "A good person is a good person . . . but there is no such thing as a good Polack."

To call Grandma a Pole would have been more degrading than calling her a yid or a kike.

Poppy had always wondered how his own countrymen—even if they had cast the first and second and third stone, even if they had called him "dirty fucking Jew," even if they had despised his people—could help send his four sisters, his father, his mother, his entire extended family, which did not exist over any light switch because no pictures of them remained, into the fires of Treblinka. His neighbors had ratted them all out to the Germans in exchange for a sack of potatoes and a few sips of schnapps. That had fueled the pilot light of Poppy's hatred.

The gentleman who honored his mother stood beside me as we watched the flames leap into the sky of Warsaw.

"You Poppy was at the Umschlagplatz, too," Grandma remembered as I read through my questions.

If the utterance of "Umschlagplatz" had pried open the Holocaust vault, the mention of Poppy threatened to slam it shut. I chose a question at random to change the subject.

"Grandma, did you ever spend any time in the Pawiak Prison?"

"I was never there."

I had figured this much as the prison was mainly for non-Jews. But it moved us away from the P-word.

"When I was in the Warsaw ghetto I walked through this park—"

"There were no parks in the ghetto," Grandma said, irritated. *What do you think the Holocaust was? Parks? The Holocaust wasn't a game of running bases.*

"I know there were no parks . . . I mean, now there is a park."

Grandma shook her head as if the rubble of the Warsaw ghetto still smoldered and the disease that had festered in that place decades ago forever made the Jewish quarter an untouchable Chernobyl.

"In this park there was this monument that had been dedicated to the Jews who fought in the uprising. It was this enormous bronze relief."

"Relief. *Oy.* This was no relief."

"Grandma. No. You're . . ." I thought of the fallen fighters and the man who clutched a homemade grenade and the others who stood frozen in the *Monument to the Ghetto Heroes*. I would never tell Grandma about the metal panel on the reverse side of the black marble memorial, where a solemn procession marched from the ghetto into the gas chambers. "At this monument, I ran into a group of Israeli soldiers."

Her weak facial muscles tightened slightly into a smile. The name of the Jewish homeland always produced at least a split-second respite from her misery. But Grandma, the living epitome of irony—a warrior in a housedress, a woman who found comfort in sadness, a survivor begging to die—smiled at the incongruity.

"Israelis? In Poland? Noiach, what should they want with Poland?"

"One of the soldiers told me that they were there to remember. First I met them at Mila 18."

"I have friends who fought with Anielewicz. You know Mordechai Anielewicz?"

I nodded. "Grandma . . . What did you do during the uprising?"

"*Oy.*" She waved off the question with a force that I hadn't seen in years, since lifting her hand to such heights off the table had become a painful chore. "Noiach, what you say to these Israeli soldiers?"

"I told them that I was there remembering my people, too."

"That's nice," Grandma said. "What else these Israelis do?"

"After I saw them at Mila 18, they gathered beneath the Warsaw Ghetto Uprising monument, and a female soldier sang the *Hatikvah.*"

"This is the Israeli national anthem," Grandma said, humming a few bars of the song. "I want to go to Israel after the war. But Poppy did not want to go. He say we go to America. We come by boat. There was such garbage on the shores. Filthy. Maybe if we go to Israel, there be less garbage and maybe Poppy be alive today."

My father had entered the room in time to hear Grandma's last five words, missing all the progress we had made. "He would not be alive today. He had a bad heart. He smoked and he was stressed. Come on, Noah, we need to go."

"He'd be alive today if we go to Israel," Grandma insisted.

"He would have died a young man if he went to Israel," my father replied. "He just survived one war. Do you think he wanted to go and die in another one? You want to go to Israel, Mom, I'll send you to Israel."

"I want to go to Israel with Poppy."

"I don't think they'll let him fly, Mom."

Grandma stroked her shaking fingers across Poppy's face in the frame, as if to shield him from the insult.

"They tried to draft Poppy into the Korean War," Dad said. "You know what he did to avoid that? He convinced the army he was insane. He was not going to fight for Israel. The Holocaust should have been an automatic pass for survivors to avoid the army. They should have been guaranteed a lifetime of peace and happiness."

"No more Poppy," Grandma moaned. "Maybe if we went to Israel, Noiach. Maybe."

"Sure," I said, giving her that.

11

THE TAPES

You see how miserable she is?" Dad said as we merged back onto the Belt Parkway. During the commute east, away from Dad's torment, I could see the drop in blood pressure as evidenced in his face.

"You didn't see her change when we talked about the Umschlag-platz."

He didn't hear me. "She doesn't stop. How long can a person mourn?"

"Where are the tapes?"

"What tapes?"

"The Shoah Foundation tapes. The ones that Steven Spielberg's people recorded back in the nineties. Who has them?"

"That's a good question," Dad said.

On a Sunday afternoon, one decade earlier, my grandparents had to unplug their refrigerator to eliminate the dim hum and disable the clock on the dining room wall so that it would not interrupt their testimonies of what life had been like during the Holocaust. My parents brought me over to see Grandma and Poppy before and after the interview, but during the marathon of questioning, we had to leave the apartment. We spent the day at Astroland Amusement Park and lunched on Nathan's hot dogs; it was an afternoon most kids would covet. For me it was misery. Poppy was back at the apartment revealing his stories about fighting Nazis in Warsaw while I was stuck in the first car of the Cyclone as it was ratcheted up above Coney Island.

Even though the stories had been recorded, as a kid, having never actually seen the tapes, I must have used kid logic and just assumed that the testimonies had been locked in Spielberg's bedroom with his E. T. outtakes. It hadn't occurred to me in all those years to ask to view them. But now, a decade later, I felt the thrill of a detective making headway in a cold case (and also the embarrassment of a dolt who had recognized for the first time that the evidence had been there all along).

"If you want the tapes, call my sister," Dad said as we entered Queens. "She probably has them somewhere."

I called Aunt Anne that evening. Her voice shook like Grandma's hands. "I really can't believe you went to Otwock. And you found Poppy's house. The tapes . . . oh, Noah." Her pause made me worry that the testimony had been destroyed—the tapes split in half in her divorce. "I'll have to look for them. I don't know where they are. Maybe in the closet. I just don't know."

Anne called back an hour later. "I just remembered something, Noah. I never told your father about this and I really don't think you should tell him either. But I wanted to tell you. When I was in the hospital with Poppy, just before he died, there was this painting on the wall. It was a landscape scene. And you know what Poppy said to me? He said that he saw it changing. I asked him what it was changing into." Aunt Anne didn't say anything else.

"What was it changing into, Anne?" I asked.

"Please don't tell your father. I think it will make him really upset. I don't know if I should say this."

In my family, it wasn't *Hey, I know this really good joke, but I can't tell you.* It was *I have this great Holocaust story, but it'll make you a head case like me, so I should just keep it to myself.*

"What did Poppy say?"

"He said that the landscape was changing. It was changing into the SS. Until the day he died, he thought the SS were coming for him. He couldn't stop seeing them. I felt so bad. I couldn't do anything for him. Oh, Noah, I should have asked the hospital to take down the picture. Maybe I should have . . ."

I listened to her compunction and then reminded her to search for the videos. She reminded me that they might be in the closet. I reminded her that the closet was in the next room. She said she would try her best. I said to start with the closet.

I spent the next day in the library, looking through their database for anything with the word *Otwock* in it. I came across a book with an excerpt from the Polish newspaper *Narod*, which means "people." The publication represented the Polish government-in-exile in London during the war, which proclaimed itself to be a politically centrist, liberal, and intellectual government. The article's hook blamed the Jews for "defecating" on Poland with their "Judaization" and accused my people of being ungrateful for Polish hospitality.

"Warsaw will say goodbye to the last Jews . . . would sorrow or tears accompany the coffins, or perhaps joy? . . . Let us not strive for an artificial sorrow for the dying nation [of Jews] that was not close to our hearts," wrote the journalists at *Narod*.

I wondered what the man who stood with me before the red candles would have said had I shown him this piece of Polish sentiment. Or Teddy's grandmother. Or Teddy. I had sent Teddy an e-mail with the information about my family. Back in Otwock, he told me that he would pass it on to his friend, who would be able to uncover facts about my family. It had been a few weeks and I hadn't yet received a reply.

I slipped the book with the *Narod* article back onto the shelf, exchanging it for Emmanuel Ringelblum's renowned account of the Holocaust, *Notes from the Warsaw Ghetto*. On December 31, 1940, he wrote, "Dozens of Jews are going on foot to Otwock and fetching meat back from there. Where exactly they go to . . . no one knows."

Podmiejska Street. It had to be my great-grandfather providing his people with meat despite Nazi decrees that banned a kosher slaughter under penalty of a ten-year prison sentence, which eventually transformed into a penalty of death. I had stood on that lawn, where a brave man had served his people even under penalty of death. To find these potential links back to an erased world made my heart accelerate. I paused to appreciate the rush.

But most of the literature offered little thrill, and it made my heart race for other reasons. I came across pictures of Germans piling onto trains on the first day of September 1939, bearing slogans: *Wir fahren nach Polen um Juden zu versohlen.* Translation: "We are riding to Poland to beat up the Jews." Three weeks later, they had arrived in Otwock and set up a Jewish council and a Jewish police force. I read the memoir *Am I a Murderer?* authored by a Jewish policeman from Otwock. He weighed his guilt as lists of Jews and their properties were collected, as the town was divided into three ghettos, as the raids began, as curfews were enforced, as merchants lay battered in the Otwock market, as orphans were executed, infants tossed into ditches, the sick and disabled slaughtered. He professed his guilt and wondered whether he was a murderer.

Yes, you're a murderer. He—a Jew—had probably shoved my family into the square with his truncheon to wait for the trains to Treblinka. He may have cursed himself as he led my great-aunts into the woods, where the Nazis would shoot them into pits that the Jews dug. "But what choice did I have?" he probably reasoned. *But yes, you're a murderer.*

Typhus spread. The death toll spiked. Carts collected bodies that lay covered under newspapers on Karczewska Street.

"Anne, have you found the tapes?"

"I didn't have a chance yet. I really need to look in that closet."

"It's not like you have to watch the videos. If you find them, I'll pick them up. Get them out of your life immediately."

Still Anne treated those tapes and whatever else lurked in the depths of that closet like an island of lepers.

The year 2004 ended.

"How's you girlfriend?" Grandma asked when I called her to see whether she might have a copy of the tapes.

"What do you think of her?" I asked.

"I like her. She's a very nice girl."

"Well, we actually broke up."

Gabriela decided that she could not make room for two Jews in her life and went with the one from Nazareth.

"Good. What were you gonna do with a *shiksah*? Poppy and I survive the Holocaust and you don't want to marry Jewish. Noiach?"

"Tell me how you really feel."

In 2005, I began work as a publicist. Five months in PR burned me out. I left to join a teaching fellowship program and spent the summer in an educator's boot camp. My typical summer day consisted of three hours of teaching high school kids, six hours of study at university, and four hours of writing papers. With lunch breaks and commuting and trying to live like a twenty-something, I was too exhausted to curl up on the couch at the end of the day with a good book on genocide.

My research into the Holocaust went cold by September. Teaching in a school that required police presence in the hallways to curtail school violence, coaching the school's track team, attending graduate school, and dating my future wife occupied most of my time. When I did visit Grandma with my book of questions, she divulged little, usually asking, "What good will come of these stories?"

But during the summer of 2006, on a surf trip down in Panama, I realized how I could get Grandma to talk.

12

PANAMA

I arrived in Panama City and boarded a bus that had been vandalized both inside and out. The commuters already looked spent, having endured only the heat of Panama's sunrise. Or perhaps they were conserving energy for a long day of work.

When the bus reached downtown, I found a dilapidated room in a high-rise hostel and spent the afternoon checking wave reports to determine where the swells would be best over the next few days.

The following morning, I jumped on a second bus and arrived in a small coastal village along the western shore, Playa Venao.

The beach was untouched. Four metal huts stood twenty feet from the shoreline. The corrugated steel walls of my hut were rusted with tetanus. Two wires that had probably been left over from some circuitry installation had been run through the door and door frame to serve as the loops for the rusted padlock. That was the security system. Inside the hut, the bed was damp with mildew, and the shower, for some reason, had electrical wires stemming from the showerhead like branches surrounding a bald flower. A dim light dangled from the ceiling, offering enough yellow glow during daytime to see the nails sticking up from the floorboards. One mile down the beach was an ecovillage where most of the other surfers stayed because it was classy and clean. And I was told that one who practiced consistent bathing did not have to fear electrocution in the shower there. But my hut was five dollars a night and sat in front of one of the longest right-breaking waves in the country. So I handed over twenty dollars and kept the room for the better part of a week.

That first full morning, I woke with the roosters of Playa Venao. The cocks had congregated before my hut. I stepped into the light. A wave had lifted in the west as if a glassmaker had stretched hundreds of yards of his medium to its limits and then watched it pitch forward eastwardly.

I grabbed my board. As I made my way into the surf, I noticed that the only people awake were the women of the kitchen standing out back between the dining area and the wave, washing their knives, pointing to the various birds in the way a *shochet* might contemplate which creature to kosherize. The women, with their knives and kitchen duties, reminded me of my grandparents, who had always shared in the responsibility of feeding a family. Poppy had butchered; Grandma had cooked.

I paddled into the ocean and in between sets watched the land. One cook crept forward, and the chickens made a mad dash. The biggest bird, the one with the jet-black feathers and Ferrari-red wattle, refused to be intimidated and continued to peck at the ground. The cook continued toward the brazen bird with her blade.

A Japanese surfer with a soul patch paddled out and introduced himself as Yoshi. He observed me watching the unfolding of this premeditated killing and decided to practice his Spanish.

"Comida," he said as the woman closed in on the bird. *Comida* meant "food." (And I quickly learned that it was one of the few Spanish words that Yoshi knew. He knew less English.) While we waited for waves and the preparation of *comida*, Yoshi attempted to tell me a story. The tale took an hour to disclose, as we did not share a common language and, like all stories told in the surf, sentences yielded to the whims of the ocean—waves produced unexpected punctuation. But as the tide dropped and the lulls between sets lengthened, there was time to sit and hear his tale enhanced by charades. Apparently, Yoshi had gotten arrested for not carrying his passport and spent a night in a Panamanian jail. Making the story most confounding was that Yoshi told it through an inexorable smile, as if prison in Panama were one notch below a five-star resort. Yoshi also inserted the word "*comida*" into every plot point. Maybe it had been a part of the story—pleading for the guards to feed him—or maybe he was suggesting that he tell it to me over lunch.

Besides Yoshi, the only two people I knew who had been arrested and had their jail story rooted in comedy were my father and Poppy. In each case, Grandma had supplied the punch line.

One summer in the 1970s, my father was traveling across the country and found himself arrested on a Friday evening in Colorado, charged with vagrancy. Grandma, operating under her preferred condition of hysteria, had wired over her son's bail. But the judge had already left his chambers for the weekend and my father was told that he would have to wait in his cell for the judge to return on Monday.

"I have a wonderful chicken soup at home for him and he's in the prison eating bread and water," Grandma said to the prison guard in Colorado, and then to Aunt Anne, and then to a Brooklyn police captain, until all could stand no more. Complementing her *kvetch* with a bottle of Chivas, she persuaded the captain to call the Colorado prison and laud my father's reputation. He was released before Grandma could light the Shabbos candles.

While mention of the Umschlagplatz hadn't dropped us into the ghettos and camps as I had hoped, Grandma had started to offer up the occasional prewar or postliberation story. In 1945, my grandparents had been liberated. But for the next four years they lived in Bergen-Belsen, the camp in which Grandma had been a slave. The Nazi barracks had just been turned over to the displaced Jews.

In those postliberation years, Poppy still found himself imprisoned for his dealings on the German black market. On the evening of March 28, 1947, significant only because Grandma would go into labor with their first child, Poppy was arrested.

Confined not in a cell but in a room on the second story of a jailhouse, he waited for the guard to leave, picked up a chair, smashed the window, and jumped to the street below. With the police searching for him, Poppy was unable to return to Grandma, who was giving birth in Bergen-Belsen. While they hadn't taken birthing classes, they did have a birth plan. Grandma had given her husband one responsibility during the labor. to keep his eye on the former Nazi doctor who now worked as one of the camp's obstetricians. He had failed.

"A Nazi does the birth?" Poppy said to his wife when he eventually made it back to Bergen-Belsen.

"Do you see first-class hospitals here?" Grandma shouted. "I had to have one of the British attendants watch the Nazi cause you wound up in jail."

When I paddled in from the surf at Venao, I walked to the kitchen. The woman with the knife told me that the lunch menu was a choice between *pollo o pescado*. She swung the blade and cleaved off the heads of a fresh catch. A second woman plucked a bird. Beside that big avian corpse was a pile of black feathers. She flipped the bird over and I saw the Ferrari wattle.

I ordered the *pollo*. The dead bird conjured that romantic image of boyhood, when Grandma rested a whole chicken on her counter and seemed to fuss over it, making soup preparation appear like a grim spa treatment for fowl.

After my meal, I sat on the dining deck with my journal and realized that there was no record of any of the stories that Panama and Yoshi had helped me to remember. As the waves continued to approach the shore with the grace of nature, I wrote about Poppy's escape from the German jail. I scribbled the Train Story and Boat Story and Barn Story, too. I even recalled the Bus Story, when Poppy had been injured on the job, was shipped for a weekend of R & R in Florida, and misinterpreted the bus driver glancing at him in the mirror. Eventually the man stopped the bus, approached Poppy, and told him that he had to move his seat. Poppy, who didn't speak much English in those early years in America, believed this to be some anti-Semitic attack. A police officer was called to the scene. The cop explained that this was the Jim Crow South, where whites had to sit at the front of the bus. Leon Lederman lost a little respect for America that day. The plight of the blacks after slavery was what the Jews had experienced before the camps. The familiarity left him angry.

I filled the journal with a few of the stories that Poppy probably thought he had taken to the grave. I wrote about the butcher shop pursuit and then covered pages with once-neglected, overheard stories and phrases from my childhood, like the tales of the sewer rat.

"My father was a sewer rat," Dad used to say of Poppy whenever anyone mentioned Warsaw or the ghetto. While both "sewer" and "rat" connote cringeworthy images in free America, the pairing was an honorific in my family and a badge of distinction in the Warsaw of the early 1940s. Sewer rats were the boys of the Warsaw ghetto who had slunk through the pipes filled with disease and excrement, risking their young lives in order to bring in near-broken weapons and rotting potatoes from the few partisans outside the ghetto walls. Poppy's blue eyes and blond hair, commonly gentile features, caused just enough genetic befuddlement to convince the Polish world outside that his emaciated frame was to be overlooked.

Pen to paper, my childhood obsessions and pastimes suddenly made a whole lot of sense. As a boy, I had loved the Ninja Turtles: a teenage, mutated foursome of superheroes who lived in the sewers. Between the turtles and my grandparents there were many parallels. My grandparents were teenagers when society viewed them as mutants. I had always viewed Poppy as this superhero who felt most at ease gliding through the sewers. Some kids dug holes to China; I had always fantasized over the horizontal mouths of sewers and wondered whether any shithole would be a portal to Warsaw, circa 1943. On top of all that, the turtles were green, and my grandparents, as per my father, were *greeners*. It gave everything a nice twist. (Though, in retrospect, it would have made more sense for me to draw connections to the turtles' mentor, Master Splinter, an actual sewer rat.)

Waves crashed in the background; the memories exploded to the forefront of my mind. I recalled dressing as a sewer rat. At five, I would sneak into my parents' room with a friend. We'd pull on pairs of my father's oversized running shorts and then stuff them with every article of clothing we could find. My friend dubbed us the *Fat Boys*, and he paraded around mocking the obese. But for me, we were the *Sewer Rats*, smuggling in potatoes, sneaking in dozens of rations to save our comrades.

Hide-and-seek had been a way to infiltrate ghetto bunkers. War games, where we would cut off traffic through my parents' apartment with intricate fortifications built from furniture, blankets, and couch cushions, were really *Warsaw* games. My friends threw grenades like GI Joe; I chucked Molotov cocktails like Leon Lederman.

I could remember the first time I read a book about the Warsaw Ghetto Uprising. I had been in middle school, and I was outraged. How the hell did it leave out Leon Lederman, who from January to April of 1943 fought alongside the famous ghetto warriors? He had been a part of that most disadvantaged group of fighters. He had been one of those unfed Jews with barely enough bullets to commit suicide. Somehow the books left him out.

I wrote and I wrote. Yoshi came over with his surfboard. "Ee Nami. Bien olas." The waves, as he indicated, were still perfect.

"Tomorrow," I told him and continued to ignore the board for the pen. By nightfall, I had a few dozen pages. All the words focused on the survivor who was gone. I thought about Grandma sitting at home, mourning her husband. These stories were a much more satisfying way to remember him. I weighed the pages in my hand. They had come so effortlessly. I could fill books, I thought. And then I decided that's what I would do. The man who had been anonymous in my middle school texts would be unknown no longer. And Grandma, who had made it her last responsibility to remind everyone of Leon Lederman, would be given one last task. Together we would create another shrine to the man she wore in gold around her neck.

A few days later, I left Playa Venao for the north. On the way, I stopped at an Internet café. My inbox contained a message from my father. He had written:

Anne found the tapes.

13

ESCAPE FROM WARSAW

"What you need to run around for?" Grandma asked after I had returned from Central America. "Poppy made a family here for you and you running around the world to do . . ." She searched for the word in English or maybe in Yiddish or Polish or Russian—all of the tongues she was able to mourn in. She moved her hand through the air once she decided that she didn't know the word in any of her languages and clumsily mimed a board on a wave, tacking on "*Oy oy oy*" to the pain she felt from wagging her hand.

On my last few days in Central America, I hadn't surfed at all. Instead, I abandoned the board to think about the importance of memory. If Panama had been the place where I had devised the whimsical idea to capture Poppy's life story, then Nicaragua had given it purpose.

On a sunny afternoon, in the main square of Granada, I sat at a table and watched as street performers shared a section of pavement with toddlers on the loose, who had grown quicker and more surreptitious than their exhausted parents. A man wearing a filthy shirt, which had shed its top buttons that might have once concealed his caved-in chest, approached me. I was accustomed to the city's beggars, but his approach was different. He stood at my table, angling his body toward me; however, he kept his attention on the band.

"This is a very famous song that I remember from my childhood," he told me, still lost in the music and unconcerned with coins.

"Which was when?" I asked, trying not to engage him, but also curious about the song.

"In '71 or '72. I can't remember. May I?" He pointed at the empty seat across from me.

"Sure," I said, not wanting to be discourteous.

He sat down and studied the architecture enveloping the square. "Do you see that building?"

I nodded. This began a lesson on the colonial-era buildings that surrounded us. I feigned appreciation at first, expecting the inevitability of an open palm. But his lecture dragged on, his voice still lost in the music. I waited for something to end—the band, his tutorial, the appropriate amount of time to abandon the scene. But then he said "war," and I was reeled in.

"Were you living here when there was war?" I asked, having seen the men with missing limbs, but having no one to ask about the time of the Sandinistas and Contras.

"I don't think you want to hear about this," he said, pointing up to the next building in order to return to the more peaceful talk of architectural design.

"I would."

"People shouldn't talk about the past," he explained. "It's hard and sad."

One day earlier, I had been sitting on the beach, adding more anecdotes into the journal, when another man approached.

"Do you mind if I join you?" he had asked, but then he noticed my notebook. "Oh, pardon me. I thought you were also waiting for the sun to set."

"I don't mind," I told him and closed the book.

"What were you writing?"

I told him about the ghettos and the camps; he revealed that he was German.

I quieted with instinct; he kept asking questions about my grandparents' lives.

"I remember learning about this in school and . . ." He stopped as if to search for the correct reply. "It was very important to me then. And it is important to me now. To know." He wiped at a few tears; I was perplexed. He continued, "I want you to know that I am so sorry for what happened. Very, very sorry."

I didn't know how to respond to his tears or apology.

"I think about it all the time," he added. "And I don't know what I can do to make it better. To make up for it. I think the most important thing is that we continue to talk about it. To never forget what happened."

One day later and here I was, in this square in Granada with a man who was hoping that we could just forget. I repeated what the German had said to me. The Nicaraguan smiled and hesitated. We spent the next two hours at that table—he sharing his stories of the time of the Sandinistas and the families brought up to the hills, while I listened.

A hand gripped my heart for the faceless victims, and I wanted to feel that same pain at Grandma's kitchen table. I wanted to remember because there was a growing population of the uninformed and, more troubling, the deniers. Nicaragua made me feel a responsibility to the past and to the vanishing present.

Days after returning from Nicaragua, I was once more borrowing words from the German man whom I had met in Central America. But this time I was speaking them to Grandma.

"I think it's important that we talk about what happened in Poland and Germany. To never forget what happened." I pulled out two notebooks: one with prewritten questions, another with blank pages for the things Grandma would relinquish. "I was thinking about writing a book about Poppy." I looked at his image swinging on the gold plate hanging around her neck. "It would be a way to keep him with us. To remember him."

She shrugged. "So what you want me to tell you. Write a book. Who's stopping you?"

I smiled. "I need your help though. I can't write the book because I don't know about Poppy's life when he was younger."

"I don't want to talk about Poppy," Grandma said.

She was the most paradoxical mourner. *Do you remember Poppy?* she would ask on each visit. Now, when I wanted to talk about Poppy, she didn't.

As a kid, I had always imagined my grandparents' Holocaust stories to be invaluable, stored in the treasure chests of their minds. But I realized that the memories were trapped behind grim ghetto walls that only the cunning of a sewer rat would know how to bypass. I had to think like those underground boys who left the safety of the murderous ghetto for the carnage of the Polish streets.

"Dad used to tell me that Poppy was a sewer rat and—"

"What?" Grandma shrieked and spat. "*Ptoy, ptoy.* Sewer? Rat? Poppy was not."

"Didn't he travel through the sewers in Warsaw to help bring food and weapons to the other Jews? Didn't he supply them so that they could fight in the uprising?"

"Of course. He fought, too. But he wasn't a rat."

"No. I mean . . ." I abandoned my explanation and did away with using that esteemed title in Grandma's presence.

"Noiach, what should I know about Poppy? We wasn't together during the war. We only met after the liberation."

This news shocked me. I had forever assumed that the houses at 15 Berka Joselewicza and 12 Podmiejska were linked, that Poppy had always known Grandma, and that their undying love had allowed them to survive the Holocaust. But they survived the concentration camps alone.

"You didn't know Poppy from Otwock?"

"I knew him, but not so much. Once, in Otwock, Poppy came to my house for a jug of wine. I had an uncle who sold wine. Our fathers knew each other from the synagogue. This is how I knew him. Noiach, what's Mommy cooking for dinner? Grandma can't cook no more." She had always attempted to distract me from my questions with the presence of food; now she was attempting to do so with the absence of it.

"So you knew each other a little then?" I asked in the hopes of steering us back on track.

"What did we know? We were kids. I had my friends and Poppy had his friends. Poppy played on the soccer fields and I did the cooking with my—" Grandma cut herself off. Conjuring up her murdered mother and dead husband at once appeared to be too much. She reached for her thinning gray hair and ran her fingers through it. For some unexplained reason, a half-smile appeared on her face, which was as rare as glimpsing the smirk of a Queen's Guard. I found the presence of this near grin most odd, considering that both of her departed loves were now circulating in her mind. She continued to comb fingers through her hair.

"This one time, it was Tishabov. You know Tishabov, it's when we commemorate the destruction of the temple in Jerusalem. A beautiful holiday." She studied my face for understanding and then scolded. "Noiach, you don't know this holiday?"

"I know it. It's when we commemorate the destruction of the temple," I said, repeating what she had just explained.

She appeared dubious.

"In Jerusalem," I added.

She glowered. "Noiach!"

"Grandma, what happened on Tishabov?"

"Tishabov, *oy*. There was me and a few girls from Otwock. We ran toward the synagogue and you Poppy was waiting in the woods. He had . . . how you say?" She rubbed her fingers together as if something sticky were on her fingertips. "How you say? From the bush. The sticky."

"Thistles."

She leaned forward. "How you say?"

I repeated the word.

"Yes. This. Poppy have *fistles* and he throw *fistles* at us." She pushed her lips together and nodded in reproach, seemingly disappointed in her late husband's behavior. "I missed services. Can you believe it? I spent the whole night getting these *fistles* out of my hair." She slammed the table with an anger that still percolated over this seventy-year-old affront. "I had to cut my hair."

Her fingers searched around for the seeds now planted as memory.

"It's true. That was you Poppy." The smile stayed. The clock by the doorway reminded us of the hour, and Grandma jumped with the chime. Did the marking of every hour in her life startle her?

"When we live in Canarsie," Grandma continued, "you Poppy had to wind the wooden clock or it would be no good. Then we move here and it goes kaput. But the day after the funeral, no one wind it, but the clock hasn't stopped ringing. This you knew?"

I shook my head.

"What you bring this book for?" Grandma asked, patting the empty pages. "You don't even write nothing. I talk and you write nothing."

Startled, I flipped the cover open and scribbled down the story of the *fistles* and the clock. Of their childhood innocence before the Nazis arrived and of Grandma's new sect of Judaism, where the Jesus Poppy that hung from her neck had the power of resurrecting a clock's chime.

"I miss him." Grandma reached out to touch the portrait of her husband, which had supplanted the gefilte fish and fare of days past. Tears usually followed this reach for Poppy's photograph, but instead Grandma said, "We were in Karczew."

"What's Car chef?"

"Karczew, Karczew," Grandma chanted. "You tell me you go to Otwock and Karczew. It was the town next to Otwock. They make it a ghetto."

The little town next to Otwock, which I had seen each of the hundred times I had consulted my map, had always sat in my brain as *Kark-zoo*.

"Karczew," I said correctly for the very first time. "That's how you pronounce it."

"How else?"

"We didn't get to Karczew. The road had flooded."

"How did you know how to go, Noiach?"

"Teddy. The man who lived on Poppy's street."

"The goy," Grandma said. "Ech. He was nice to you?"

"He helped me find Poppy's house."

"Okay, then let him live and be well."

I wasn't sure, however, that I agreed with Grandma's generous pronouncement. It had been two years since our meeting on Podmiejska Street, and I hadn't once heard from Teddy or his expert friend. My e-mails to him went unanswered. Teddy had been nothing but kind in Otwock, but now, with distance between us, he was unreachable.

Had there been something that he was trying to hide? How had Teddy's grandmother truly acquired the house? Or maybe he had been disappeared for talking to the wandering Jew.

"What happened in Karczew?" I asked Grandma, trying to stay on the path lined with the *fistles*.

"After they kill my mother, there are no more Jews in Otwock, but there were four hundred Otwock boys in Karczew. My brothers—Shmuel and Shama—they were in Karczew. But this was a boy's camp. Girls are forbidden. A Polish man, who used to purchase sandals from mine uncle in Otwock, helped to sneak me in. He tells me to walk in the back, in case we are caught. You know, he don't want to be punished.

"When I enter the camp, I find my brother Shmuel and I say to him, 'Shmuel, Mommy was killed.' I cry, but my brother did not cry." Grandma smashed her knuckles upon the table. "I say to him, 'Shmuel, why you don't cry for Mommy?' He tells me he cannot cry because he just buried four thousand Jews. He says 'I will cry. But I cannot cry now.' This is what they did. They buried our neighbors."

First *fistles* and young Poppy's mischievousness, then this. My jaw unhinged. I looked at my book of questions, searching for something that could have passed for a follow-up. "Umm . . . Umm . . . What did you do?"

"I hid in the bunks, when the boys go to work." Grandma stopped to think. "Noiach, I saw this boy hiding in the bunks, underneath the blankets, and I whisper to him like this"—she leaned toward me as if I were the child. "'Boy, boy.' I say this because I see that the Nazis are coming. I go to hide by the river.* He didn't follow me." Grandma stopped again and looked off into the distance of memory.

I swallowed hard knowing that she was probably looking back into the bunk from her hiding place beside the river.

"They killed him," she said. "Noiach, no more." Grandma placed a hand to her heart and nodded at the events of her teenage years. I closed

---

* Most likely, when she says "river," Grandma is referring to one of the canals that the four hundred Jewish boys and men imprisoned in Karczew had been forced to dig.

the books, but Grandma kept talking. "The next morning, the Nazis search the bunk. Again I hide. This time beneath a wooden crate." She reached for her back, but she couldn't even lay a hand on her shoulder. "I had such bad sciatica. I sat like a hunch for so many hours."

"Where? Beneath the crate?"

"Where else?" she said and looked at Poppy's image. "When the boys were on break, I could see through the crate. It was like a bazaar. And I see this one boy like this." Grandma rubbed her fingers together in the way that a sarcastic person would offer up a tune on the world's smallest violin. "He was making cigarettes. And I say through the crate, 'Leon. Leon.' And you Poppy tell to me *shhh*. Is that right? Is it right to tell to Grandma *shhh*?"

"How was Grandma?" Dad asked after I met him on the boardwalk. He had no interest in spending the beautiful fall day pacing her apartment, stewing like a twenty-four-hour pot of cholent, which she no longer cooked.

I had left her apartment bemused. I had entered earlier that day hoping to capture Poppy's stories. But Grandma *was* the story.

Growing up, the woman had seemed to only cook and clean, *kvetch* and *kibitz*. Poppy, on the other hand, had been an upriser who took no credit, a Nazi killer who refused to recount his heroics, an anonymous sewer rat missing from the books that praised Anielewicz. He had always been my protagonist. And I, apparently, had always been the stupid boy who never fully realized that Grandma had survived with her own horrid collection of Holocaust stories.

"How much did she cry?" Dad asked after I let his previous question go unanswered.

"She didn't really cry," I said.

"That lady hasn't stopped crying for almost seven years and you're telling me she wasn't really crying. What was she doing instead? Choking?"

"We talked about Poland."

"Poland? Poland made her stop crying. She's insane."

I told him the stories about the crate and the thistles as we walked toward the orange, defunct parachute jump that mushroomed over Coney Island like a small nuclear explosion frozen in time.

"See? Poppy couldn't stand her during the Holocaust, too," Dad joked. "He used to tell Grandma that he would put up with her for fifty years and on the fiftieth anniversary, he was cashing out. Do you remember the fiftieth anniversary, when we celebrated at the National, that Russian nightclub underneath the train?"

I nodded.

"Poppy went up to her that evening and said, 'Tonight's the night, baby!'" Dad brushed his hands together like a ballplayer after sliding head first into second and placing himself in scoring position. "Tonight's the night."

"I remember." I looked at my father, staring toward Coney Island as if searching for another memory. "You never heard the story about Grandma hiding under the crate or Poppy and the thistles?"

"I must have," he said. "Like I said, I always tried to forget."

This was the problem. Everyone was trying to forget. It seemed the sympathetic German in Nicaragua and I were the only ones dedicated to remembering.

Remembering was the only thing that felt natural, the only way to piece together a past that had been so torn apart. The story was my way to make my family whole.

That night, I parsed the little information that I had on Poppy and started outlining the book that I had hoped to write. But Poppy read flat. Also, I could trace his timeline through most of the Holocaust, but of the camp from which he was liberated, Klein Webber, there were no records. Of all the camps, why did it have to be the one to have no records? I could imagine how a story without closure could become the fodder for deniers.

On my next visit, I kissed Grandma at the door and looped my arm through hers as we walked through the kitchen to the dining room table.

"Noiach, I ordered in gefilte fish."

I smiled at the irony. Opening up the Holocaust—this most sickening event—had been the very thing to bring Jewish cuisine back to her table. She removed the lid from the Tupperware, where she was keeping the long, pallid slab. I had never seen gefilte fish in bar form before; Grandma had always shaped hers to resemble hamburger patties.

"You remember when Grandma cooked for you?"

"Of course." I sliced a section from the hunk of fish and smeared it with horseradish so that it looked like a gray-bodied, purple-haired Chia Pet.

"How is it?" she asked.

"Not as good as yours,"

"*Oy*, Noiach, I can't cook no more."

There never seemed to be an appropriate transition into Grandma's past, so I just flopped in with my questions the way a gefilte fish might attempt to return to the sea if it were magically animated.

A yearbook photograph of schoolchildren in Otwock. Front and center, leaning against one another, are two of Poppy's four sisters: Esther and Anja. (Esther, according to Poppy, was quite intelligent and had skipped a grade.) Both sisters, and most likely the majority of these kids, were murdered in Treblinka or in the forests around Otwock.

Grandma and Poppy walking Helen down the aisle at her wedding in New York. None of the survivors had living parents to give them away.

Poppy somehow acquired this convertible when they were living in the displaced persons camps at Bergen-Belsen.

Poppy and Grandma's fiftieth anniversary party at the National nightclub in Brighton Beach, Brooklyn. This is when he shouted, "Tonight's the night."

Some of the women from that group of nineteen girls who survived Auschwitz with Grandma, as well as other survivors. From left to right, beginning with those standing: Herman Jurish, Helen Jurish, Poppy, Ruth, Yadja, Grandma, Schmulich, unknown, unknown, unknown. From left to right, for those seated: unknown, Esther, unknown, unknown. This is at Dad's bar mitzvah.

A few of the survivors from Otwock: Genya (top row, far left) and Morris Pilberg (beside her), Grandma (third from left), Poppy (in the middle). Of those seated, on the far left to right are the Szafranskis. (The rest of the people I don't know.)

Helen and Herman, along with their children Alice, Susan, and Mark, posing with Poppy, Grandma, Aunt Anne, and Dad at his bar mitzvah.

Poppy is in the middle wearing the tank top. Helen and Grandma are behind him. Bergen-Belsen displaced persons camp.

Poppy with Anne in the Bergen-Belsen displaced persons camp.

Poppy, me, and Grandma at my high school graduation. Poppy would die later that year.

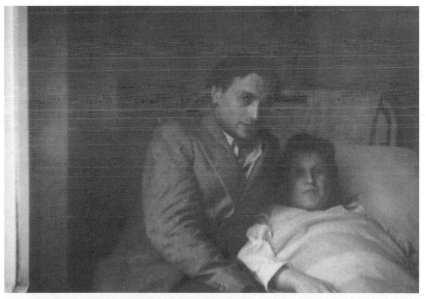

Poppy and Grandma in the hospital at the Bergen-Belsen displaced persons camp either before or after she gave birth. He missed the birth because he was arrested for dealing on the black market.

Aunt Anne as a little girl in the displaced persons camp, playing with other children who were born into Bergen-Belsen after the war. She's the little girl on the bicycle holding her friend.

Grandma in front of the bike, Helen behind. Bergen-Belsen.

Poppy outside the Bergen-Belsen displaced persons camp barracks. The picture that I pondered over before I closed the box of photos.

Poppy and Grandma gazing at their newborn just two years after liberation. Bergen-Belsen.

Aunt Anne, Grandma, a bear, and Poppy in Bergen-Belsen.

A funeral procession in Germany. The people are carrying either dug up bones or a body. One of the many pictures in Grandma's box of photos of which she didn't remember the story. One of the many stories that I couldn't learn.

Poppy, Jake, and me on the couch in their television room, most likely watching wrestling.

Poppy and Grandma in Israel, 1972, in front of the Otwock plaque at Yad Vashem.

Poppy and Grandma in Bergen-Belsen's displaced persons camp.

Rachmiel Eisenberg on the left and Poppy on the right. It's unclear how soon after liberation this photograph was taken, but Poppy quickly acquired a watch and clothes. There are rumors in the family that he took it off a German.

Poppy's sister, Esther. She was most likely murdered in Treblinka or in the forests around Otwock.

Grandma's family at the Seder table in Otwock. The photograph above the light switch. The boy standing tallest on the left of the photograph is Grandma's oldest brother, Shmuel. At the head of the table sit her father and mother. The father is holding a photograph of Grandma's grandparents, who are in Israel. Grandma is just behind her mother. She is clutching the arm of her youngest brother, Shama, who is likely standing on a chair. Everyone else, from the infant on the left to the little girl on the right, are cousins, aunts, uncles. They were all murdered in the Holocaust. Only Grandma survived. (*Note:* Just before this book went to print, my father told me how the infant was killed. The Nazis threw the baby off a roof and caught the infant on a bayonet.)

"Grandma, what do you remember about Warsaw? Were you ever in the sewers?" If I couldn't track Poppy through Warsaw's filthy tunnels, maybe Grandma's stories would lead me to him.

"Eat more gefilte fish."

"I'm still—"

"I get a whole gefilte fish for you and you only eat one slice." She picked up the butter knife and carved the fish with such jerky movements that flecks of white shot off. Grandma plopped the piece down on my plate, atop the one that I had yet to finish. I ate the two slices and then moved the Tupperware to the refrigerator to avoid further distractions.

"Were you ever in the sewers of Warsaw?" I tried again.

"You know, each day they send thousands of Jews to the concentration camps. Bodies and luggage everywhere. In winter, just before the uprising, I go into the sewer with a group of people. People from my bunker. Filthy. Water—I say water, but it was not water—came up to here." She placed her hand over Poppy's golden image and beneath her chin. "We sat there in . . . in . . . in shit. It was shit. What else can I call it, Noiach? This is what it was," she said apologetically, as if the cursing were the worst part of her story. "Down there we hear Polish children playing above. And rats. Big rats. *Ptoy, ptoy.* All around. We wait for a long time and then the leader for our group he climbs the ladder and takes off the . . . How you say? The round metal."

"Manhole cover."

"Yes. He takes off the cover and they kill him." She shrugged and collapsed her arms to the table. "They shoot him and his body falls into the shit. We run and I get this sewage splash in my face. But I'm not thinking about this because I know they gonna throw a grenade. But they don't throw one." She turned in her chair toward the refrigerator. "Noiach, Grandma can't eat the fish. You gonna have another slice?"

"I'm . . ." Who could think of food at a time like this? But this was a consequence of having starved through one's youth. Loved ones were to be fed, always, especially when the refrigerator was filled with fish. "I'll have another slice later. Let me digest."

"Noiach, I go back into the ghetto," Grandma says, moving from fish to hell. "I come out through the . . . the . . . How you say again?"

"The manhole."

"Yes. This. And I'm on Ostrowska Street. Suddenly, I remember what my father said to me. Feathers. Look for feathers."

"Feathers? Where?"

"On a door," she said as if that were the universal place for storing feathers. "Feathers is where there is a hiding place. It's like a secret code. I go into a room with the feathers and I know I have to move this big dresser. You know what I find there?"

I shook my head.

"The bunker," she said. "And I find my father and sixty-five other Jews. Very smart people. We had engineers in the bunker. You know what they do?"

I shook my head. Partly because I did not know the answer, but more so because I had spent an entire childhood misjudging this woman.

"They make the smoke from the stoves here." She pointed to a spot on the tablecloth and then zigzagged her finger away from the original point. "And then the smoke come out here," she said, explaining how they rerouted the chimney lines, causing the emissions to spill out a few doors down instead of rising up above the occupied spaces in the ghetto. "So the Nazis don't catch us. We live like that for months. But the Nazis find us in April—the last day of Passover—and that's when they bring us to the Umschlagplatz."

"The Umschlagplatz." It had been the key to all of this. "Last time you said many things happened at the Umschlagplatz."

"Of course. Many, many things." But she took it no further, and I didn't press her. "Noiach, *oy oy oy*, I can't talk no more. No more about Warsaw. I need to take a tranquilizer."

14

REVISION

I can't believe what she went through," I told Dad.

"She might be crazy, but she's a tough lady."

I wondered how often Grandma saw her dead comrades fall from above into the piss and shit of the sewer. What did she remember when the word "Umschlagplatz" scrolled through her mind?

I had set out to write Poppy's Holocaust biography, but instead unveiled my own ignorance. Grandma had survived the same atrocities as he had. In fact, if I had been given a choice between Poppy's Holocaust, in which his entire family had been lost in one faceless transport to Treblinka, or Grandma's Holocaust, where her mother was killed while they held hands and her older brother was murdered by a Polish police officer weeks before liberation, I would have chosen Poppy's Holocaust as the easier struggle.

"That's a weird thing to think," I said to Dad after revealing my own thoughts. "Trying to figure out whose Holocaust was worse."

"You're not a survivor; I'm a survivor. No, I'm a survivor," my father quipped, quoting from *Curb Your Enthusiasm*'s infamous scene between a Holocaust survivor and a former cast member of the show *Survivor*. "Poppy did the same thing—decided whose Holocaust experience was worse. You know what he always said. He considered himself to be among the lucky ones because he hadn't been a parent during the war. He didn't have to watch his children die. Parents had it the worst." Dad gave two smacks against my leg, as he was left with the thought.

This was another check in Grandma's column. While she hadn't been a mother during the war, after her mother was murdered she took on that role for her youngest brother, Shama. And when they wound up in Maj-danek, she was forced to watch Shama and her father wither away on the other side of the fence before they would be buried in mass, unmarked graves. Still, Grandma found a way to survive.

I knew that the book had to be about both my grandparents.

That night, I watched the tapes that Anne had found in her closet.

Grandma looked like a younger, healthier version of her feeble self. Flat gray hair had been sculpted back into a blond-tinted perm. She was the grandmother of eleven years earlier, the one who had been strong enough to protect her expensive permed hairdo from grandsons who wanted only to compress this coiffure to her head; the one who obliged my requests to march down fifteen flights of stairs in her apartment building while she *oy, oy, oy*ed all the way down; the one who would sit for hours, in between cooking and cleaning, to watch closed-circuit building security and worry about trespassers because it revitalized her; the one who would snarl at me and my brother when we wore her housedresses, pushed about her brown carpet sweeper, and mocked her *oy gevalt*s and *oye broch*s; the one who would mutate into a biased film critic, rate our parody as a thumbs-up performance, and then quickly shift into the Academy to award us with pinches on our cheeks.

I couldn't believe that I had spent a childhood lovingly mocking her, viewing her as a stereotype of a Jewish grandma, which was the guise that she had always presented. This was a woman who should have earned the world's respect, or if nothing else, at least her grandson's.

The Grandma on Steven Spielberg's Shoah Foundation recording spoke about family, school, and the anti-Semitism of her childhood. She detailed for the camera the murder of her mother and her time in Karczew. I worried that I would burn through the film because I kept rewinding to the moments when she spoke of that young girl who would go on to sur-vive three ghettos and three camps and then rattle the mind of one feckless grandson.

In minutes, she had brought the interviewer from the barn where her mother had been shot to the time she had left her brothers in Karczew for Mrs. Tzowzkowska's damp and dark attic, where rats half a meter in length crawled across her in hiding. But the rats were less disconcerting than Mr. Tzowzkowski, who had discovered her in a dark corner and said: "You dirty Jew. I'm going to kill you if you don't leave."

I choked up when she spoke of the camps. She recounted the pain, yet there seemed to be something cathartic in remembering these terrors, even at a time when the stories were not told to supplant the depression of having lost a husband.

Video had stolen something from death when it became Poppy's turn to sit before the lens. He did so with a sneer that said *let's be done with this* even before the interviewer proposed his first question. Unlike Grandma, who disregarded chronology, Poppy told his story from beginning to end. And when the interviewer moved him along or failed to ask a pertinent question about the event or date just discussed, Poppy moved on, too, refusing to go back, abandoning one tragic scene for the next.

While Poppy was telling a story about Warsaw, the interviewer pushed him forward to Majdanek. I begged to history that Poppy would interrupt Spielberg's man to tell him that he could talk for days about the uprising, his time in the sewers, how to measure out the perfect amount of fuel for a Molotov cocktail. But we had left Warsaw all too quickly, and there was no return.

At the end, the interviewer asked Poppy whether he would ever bring his family to Otwock. He responded with a story of a Polish man whom he had spoken with after the war. The Pole had asked Poppy: *If it had been the other way around, would you have risked your family and your life to help us?*

"Maybe I wouldn't," Poppy told the camera. "But I wouldn't sell you [out] for a pound of sugar or a million dollars."

"Do you still have anger?" the interviewer asked.

"I let it sleep, you woke me up . . . but I don't forget."

At the high school where I taught, I realized that I had a bit of waking up to do myself. My students—some of them descendants of slaves, others victims of Central and South American murderous regimes—had little to let sleep because they had nothing to remember. They knew nothing of their roots and even less about the Holocaust. This was presented to me most clearly during final exams when one of my students stopped me in the hallway after he had completed his global studies test. He wore a celebratory smile as if this one test were going to mean a scholarship to Princeton.

"I did great, mista," he predicted.

"What did you write your essay on?" I asked.

"Uhh . . . What's his name? John Hitler," the kid said. "You know, and how he freed the Jews."

There was work to be done.

The semester after the John Hitler conversation, I searched the book room for my English class. I wanted to teach the Holocaust. Though we only had three complete sets of books, other than the ones about gangs and amateur boxing, option three was an untouched class set of *Night*.

The next day, I spilled the Holocaust onto my students' desks, just about one hundred pages of it.

"Who Elie *Weasel*?" asked a student. I'll call him Winston.

"It's pronounced Wiesel. He's a Holocaust survivor."

They stared at the cover of *Night* and at the boy who stood in the blue haze and black tangle of barbed wire.

"Looks boring, Mista," Winston declared.

"What do you guys know about the Holocaust?" I asked the class.

After a long silence, one kid raised his hand.

"That Jewish thing, right?" He looked around and the other students shrugged. For all I knew, he had stopped off at a kosher bakery before school and overheard the Orthodox Jews in the neighborhood. *How much that challah cost?* How much that Holocaust?

Yeah, that Jewish thing. Jewish bread. Jewish dead. Whatever.

The next day I moved the desks so that the front edges formed a rectangle in the center of the room. I asked my students to stand within the boundaries. My fourteen students *kvetched*. There was shoving and groping and blaming. "No homo." "Fuck you, nigga." "Don't step on my shoes, yo." "Get off my shit."

"This is about the size of a cattle car," I said, interrupting the mostly harmless melee.

"What's a camel car?" one kid asked.

"Cattle car, dummy," said Winston.

"It's how they transported the Jews to the concentration camps," I explained.

"Like the Underground Railroad," someone else said.

I spent the day clearing up confusions about slavery in America and then moved on to the Holocaust in Europe. We talked Nuremberg Laws and ghettos, liquidations and camps. I showed them pictures of the exposed rib cages and protruding hip bones and swollen knees that hunger had set into the emaciated.

"This shit's real," a kid said.

"That's my intention."

When one kid tried to be flippant, I didn't have to rein him in; the class did it for me: "Be serious, nigga."

My life had become infused with the Holocaust. Before work, I pored through the Holocaust texts that inundated my dining room table, searching for Poppy's mystery camp, where he had been liberated. Other mornings, I attempted to connect Grandma's disjointed memories with time and place. By the third period in my teaching schedule, I was digging into *Night* with my students. Then I'd leave class with assignments from these kids.

"Grandma, my students wanted me to ask you another question."

"Please, Noiach, I don't want to talk about it." She breathed into the receiver and the phone crackled like tin foil. "I need to take a tranquilizer." It was nighttime. Her *Night*, where she would see all of the gaunt faces, dead kin, grim reapers, the gnashing teeth of the dogs, the smoke, the gray—the elements of a memoir never to be written.

"Sorry, Grandma." I was always shuffling hats at her expense: the teacher, the writer, the investigator. Sometimes I simply had to realize that she needed her grandson. "Have a good night, Grandma."

"*Oy*, Noiach," she replied and hung up the phone.

As my students and I read Elie Wiesel's book, the kids demanded more of my grandparents' stories. When we read about the tattoos, Winston wanted to know my grandparents' numbers. He scribbled them in the margins of his notebook. When Elie first saw the smoke, the kids begged me to ask Grandma about the first time she watched the sky turn gray. (I couldn't.) Even though Wiesel had been writing about a kid their age, my students seemed to cherish their one degree of separation from that old survivor in Brooklyn. Consequently, my class often confused the book with the stories not yet written. On exams, the questions about *Night* received answers closer to home.

> *Describe Elie's relationship with his father before being sent to the concentration camps.*

> *His father would need the blade for killing the cows because it was illegal to use that blade because being a kosher butcher was illegal and Elie would run that blade to his father so he could do his thing. Elie and his father tight.*

They didn't understand that Froyim Richner and Yankle Yeblanche—two Jews from my grandparents' Otwock, men who had warned their neighbors that they had built Treblinka—were different from Elie's mentor, Moishe the Beadle.

> *This Jewish plumber told the Jews about Treblinka and nobody listened. Where do you think those three hundred dudes rounded up went? Then this other Jewish guy comes back and says the same damn thing. That he built the gas chambers and got out by hiding in all the dead people's clothes.*

They confused Elie's childhood with Poppy's.

> *In fact, Elie was selected for Treblinka, but this big German named Ditz for some reason told Elie to go back to the ghetto. Elie have no clue why they let him go. And still the people in town don't believe Moishe and The Beadle. They kept saying they all dead. I woulda believed him.*

They mistook Elie's visit with the dentist for Poppy's stay at the Buna infirmary.

> *Elie went to this big Nazi named Stolp and says that his leg is infected and that he needs to go to the infirmary. Yeah you might rest for a bit, but you might also go to the gas chambers. But the Nazi sorta likes Elie and tells him that you better not go because they gonna burn everyone in the crematoriums. Luckily Elie listens because they burn everyone.*

When I asked them about Elie's run-in with Mengele, one student wrote an essay about Grandma's two encounters with the infamous sadist.

While my students may have been confused between the characters of *Night* and *My Grandparents' Holocaust*, they understood the genocide. They knew that everyone was humiliated, that they were swollen with hunger, that the smell of burning flesh filled the skies above the camps, that showers weren't always showers, that people were stripped of their identities. More important, they understood how it connected to their lives.

"Yo, leave that nigga alone," Winston shouted when another kid bullied his classmate in the hall. "You better read a book."

I tried to get them to see text-to-text, text-to-self, text-to-world connections, but they often interrupted for text-to-Poppy and self-to-Grandma links.

When Elie entered the Buna, I fed them statistics: "Doctors calculated that if you ate the Buna diet, you'd only live for three weeks."

"Grandpa in Buna?" Winston wanted to know.

"He was," I said.

"What unit?"

"The construction unit. He was a slave for this German corporation, IG Farben. He was lifting hundred-pound bags of cement to help build the factory."

Winston opened up to page 45. "That like the building unit then?"

"I think it would be the same thing."

"Shit. Grandpa in the unit that Elie say 'important thing not to get transferred to.' And how long grandpa in the Buna?" Winston asked.

"More than one year."

"So how'd he do that?"

"He had to be clever. He traded extra shirts for bread, whatever else he could acquire. Look, when I went to visit Auschwitz—"

"Whoa, whoa, whoa. Hold on," Winston said. "You tellin' me you went to this *Ow-shits*, where Elie been, where they killed like a million people?"

I nodded.

"Why would you go to this place? Aren't there ghosts and stuff? Everyone trying to get outta *Ow-shits* in this book and you tryin' to go in. Strange Mista."

The bell rang.

"How did he carry those bags?" Winston asked on the way out while simultaneously attempting to lift one of his ninety-pound classmates. Winston grunted a few times in his failed effort to bring the smaller boy's feet off the ground. "I can't even lift this nigga, and Grandpa, nothing to eat, nothing to drink, no rest—you know how I need my nap—he lifting hundred-pound sacks of cement to build a factory."

"I don't know how he did it."

The next day, we succeeded in focusing on the memoir.

"Man, this is a good-ass book," Winston shouted at the end of the chapter. He placed *Night* into his backpack and shook his head as he exited the classroom. "Never read a whole book before. Might read rest at home, Mista."

I smiled; Winston stopped in front of my desk and placed a hand on my shoulder.

"Mista, give Grandma hug for me. Okay?"

"Okay, Winston."

15

A BOX OF PHOTOS

That's a Russian," Grandma said after I had entered her apartment and given her Winston's hug. The Russian that she was referring to was the woman who had ridden up in the elevator with me and followed me down the hall to enter the apartment two doors down from Grandma's. Her comment was the equivalent of walking around the Brooklyn Aquarium, pointing to the creatures on display, and saying, "That's a fish." Brighton Beach was Little Russia. She revealed more of the obvious: "The Russians are everywhere."

The Russians were also on my mind. Earlier in the day, I had replayed the tapes and listened to Poppy tell a story about two Russian soldiers, prisoners of war, who were also in the Buna. The Russians had taken a liking to him and invited Poppy to escape with them. I recounted the story for Grandma to see whether she had anything to add.

"The tapes? With Spielberg?" she asked, as if the famed director had been the one who helped unplug the refrigerator to eliminate the ambient noise and then sat down to interview her and Poppy.

"Right. With Spielberg."

"Poppy didn't go with no Russians."

"I know, Grandma, they invited him to escape, but he chose not to." On the night he had to make his decision, he had witnessed his first hanging in the Buna. "I just wanted to know more about that story."

"What happened to the Russians?" she asked.

I shrugged. She shrugged. I allowed the question to die and laid my hand on her arm, over the numbers.

"Two girls escaped from Majdanek and they hung them." Always with new and grim facts, that was how she broke long silences these days.

Even as she grew weaker and the tattoo faded with the years, she managed to show more strength, which I had overlooked for too long.

I lifted my hand off the numbers, as if rubbing them had conjured up the story in the same manner that a genie could be summoned from a lamp.

"They told to us, 'You will watch this execution. This is what happens to those who try to escape.'" She smashed her knuckles against the glass table just as the ropes snapped taut in her mind. She stared off from her Brighton Beach window.

"Noiach, go look in Poppy's drawers. I buy him such beautiful clothes and he can't wear them no more. Please, take some of Poppy's clothes."

And that's also how she left tragedies, with sudden little non sequiturs.

I dug through Poppy's drawers. She stood behind me, watching and interrupting as I passed over one sweater that looked like a swirl of cat-vomit green, corpse gray, and mustard yellow. Some failed design for army fatigues that might have been considered for combat held on frozen grassland.

"I buy him the most beautiful clothes. He was so handsome in this sweater."

"It is beautiful, Grandma."

"Take."

"Sure," I said, adding it to a hideous fashion statement that was piling up on the bed.

I opened up the closet and found Poppy's old shoes. I held up a brown suede pair. "Can I take these?"

"Noiach," Grandma shouted, ripping them from my hand. "You cannot wear a dead person's shoes!" It was as if Jewish laws had been adapted from platitudes—*You could never fill his shoes.* "This isn't Bergen-Belsen."

We had progressed far enough into the Holocaust that I even understood statements that would have seemed confounding only weeks before. In the camps—where shoes were holy, currency, inheritance, lifelines—someone had once taken Grandma's shoes. She spent an entire winter day working on frozen ground, her feet blackened with frostbite. Later that night, in order to survive, she found the one girl in the barrack who had failed to sleep with her shoes. Grandma had passed on the death sentence.

"*Oye broch,*" she said, returning us to our present rummaging. "You Poppy had so many beautiful clothes. Noiach, take the sweaters."

But I was still in the shoe closet, where a brown shoebox, bursting with its contents, grabbed my attention. "What's this?" I asked as I lifted the box that contained more than loafers.

"Pictures," Grandma said, indifferent to items that could not be worn.

"Can I look at them?"

"Who cares?"

I loved how she said the word "cares"—Who *cay-yes*? I took the box of photographs back to the kitchen table. Grandma followed me with the bundle of sweaters. I lifted the box's cover and stared into a history reel of black-and-white images. Hundreds, if not thousands, of survivors were piled inside.

On top, Poppy nestled himself into Grandma's side as she sat up in a hospital bed with legs outstretched. The photograph from 1947 had them packed tightly in a twin bed at Lohheide-Hohne, a part of the former concentration camp Bergen-Belsen. A placard above them read LEDERMAN, and on the line below, POLISH JEWS was noted. Grandma sat stiffly, with the sheets tightly drawn around her. Grandma's curved nose, teardrop eyes, and cherubic cheeks revealed no emotion. Poppy wore a pinstriped suit, a wild mane of hair parted on the left, a sharp tie, and penetrating eyes. The Holocaust appeared too fresh in their eyes to allow them the normal fears and joys shared by expecting parents.

I held hundreds of black-and-white photographs from Germany, taken in the years after liberation.

"I can't believe you didn't tell me about these photographs." I wasn't upset with Grandma, only chagrined at having discovered the box years after starting this journey for answers and having learned that I had been a shitty child detective.

"What's to tell? They pictures. You tell me about the things you have in boxes?"

"I guess now I'll start." I shuffled through the photographs. "Who's this?"

Grandma studied the photograph of Poppy sitting beside a stranger. "This a German man. A Nazi."

"Why is Poppy sitting with a Nazi?"

"There were some good Nazis."

Good Nazis? I would have previously wagered my life against Grandma ever marrying together the words "good" and "Nazis." But she said it, right there at her dining room table.

Grandma added: "This Nazi treated Poppy well in the camps and when you Poppy discovered the British were holding this man after our liberation, Poppy went to the British and got him out."

"Who's this?" I held up the next image.

Grandma squinted. "I don't know."

I flipped through the photographs, and Grandma commented: "This one I don't know . . . Who remembers? I don't know . . . Wait . . . This one I remember. This man was Abrashka." Abrashka had brought a smile to her face. "You Poppy was one of the first butchers in Bergen. He bought meat from the Germans and Abrashka was Poppy's assistant." Grandma chuckled and stroked the ugly sweater atop the pile. "They used to push cows up into the attic of the Nazi barrack where we lived after the war."

"Poppy brought cows into the attic?"

"Everything. Cows. Maybe twenty lambs." She stuck her arms out. "I remember the two of them. A man drop off some lambs and Poppy and Abrashka say, 'Come lamb. Come lamb.'" She made the face of a dolt as she imitated her husband and Abrashka chasing lambs around the former concentration camp. "They use the attic because Poppy didn't have no license to be a butcher. It don't mean he wasn't a good butcher, but he didn't have no license. You understand?" she said, in defense of his reputation.

"I do. It's because he was a Jew."

"Do I know? All I know is that they pushed cows up into the attic. I work downstairs, cleaning the blood off Poppy's clothes, and I hear boom. Later, I see cow blood dripping down onto my ceiling. Then the police come. They look for Poppy because he would get me all sorts of jewelry."

"Where did he get you jewelry?" I asked.

"Eh. He got. You should get jewelry, too, for you *geelfriend*."

"I do."

"A ring."

"Tell me about the police."

"I had to tell them you Poppy left me, even though he's hiding in the attic."

Grandma smiled, the police vacating her mind without their suspect. I shuffled through the photographs like one cranks the reel of a silent movie—open with a funeral procession, a casket weighing down on the shoulders of Jewish men; then cut to Poppy seated behind the wheel of a dark convertible, the roof rolled back like the lid of a sardine can; close-in on Poppy smiling alongside friends, a thin cigarette hanging from the left side of his sneer; the camera lens collides with his lean face and cut chin. The remnants of war—army trucks and barracks and miles of wire—infiltrated each photograph.

The box didn't contain all of the pictures. On the Shoah Foundation tapes, Grandma had held up a photograph of two thickly bearded men in front of the camera. Rabbis from Otwock. The men wore white prayer shawls and black yarmulkes; they had long *peyot* winding down their cheeks. The pious Jews were a typical prewar snapshot of the Jewish streets of Poland—two rabbis perhaps debating the nuances of the weekly *parshah*. But there were two things in the photograph that communicated the evils of the time. First, the Nazis had surrounded them. But there was also something else, something that Grandma had struggled to explain.

"They were forced to hang their penises from their pants," she eventually told the camera.

These were photographs that I would never find, just as there were certain facts that I would leave to rest. Things a grandson would never ask of his grandmother. I sealed the box.

I glanced up from the 1940s and stared at Poppy's image hanging in the gold portal around Grandma's neck in this new millennium. Her thick, arthritic fingers drummed the glass table. I wanted her to feel at least a modicum of happiness in the time that she had left. I reached for her hand. Should I stop digging up her past? I wondered. To let her—and it—rest? Then again, the rare smiles and breaks from mourning had started to occur only when we returned to the Holocaust via the Umschlagplatz. This time spent remembering felt cathartic. We sat there holding hands.

"I woke up this morning at three thirty and I reached for him," Grandma said. "I do this every morning. And you know what I think? My husband will be there." She inhaled the room and then slowly exhaled. She touched the golden likeness of Leon Lederman hanging from her neck. "I tell myself that he got up already for work. I tell myself, the next morning, I'm gonna wake up earlier. That way I'll see Poppy."

That knot from the gravesite reemerged in my throat. The fibers were compressed so tightly that air pockets between the individual threads would have been choked out, too.

When I left for the evening, I kept recalling one photograph of Poppy. Just before I had settled the lid over the pictures, the final image was of Poppy sitting outside of barrack L-8, a wedding ring fit to his finger and a watch fastened around the same wrist. In his right hand, below his knuckles, a cigarette dangled. His jacket was off, and his dress socks sat bunched at the ankles. An empty stroller was in the background. A man focused his attention on Leon Lederman—maybe Abrashka or the good Nazi. From a tree limb, clothing dried. Its trunk and branches were silhouettes upon the white walls of the barrack. Like the solid tree casting its outline on the building, Leon's lower lip placed a dark shadow over his chin. His nostrils flared. I couldn't stop seeing his aggrieved eyes.

What was he thinking at that moment in time with everyone dead and a war behind him?

At home, I replayed the interview, pausing it after Poppy had been asked about God. His tone sounded foreign and indignant.

"I was dark about God," he said. "I had doubts . . . many doubts."

16

THE FOUR QUESTIONS

And they were all saved," Mrs. Sussman exclaimed, closing the book and knocking on the cover as if her rapping knuckles were strikes from a judge's gavel. The case of God splitting the Red Sea had been decided in the Hebrew school classroom in the year 1992. My Hebrew school teacher pressed the age-old story against the life bulging in her belly and smiled at the class with a self-satisfied smirk at having prepared us once more for the Passover holiday, which was quickly approaching. "Isn't that a beautiful story, children, how God helped lead the Jews of Egypt to freedom by parting the sea and allowing Moses and his people safe passage?"

Mrs. Sussman scanned our faces, and when her eyes fell on me, I guess she had sensed a doubt that required extinguishing. "What do you think about this, Noah?"

"I don't believe it," I told her.

The Moses faithfuls up front gasped.

"Excuse me?" she said, placing her hands on her pregnant hips.

"How could God split the sea? Why would he do that?"

Mrs. Sussman's complexion was always paper-white, but after that remark, her face became so flushed that even the Red Sea would have been envious.

"What do you mean, *why would he do that?*" asked Mrs. Sussman.

I thought about my grandparents crouched in the Warsaw ghetto, stuck in the bunkers and the sewers as their people were led to the death camps. Where were the miracles then? Was it the flume of gray smoke to the heavens? "I don't think that God cares about Jews."

The gasping section grew wheezy and Mrs. Sussman leaned back in disbelief, lifting the book up as if to shield her unborn progeny from my heresy. She kept wriggling around on the corner of the desk, as if my doubt had induced early contractions. But the discomfort evolved into anger and she sent me to the principal's office.

"You again," the principal bemoaned in her gravelly voice. Her unadorned office looked more like a supply closet. Boxes of staples and pushpins and pencils cluttered her desk. *Haggadahs* were piled on every conceivable surface apart from the floor. "And what did you do this time, Mr. Lederman?"

"Nothing," I told the principal.

"I'm sure you did something." The principal watered a small plant on her desk, using water from a Styrofoam cup stained with lipstick.

I did what God did for the Jews in Egypt and Poland. Like I said, "Nothing."

"Sit there, I'm going to call your father."

A few more weeks of Hebrew school preceded the Seder. Mrs. Sussman continued her dogmatic series of Passover stories as if that ancient enslavement and journey had been the only place in Jewish history in which to find guidance for our lives. I shook my head in quiet protest. However, the real excitement during those weeks were the code Josephs. A code Joseph was something I made up, like a code blue or yellow for organizations enacting some emergency plan, but more apropos for Hebrew schools. In my estimation, Hebrew schools could use code Josephs to alert the staff to a missing child, named for the Joseph of the Bible whose brothers disappeared him. The code should have been called for my brother, who, after each of his first few days of Hebrew school, ran from the classroom and hid in the parking lot.

"You'll go back when you're older," my father told him on his last car ride home from the temple.

"Please," Jake cried. "Can we just convert to being Catholic?"

When the Seder of 1992 arrived, the family gathered at my grandparents' dining room table. Everyone had lost interest in the *haggadah* well before we had dipped the bitter herbs into saltwater. My cousins had closed their books. Grandma sat at the table (only for the Seder portion), though she rose every few minutes to examine the brisket in the oven. My father told his Passover jokes—"An erection on Passover? A Pesach dick."

Despite Jake's lesser age, when Poppy asked for the youngest male to recite the four questions in Hebrew, the task fell to me, the child who hadn't fled from Hebrew school. (Though to my brother's credit, the school did feel like Egypt post-plagues.)

I fumbled over the serpentine letters and the speckish vowels that looked like they had been defecated by the Hebrew consonants above.

And Poppy, who normally had endless patience for his grandchildren, had none on Passover. He corrected me before I could self-edit, diminishing my small contribution to the Seder.

"Sit like a *mensch*," Grandma shouted at Jake, who was crawling about under the table. My aunt's daughters rolled their eyes. "Why on this night do we eat cardboard?" my father asked.

Nobody really noticed how I messed up, but I shrank down at the table and then left for the silence and solitude of the television room. I had never been angry at Poppy before that Passover.

One spring led to the next, and it was time yet, again, to perfect the reciting of the four questions in Mrs. Sussman's prolific presence—once more, she was bursting with child. I avoided being the contrarian and dedicated myself to mastering the four questions.

In that year, I had realized that I was not angry at Poppy, but rather with myself. Poppy had needed to tell the Jewish story of slavery correctly; a story he had written with his own blood, sweat, and tears; one that he stopped telling to his children because the words had forced my father to keep a packed suitcase beneath his bed and gave my aunt an eating disorder; one that he concealed from his grandchildren in an attempt to preserve our innocence. Passover was a reprieve from his sequestered past. A way to tell of his suffering and survival in code. And by messing up the four questions, I had put a snag in the tale that he used to convey his truth.

On the Passover following the failed four questions, Grandma stood over the table and dipped her finger in the saltwater to check whether the amalgamation approximated Jewish tears. She poured in more salt.

That first Passover after liberation, in the former concentration camp Bergen-Belsen, Poppy and Grandma had sat around the table with their friends, the other survivors, and cried. They did not have to make saltwater for the eggs; they produced the symbols. I wondered which survivor had the honor of reciting the four questions on that sacred day, what plagues they had recounted with each finger dipped into wine, how they handled praising God with *Dayenu—If He had taken us through the sea on dry land and not drowned our oppressors in it, it would have sufficed.*

But He did not.

Grandma finished with the saltwater and commanded us to shut our eyes so that she could hide the *afikomen*. I had read somewhere that Holocaust survivors had a habit of hiding bread around their houses, conditioned from the camps to squirrel away their calories. But not Grandma. The idea of bread sitting around her house, shedding crumbs in closets or drawers, would have made her more mental. Even the hidden *afikomen*, which would be found in no time at all, probably induced anxiety.

Poppy began, davening the Seder, muttering Hebrew with fiery anger, and then nodding at me to ask the scripted questions.

I cleared my throat and looked over at him. He smiled and I sighed, prepared for regret. Then I began, singing the query with the rhythm learned in Hebrew school, along with the secret coda not revealed in the Maxwell House *haggadahs*.

Poppy responded in his gentle baritone and looked up with quiet, pleased eyes when it was time to commence with question two. Our call and response across the table felt like a Jewish slave's work song. He preached his coded Seder and I asked my ciphered questions—*What was your role during the Warsaw Ghetto Uprising? Did you watch our family get sent to the camps? What did you dream about each night beside the crematorium? How did you survive?*

We continued with the sad hymnals percolating from the Maxwell House *haggadah*—the saddest coffee advertisement in the world.

Poppy flicked drops of wine on his plate for each of the ten plagues. I watched as his six green numbers pulsed with each red droplet that exploded onto the china. Did he think of frogs, boils, locusts? Or was it darker—crematories, chambers, cattle cars, Warsaw?

Poppy closed the *haggadah* and Grandma raced into the kitchen to slog the table with trays of meats and fish and starches. Poppy reached out and touched my cheek. "*Tateh sheine.*"

I was relieved that I hadn't let him down.

"When Moses was a boy, he put a coal into his mouth," Poppy said to the family after the Seder had lost its gravity to the feast set before us. "This left him with a stutter. When God asked of him where you should like to take the Jewish people, Moses tried to say Canada. But it sounded like he says Canaan. In Ottawa, we'd have been better off."

The joke and the weeks spent preparing for that Seder had left me with a fifth question: If there was no God, what made me Jewish?

17

ISRAEL

In 2007, in the land of Canaan, as a participant of Birthright Israel—when young Jews from around the world travel to Israel to better connect to religion, culture, and the Holy Land—that question of doubt, which had formed years earlier at that Seder, was asked of me daily as we toured the country.

"What makes you a Jew?" our tour guide, Yoni, would challenge in the places where Jews fought to their death—at Masada, and during the War of Independence, the Yom Kippur War, the Six-Day War. "What makes you Jewish?" he asked at the scenes of more recent homicides—outside storefronts that had been reconstructed after bombings on Ben Yehudah Street, in towns near the border with Lebanon, where the residents checked for rockets the way most check the weather, in Rabin Square, where its namesake had been assassinated. "What does it mean to be Jewish?"

Some had answers. Some shrugged.

We were a mix of secular Jews, temple-going Jews, just Jews, and maybe even non-Jews, as some liked to speculate.

"What do you think about that one?" one girl asked me as we walked through an ultra-Orthodox neighborhood. "I think that girl and her husband are faking it. They're as Christian as they come. They just wanted the free trip. Fucking fake Jews."

Meanwhile, a few ultra-Orthodox men had stamped out of their apartments and begun castigating the females in our group, accusing them of showing too much sexy shoulder skin. None of us were Jews to them.

"They shout at you, the bastards. They don't even fight for Israel and they cause most of our problems with the settlements," our Israeli medic said, pulling his rifle off of his shoulder and holding it at the ready in his hands. "Fucking Orthodox. What kind of Jews are they?"

Defining Judaism, for me, had never involved temple or God or accepting the biblical tales as even figurative truth. Yet I had always identified as a Jew. I realized that my Jewishness was linked mostly to the numbers on my grandparents' arms.

Sure, like most Jews, I enjoyed the miracle of Hanukah, the Passover Seders, the reprobation of Haman, but only because they served as allegories for my grandparents' Holocaust: Hanukah adumbrated those brief moments of luck inside the camps; Passover symbolized *their* story of slavery and liberation; the denunciation of Haman proffered a merry *fuck you* to Hitler. At the same time, the event that linked me most to my Jewish roots was also the very thing that had removed the "Judaism" from my Judaism. Never again could I believe in a God when babies were burned in pits because some religion had been assigned to their births. Never again could I believe in a God when entire families were gassed together.

Still, I was a Jew.

"You're not a Jew if you don't do Jewish things," I had been told by a *real Jew* who denounced bacon (but who then broke from reprimanding me to tackle the peel-and-eat shrimp at little David's bar mitzvah).

"If you refuse to hang a mezuzah on your doorframe, how are you a Jew?" asked a *true* "chosen person" who kept a kosher home (but who used paper plates to eat *traif*).

In the Old Testament, God had promised to spare a town as long as there were ten righteous men there. Did that mean that Otwock, a town of fourteen thousand Jews, hadn't met the quota? The ground had to be filled with at least ten. And if not Otwock, then there had to be one town, one fucking town in all of Europe where people were incinerated despite God's promise.

Anyway, what was a God whose guarantee had less credence than Hitler's?

If I had been born in the 1920s or '30s or '40s, Hitler would have stayed committed to my annihilation whether I had fasted on Yom Kippur or ate bacon-wrapped oysters with the Führer off of the Torah. In a sense, it is Hitler's failed promise that makes me a Jew. (In fact, Birthright had used Hitler's pledge when selecting participants for trips to Israel: *Do you have at least one Jewish grandparent?*)

However, I was also not a Jew whose identity was rooted in victimization; I found my connection to Judaism in the stories of revolt and survival.

Though I wasn't inclined toward prayer, in Israel I went through the motions. I didn't object to placing notes in holy edifices. On a slip of paper no bigger than a fortune cookie I wrote a wish for Grandma and crammed the note between the square boulders of the Western Wall. Two images of Grandma flashed before me as I closed my eyes and pressed my head to the beige stones littered with weeds and paper prayers. I saw the young girl who had witnessed her mother's murder and the old woman wading through depression, waiting to join her husband. But then I saw this third form—a chimera of the two. An old, depressed woman finding catharsis in resurrecting the terrors of her past with her eldest grandson. I smiled at this image, an image that would have been impossible without that trip to Poland.

Here, in Israel, I was hoping to stumble upon another key—another Umschlagplatz. Perhaps it was at Yad Vashem. I needed to find the mystery camp. I hoped to uncover some long-lost relative. Maybe I'd get lucky and come across an artifact that linked Poppy to a revolutionary Warsaw ghetto bunker. For the past few months, I had found no new information, and Grandma had gotten in the habit of repeating her stories. Our journey into the past had plateaued, and the stretch forward appeared barren.

After I took my distance from the Western Wall, one of the more observant Jews on my trip approached me. "If you don't believe in God or prayer, why did you shove a prayer into the Western Wall?"

I was tired of this perpetual identity challenge. But he did make me think. I thought mostly of Poppy and the thousands of deaths that had inculcated doubt in him. At the Western Wall, I could still see his expression when he was asked about his faith during the Spielberg session. Poppy's response was the only one that could answer this question.

Poppy's left eye had closed, and his head lowered. That eternal smirk deconstructed. He had had seventy years to ponder this question.

"The Nazis found the Otwock rabbi being led to Sobienie"—a town near Otwock—"by a Polish *shiksah*," he said, his voice growing most serious after mentioning the non-Jewish woman. "They made him put on his *talis* and *tefillin*. They said to the rabbi, 'Pray to God that we won't kill you. Pray to your God that maybe our hands will fall off and you'll be able to live.' He prayed. I saw they killed the twenty others, then the rabbi, and then the *shiksah*. Then they threw the rabbi into the grave with the woman. I buried them. Then, after, we took the *shiksah* out and put her in a separate grave."

Maybe Poppy had been unhappy with his explanation because he continued: "God says we don't kill the mother cow and calf on the same day.

Are you listening? Nazis killed mothers and children in the same day. A boy before he is thirteen has no sin; a girl before her wedding day has no sin."

One and a half million children were killed. Mothers walked with their sons and daughters into the gas chambers.

"I'm not an atheist," Poppy added, "but I had doubts about it. Many doubts."

But I didn't tell the guy from my trip about Poppy. I just lied to him: "I shoved in a gum wrapper."

Or maybe I placed the prayer in the wall because in the land of Canaan I was giving God one more chance to prove me wrong; maybe I was making a gesture to my grandparents; maybe I wanted to find something familiar in this foreign place. Maybe I just missed Poppy and hoped that Grandma would still be well enough to return to our sessions after my three weeks in the desert.

On the bus ride from Jerusalem's old city, the wall had placed its weight on some of the Jews in my group. The conversations had switched to *aliyah*—the immigration of Diaspora Jews to Israel.

"I'm thinking about making *aliyah*," one of the American Jews said.

"Me too," said another.

"Oh my God, me too," said a third.

Aliyah, in Hebrew, means to go up, to ascend. I wondered how the Zionists ever could have chosen that term for Jews wanting to make Israel their new home. Jews *going up* or *ascending* didn't connote a stronger Israel; it was the consequences of the crematories. Six million Jews made *aliyah*. Hitler, if he had spoken Hebrew, would have called his Final Solution "Making *Aliyah*."

Later that evening, we joined four thousand Jews from around the globe at the International Convention Center of Jerusalem, where Brazilian Jews and Canadian Jews and Argentinean Jews and American Jews and Russian Jews and Georgian Jews had gathered in an auditorium in segregated units, chanting nationalistic slogans and waving their countries' flags. The divisiveness bordered the insanity of a tied soccer match approaching the ninetieth minute between Manchester United and Real Madrid.

But it took only one Israeli song pumping through the speakers to affect the atmosphere. The Jews of the convention center suddenly exchanged their country's flags for the small plastic Israeli ones we had been given earlier. Netanyahu and Olmert asked us to be their countrymen. Four thousand people sang *Adon Olam* and *Shalom Aleichem*. We shook the blue-and-white flags; it looked like rough seas below the balcony seats. We were engaged in some reverse Diaspora.

The plastic pride looked so beautiful, and it filled my heart with its ripples. I wondered what my grandparents had felt as they prepared to fight to the death in Warsaw.

Then the *Hatikvah* echoed through the hall. Each person grasped the shoulder of the Jew beside them and swayed like a slow swell in the ocean. Everyone still held on to their plastic flags. Those four thousand flags with blue Stars of David fell onto every neighbor's shoulder. In this mass fraternal clutch, arms that were overlaid with the blue star looked like the identifying yellow armbands that the Nazis had forced on the Jews before the camps. But in Israel the stars-on-shoulders embodied unity. The national anthem played like our redemption song.

I thought back to the Israeli soldier, the one who sang the *Hatikvah* in Warsaw in front of the statue that honored the ghetto fighters. The message in Poland, just as it was here in Israel, was *Never again*. And in both instances it finally seemed to convey credence.

Jerusalem. Warsaw. The two cities intertwined in me. These were the two strands that formed the double helix of my Jewish identity. Israel would always be a home born from the pact of the Warsaw ghetto heroes. And that's how and why I was a Jew.

18

RESEARCH AT YAD VASHEM

When the Birthright trip ended, I extended my time in Israel and returned to Yad Vashem to use its research facilities. Two questions had bothered me the most: Where had Poppy been liberated from? And what were my grandparents' stories on those heroic grounds of Warsaw?

I sat down at the database and plugged in all of the names and towns connected to my grandparents' pasts, spelling persons and places phonetically, then correctly, and then Germanically. Poppy's four sisters and Grandma's two brothers as well as all the great-grandparents and great-great-grandparents were expunged from the earth and the records, too, floating similarly through the world and cyber-universe like dust. When I punched in the names *Leon Lederman* and *Hadasa Zylberberg*, what turned up were the doppelgangers that my grandparents had invented.

Grandma was Chadasa and Hadasa and Zylberberg and Silberberg. She was born on the fifth of April and the fifth of May and also the fifth of November. The discrepancies and contrary facts belonged to only one person as the other information listed—parents' names, concentration camp dates and numbers, and other biographical details—was all the same. None of this surprised me, not the way it had shocked me on an April 5 morning fifteen years earlier.

"We're going to Grandma's today," my father had told us then. "For her birthday."

"But Grandma's birthday is November 5," I said.

"Tell her that," said my father. "It's news to me, too."

"What does that mean?"

It meant that in 1949, when Grandma had stood on the immigration line, she panicked when the agent had asked her for her date of birth. She gave the first date that came to her mind, a merge between the birth month of the stranger entering America just before her and her own date in April.

Grandma was older than Poppy. She had been born in 1923, he in 1925. So, like any age-sensitive wife who was creating a new identity, she also swapped birth years with Poppy and left it at that.

The falsifications of and inconsistencies in records made the search for facts more like espionage rather than piecing together a jigsaw puzzle. And if I weren't running into the clans that they had created for themselves during the years surrounding the Holocaust, I was chasing ghosts. As I continued through the records, Yad Vashem delivered Ledermans from Otwock whom I had never known before. Samuel Lederman, for instance, shared Poppy's father's name and my father's name but had been too young to father Leon and too old to be his son; he was just another Jewish Lederman from Otwock. But the most confounding phantom was the Leon Lederman with a different six-digit concentration camp number. While there were plenty of documents that did match the number on his arm, I couldn't get over this one document that was also unmistakably Poppy's, as all of the other details matched up. Why did the tattoo that I had committed to memory not match this second number assigned to him during the war? Had Poppy been tattooed twice?

Though I hadn't made any great discoveries at Yad Vashem and probably left more confused than when I arrived, I was uncovering facts that had been condemned to obliteration twice: once as failed aspects of the Final Solution and again as historical notes that would have sat buried in this massive archive.

Yet by digging up these documents, I felt a small victory. I was taking something back from the past, preserving facts that the world and my grandparents and my father had laid to rest. In the way that a scientist might dedicate an entire career to studying a small area of research yet still end up satisfied with answering only one part of a bigger question, I felt a catharsis in finding these falsified birthdates and bemusing numbers. It meant that there was more out there: trivia that could lead me to truth. I was closer to the stories that I was never supposed to have. Closer, maybe, to Klein Webber and to Warsaw.

From Yad Vashem, I walked over to the bus stop enervated and satisfied. Jerusalem seemed at peace. The awaiting commuters moseyed about in the heat. Others struck up conversations. I stood and wondered over the details of two puzzling lives. When the bus pulled up, instead of a line, the throng of once-civil Israelis began to box each other out, placing their hands on the bus as if the year were 1969 and a car shuttling the Beatles had just pulled up in Jerusalem.

I watched the disorder as the Jews vied for position, refusing to form that civil construct learned in kindergarten. Religious men barked at Gothic teens who pushed off of old women who used their groceries like clubs on the rabbis. I was forced to elbow my way onto the bus, too.

When I returned home from Israel, a packet from the International Tracing Service had arrived with more enigmatic documents: Poppy, who was born on February 3, had had backup births scheduled on May 2 and May 5. Grandma, on the other hand, broke away from the fifth of the month and opted to have a birthday in the middle of June.

"Did they send anything on Grandma's Aunt Bruder?" Dad asked. She had been a key donor to the Polish army during World War I, and Great-Great-Aunt Bruder had never been repaid.

While I was unable to find documents that would bring us closer to restitution, I found facts that felt as pertinent to me as my genetics.

The papers indicated that Grandma had been tattooed in Auschwitz on June 26, 1943. Poppy had been transported from Dora-Mittelbau to Ravensbrück in April 1945, when he was issued another prisoner number, 14477 (which was different from the second string of numbers that I had uncovered in Yad Vashem).

Inside the packet was my aunt's birth certificate from the Lohheide-Hohne camp, formerly known as Bergen-Belsen. Documents that originated from a time when Grandma could sign her own name without my father's help were inside. Records from the *General Howze*, the ship that brought my grandparents to America, indicated that Poppy had committed, in writing, to his father's job. His profession was listed as butcher. Grandma, it read, was a housewife.

The Auschwitz Chronicles revealed that Poppy had entered Auschwitz on July 8, 1943, on a transport that sent 1,500 Jews from Majdanek for slave labor. Five women had died on the train. Many of the other people had scabies. Four hundred twenty-four men were deemed healthy enough to work and were thus selected for quarantine. The rest—more than two-thirds—were sent to the gas chambers.

The discoveries were tragic, but exciting. The puzzle started to look a bit more complete. I was getting a taste of data that delivered results. But I still hadn't answered the questions I had hoped to answer at Yad Vashem.

19

NEARLY UNRAVELED

I brought all of the documents to Grandma's apartment, hoping that she could scan them and separate fact from fiction. She looked at the dates, names, and descriptors. With a few words and one swipe of her hand, Grandma brushed everything to the side.

"Noiach, what's the difference? I was born. I had a name." She shrugged. "Israel was nice?"

"Beautiful," I told her.

"Sure. What's not to like?"

"No complaints of me traveling the world," I joked.

"Go. Travel. Who cay-yes? You go with you geelfriend, Marissa?"

"I did."

"So maybe you should get married already."

I needed an exit strategy from this conversation. So I relayed a question that my latest group of students had asked of me as I introduced them to the Holocaust by way of Night. "Grandma, did you ever meet any good Germans?"

"Good Germans?" The oxymoron from her moron grandson had unsettled her.

"You once told me that Poppy knew a good Nazi."

She looked stunned. "I wouldn't say this. Good Nazi? Good Germans? Noiach, please." She stopped and sat there shaking her head. "I remember this one."

"This one what?"

"Noiach," she reproached. "I was in the fields in Auschwitz. Lots of snow. A Wehrmacht soldier walking around. Not a Nazi, but a German. And when he move away, I say to Yadja . . ." Grandma paused. "Noiach, do you remember Yadja?"

It had been years since her friends had died. All of those survivors who had gathered around my grandparents' living room, and only Grandma still clung to life.

"I remember Yadja."

"Well, I say to Yadja, 'When this is over, I'm gonna make such a good meal for us.' But, Noiach, now what can Grandma do? *Oy, oy, oy*," she chanted, mourning her renounced skill.

"That's okay, Grandma."

"Anyway, someone whispers, '*Machshifa* is coming,'" Grandma said.

"What's a *mock shifa*?"

"*Oy*, Noiach, you speak no Jewish. You need to learn Jewish."

"You want to teach me Yiddish now."

"Noiach, I'm too old. I don't have patience. You need patience to speak Jewish."

"Fine, what's a *mock shifa*? Teach me something."

"*Machshifa*, this mean vitch."

"Vitch?"

"Vitch. Like a evil voman."

"Witch."

"At least I can speak Jewish. Listen, there *vas* one SS *voman* who *vas* a *vitch* and she come past that day, angry, checking to see our *vork*."

"Who warned you?"

"This is what we want to know. And then we realize that it had been a man. But what man spoke Jewish? The only man was the Wermacht soldier. So we look at him and he smiles. This German smiles at us. We're scared now. He sees us see him. So we dig faster and faster. We don't want he should see us seeing him. And then he comes over. But he says to us, in Jewish"—she stressed those last two words—"'Don't worry, children, on the Sabbath you will soon eat delicious fish again.' Even he, a German soldier, can speak Jewish, Noiach."

"Did you teach him?" I teased.

"I didn't teach him. He was a good man. Remember when Grandma could cook for you and make delicious gefilte fish?"

"I remember. Grandma, didn't you find this guy a bit creepy? It's a strange thing to say: you will soon eat delicious fish."

"Creepy?" she threw her arms up. "Who knows from this? He spoke human to us. The only German who ever spoke human to us. What else should he say?"

"I guess. Do you remember any other Germans?" I asked, looking to plunder more stories with the vault door open.

She paused and exhaled.

"I remember the worst two Nazis. In Warsaw. Klaustermeyer and Blosche."

Anytime Warsaw was mentioned, my heart seemed to flutter with excitement. I leaned forward and readied my pen. I actually knew the names of these Nazis from Poppy's tapes. When he had entered the Jewish compound in November 1942, Poppy contracted typhus and left his cousin's ghetto apartment to recover in the Czyste hospital. But after four days inside, he had learned that a selection would empty the hospital. He stole clothes and returned to his cousin's apartment. But his cousin turned him away.

That's when Poppy ran into Klaustermeyer and Blosche. The pair was notorious for their barbarism: shooting babies, smashing infants' skulls against brick walls, throwing the disabled from the top floors of buildings. The two would release their victims only to gun them down as they fled.

The pair circled Poppy on bikes, laughing sadistically. He knew that life was over, so he just walked, looking straight ahead, allowing the Nazis to ride and laugh and plant a bullet in his head.

But they let him go.

Nicknamed Frankenstein, the barbaric Blosche is portrayed in one of the more infamous Holocaust images: Women and children from the ghetto hold their hands high above their heads; but the camera is focused on one boy wearing knee-high socks, a cap, a dark coat, and a frightened expression. Behind the boy stands a Nazi with a submachine gun trained on the boy's back. The man holding the gun, wearing a steel helmet and motorcycle goggles, is Blosche.

I couldn't understand why they hadn't shot Poppy. Maybe they saw something in him. Maybe they had had a good breakfast that morning.

"What do you remember about them?" I asked Grandma.

"Me, my father, and Shama were out past curfew in the ghetto. Those Nazis yelled 'Halt! Halt!'" Grandma shouted their commands. "We ran. What can you do? And they chase us down Ulica Mila. I was very ill with typhus then. Very bad fevers. My father, he finds an open door that go up into a ghetto apartment, but the door is . . . how you say?" She touched the tips of her thumb and pointer together and slid them back and forth.

"Bolted?" My heart raced with her telling.

"The door is bolted. So we hid in this little hole. My father drags a small closet across the floor so the bastards can't see us."

"How do you drag a closet?"

"You drag."

"An armoire?"

"Yes. A closet. I hear them stomping up the stairs. Noiach, I was so scared. I could hear them outside. They do this to the handle." She jiggled an imaginary handle and even when she stopped, when she placed her hand back on the table, atop her case of tranquilizers, it still shook. "Then they went away. They killed Jews for looking at them wrong and us, we run from them. They know we are in the apartment hiding. They could have break down the door."

I swallowed hard at the realization that two murderers—twice—had nearly stood in the way of my existence. As much as Warsaw and Israel had a hand in spinning my DNA, Klaustermeyer and Blosche could have unraveled me before I was ever a consideration.

Grandma took a pill. I sipped some water. I thought about stopping the questions, but realized that we were back inside the gates of Warsaw.

20

THE BOY AT
THE GATES OF WARSAW

There was another Nazi from Warsaw that I remember," Grandma said after the pill had calmed her and I pressed farther into the ghetto. "He finds me in the street and tells me to follow him. I do. I feel a heat coming from around a building. I turn the corner and there's a big *barn fire*. The Germans were burning books. Jewish books. Right there in the street." Grandma squeezed her lips together and nodded with disbelief. "Can you imagine?"

I could imagine just as the German poet Heinrich Heine had imagined well before the camps: *A society that burns books . . . will eventually burn its people.*

"The Nazi told me to go up into the apartments. To throw down the books. He tells to me 'If I see one book left up there, I'll throw you into the fire.' This is what he said."

Grandma climbed the creaking staircase, opened the door to the top-floor apartment, and entered the empty room. On a small wooden mantelpiece stood a modest collection of religious texts. She lifted the *siddur*, *Humash*, and *Gemara* and flipped through them, noting God's name on each page.

"I could not throw the books from the window, Noiach. So I picked up a string on the floor, like a string a baker uses for a babka, and stacked the books up. I made like this." Grandma wrapped the imaginary books with the invisible string, creating a mirage of the righteous bundle. "I walked over to the window and looked down at the *barn fire*. These Germans are burning Bibles and Torahs. *Ptoy, ptoy.* And the German who tells to me to go up into the building sees me. He says throw down your . . ." Grandma paused and looked at the imaginary pile, as if from it God had sprouted ears. "He said 'shit books,' Noiach. He says this about sacred books." She tapped the table with each syllable. "So I turn from the window and walk down the stairs. Do you think I'm gonna put the books in the fire?"

Her question wasn't rhetorical, and she waited for my response.

"N . . . No." Who was this woman who sat feebly before me now? Why had she risked her life for books that named a God who had allowed all thirty-plus relatives in that picture above the light switch to perish? "I don't think you would."

"Well, I didn't. When I come down the stairs." She cleared her throat so she could raise her voice like the Nazi. "'I told to you to throw the books down.' He's spitting on my face. I reach out to give him the books. But he puts his hand on his rifle. You know what I do? I close my eyes." Grandma closed her eyes and told the rest of the story from the haunting memory playing out across her shut lids. "Let him shoot me, I think. But instead, he rips the books from my hand and probably walks with them to the fire. I don't look. I just run. I don't want to watch." Grandma shivered and left the table, limping from the conflagration she had set.

She was starting to fill those unwritten chapters about my heroes of the Warsaw ghetto. I was too shocked to write.

Eventually, she returned, lips still pressed together, thinned eyebrows still lifted in horror over the burning books. "Noiach, you wanted to see Holocaust books, right? Well, they in the china cabinet."

I got up and opened the drawers. I hadn't dug through the china cabinet since before Poppy had died. And when he had been alive, the only drawer that I ever explored in the china cabinet was the one with his cigarettes and playing cards. (Yes, I concede again, I wasn't much of a child detective.)

The Holocaust books that Grandma owned were mixed up with year-books from survivor conventions in Washington, DC, and Miami. Inside the books were newspaper clippings of Grandma flashing the numbers on her arm to a photojournalist. The blurb beneath the photograph noted that Hadasa Lederman had survived Auschwitz, as if Auschwitz were the only camp worth remembering.

"What's this?" I held up a Hebrew text that had to have been similar to the ones that Grandma had refused to burn in Warsaw. The cover, which had most likely once been the color of coal, had faded to brown and been speckled with white patches. Inside the musky book were the signs of a preteen vandal: cartoon drawings and sacrilegious scribblings.

"It was you father's," Grandma said.

"Can I take it home?"

"Take whatever you want. What am I gonna do with any of this stuff?" She said this to the heavens and threw her hands out, asking her omniscient watcher once more why He had taken her husband or why He hadn't sped up her demise.

How did she find a way to forgive God for any of this?

I returned to the table and flipped open one of the Holocaust history books to a few images of Warsaw—suffering children, piles of carted-off bodies, a moribund population.

"What did the Warsaw ghetto look like to you when you first arrived?"

"My father, when I see him in Karczew, he knows that it isn't safe for me there. So he sends me with a Pole he knows to the Warsaw ghetto. My father gives me a five-*zloty* coin with Piłsudski's face."

"Who's Piłsudski?"

"A man. A general. My father tells to me, if anyone looks to give you harm, you give them this coin. So the Polish man takes me to the trolley, but you know, Jews cannot ride the trolley anymore. It's illegal. On the trolley, I remember there was this Polish boy. He stands up and points at me. 'You Jew. You Jew.'" Grandma shrugs and nods. *Can you believe it?* said her expression.

"What happened?"

"What happened. Nazis outside. The conductor comes at me. '*Yakim provim?*' This is what he shouts."

"What does it mean?" I asked.

"Like, Where do you get the nerve? Something like this. I don't know what to do. But then I feel the coin in my pocket and just like my father tells to me, I place Piłsudski's coin in his hand. And we go to Warsaw, where I'm supposed to meet a group at the gate. A cousin. But nobody was there. This Jewish policeman, he sees me and he tells me to join this group entering the ghetto. He pushes me in. That's how I get in. I was lucky. Some weren't."

"Like who?" I asked.

But Grandma didn't speak right away. And we sat with the silence. Then she spoke.

"There was a young boy there. It was on a day when I was coming back from work outside the ghetto. He just wanted to enter the ghetto. He knocked and knocked on the gate. He wanted to come in. He said to the

Nazi outside to let him in please." Grandma's eyes grew foggy. How often in the past sixty years had she heard that knock?

"What happened?" But I knew the answer well before her knuckles struck the table.

"The Nazi shot him in the face. A young boy. His face on the wall. A young boy." Grandma shook her head. Knuckles to table. We both needed a break from Warsaw.

21

LIGHTNING LAD

At home, I showed Dad the Yeshiva book he had marked up.

"Where did you get this?" I asked him.

He exhaled with nostalgia and rubbed the graying circle of facial hair hiding much of his expression. He flipped through the first few pages, examining the ancient letters and his past mischievousness. "You know what? This was the *Gemara* that Poppy brought over to America from Germany. It's a book of laws, ethics, and morals governing Jewish life. Stuff about lox and bacon, I think."

"I'm sure there's a law in here prohibiting the doodling of Archie cartoons and scribbling notes to friends."

"Now you know why the rabbis hit me. But only once. I told Poppy, he went in there, and after that the rabbis were too scared to even look at me."

"What did he say to them?"

"It was probably more than words."

Dad studied his old notes scribbled in the *Gemara* and read some aloud. *"Be 12 this coming January in the year 1963.* I told you English wasn't my first language. Poppy gave this to me when I started Yeshiva. This book was very important to him."

Alongside my father's grammatically flawed pronouncements, he had covered the moldering pages with his address, phone number, math equations, and acrostics for "Sam," "America," and "Israel." But my favorite project was his alphabetized, incomplete list of superheroes: *A* was for Aquaman, *B* for Batman, then Cosmic Boy. He couldn't come up with a protagonist for *D*. There was Flash and Hawkeye, Krypto, and Superman.

"I can't believe I did that."

"Who gave this book to Poppy, anyway?"

"After the war, Poppy wandered the German countryside trying to figure out where he should go next. He had nobody left. His entire family was killed in Treblinka. Poppy had come across this group of rabbis in Germany. They were studying the *Gemara*. He heard them praying in this deserted temple and he sat down to listen. The rabbis took one look at him—at the time he had this wild hair," my father said, making a mess of the hair he didn't have. "Poppy looked like a hooligan. They said to him '*Vous viste.*' Kind of like, 'What the hell do you want?' Poppy said that he wanted to join them. So they laughed. 'What do you know about what we do?' they asked. So Poppy walked over to them and they handed him the book, doubting he could even read it. Not only did he read it, but when they asked him to interpret the text, Poppy blew them away. Anyway, that's how he told me the story." Dad stopped to think. "Poppy never had the chance to go to high school, but he was a scholar. And the rabbis could sense it. They liked him so much, they gave him this book."

I thought about what Poppy had said on the Shoah Foundation tapes—the story of the Otwock rabbi praying before his murder, God's pronouncements that forbid the killing of the mother and child on the same day, his darkness about God. Had the *Gemara* been the one physical cord that he had allowed God, whom he doubted and hated and adjudicated and missed, to attach to him? It was a book that questioned right and wrong, just as I was certain he had done every day after the Holocaust. Poppy must have needed the *Gemara* like a superhero in need of a rival.

I flipped open to my father's superhero acrostic. "Why did you write Lightning Lad for the letter *L*?"

"Who else could I have used for the letter *L*?"

22

ESCAPE FROM TREBLINKA

A few days after finding Poppy's *Gemara*, a book that I had ordered online, *Cyanide of Potassium*, arrived in the mail. The author, Roman Grunspan, had lived in Otwock with my grandparents. Though the book wasn't a gripping read, Grunspan had done what those Warsaw accounts had failed to accomplish. He had mentioned Leon Lederman. Poppy had a small role in the memoir, appearing like a minor character in a movie. But he had received a credit nonetheless.

"Do you know anything about this day?" I asked Dad, foisting upon him the photographs and pages of that tragic day in Otwock, the one that Grunszpan had linked Poppy to.

"How many books are you going to show me?" I was exhausting him with the Holocaust. Each question was a pickax. And I was constantly demanding that he break through to the gems deep in his subconscious. But he looked at the book and read.

"This is the liquidation," he said, deep in the cave with those memories.

Dad's story played out like the pages that Grunspan had never written.

On August 19, 1942, the Germans had commenced with the liquidation of Otwock. Eight thousand Jews would be shipped by cattle car to Treblinka. Four thousand more were marched into the forest where, in the days before, trenches had been dug.

Leon Lederman was one of the few hundred boys who would be saved by labor: he was tasked with filling mass graves with the bodies of his four thousand neighbors, and perhaps family, and then dirt.

Before the transport, talk in the small camp at Karczew spread. Rumors taught the boys of their people's fate. Four boys departed Karczew under penalty of death for Otwock.

It was a sweltering morning as Leon dashed through the woods with his three friends. They knew nothing more of their plan than to reach the perimeter of the deportation square. The road crawled with Ukrainian militiamen, drunk with laughter and firing celebratory gunshots into the air. Their Polish neighbors had already gathered in the streets, wielding axes to hack down doors and loot the homes of the not-yet-murdered Jews. Abandoned suitcases and the heirlooms belonging to those without heirs littered the street.

From the cover of the forest, Leon Lederman found his eight thousand Jewish neighbors at the mercy of the heat and the German and Ukrainian guards. The Nazis and their volunteers drank liters of beer, waiting for that cocktail of power and booze to thrust them into the crowds and beat their prisoners for sport. Leon tried to devise a plan.

But the cattle cars filled before anything came to mind, and he watched as bullets and lime were sent through the windows of the cars.

"Leon," the three boys yelled in a whisper.

But he didn't stop. Leon ran into the square and got himself lost among the rounded up Jews. He searched for his four sisters and parents, but they were lost in the crowd or already devoured by the hundred-person coffins standing upon the tracks. Treblinka served only one function; there were no laborers there.

Leon was forced into the cattle car. The doors slammed shut. Inside was darkness. The heat was unbearable. He squirmed to reach the window. Wiping his brow, he waited for the trains to depart. The most important thing was to not lose consciousness, to not succumb to the heat.

When the trains did move, hours later, Leon reached down to his waist and unfastened a wire that he had worn like a belt. He wrapped the wire around one hand, fed it through the bars of the window, and then raveled it around his other hand. It was difficult to move his arms, but he managed and used the wire as a saw on the bar. The train progressed toward Treblinka.

As night fell, while the unconscious bodies around him could not collapse—the masses even kept the dead standing—the wire severed the bar. His arms burned. Leon punched at the bar. It clattered to the tracks below without sound. Treblinka was coming.

Struggling to pull himself through the small window, he eventually managed to get his head through and then his body. Leon was draped from the window by his waist like clothing on a line. When strength returned, he righted himself and released his grip.

Leon fell to the earth, missing the metal wheels and the bullets from the Nazis atop the roof. He lifted himself from the dirt and stood in the darkness of that Polish night, stood somewhere between Otwock and Treblinka, and watched his sisters and parents continue toward the gas chambers. He was alone in the universe.

"He was seventeen when that happened. This is the one story that I really remember well." Dad handed me back Grunspan's book. "I haven't thought about that story for all these years. I miss Poppy."

"I miss him, too," I said, eyes still wide at having heard the Train to Treblinka Escape Story.

"What you're doing with Grandma, learning all these stories, it's a good thing."

"Thanks." It meant a lot coming from the generation that had always wanted to forget.

"Plus, she hasn't cursed me out for a while," Dad added.

I returned Grunspan's book to the shelf, beside the *Gemara* filled with my father's superhero acrostics. *Lightning Lad. Really, Dad?* There had always been a much better choice for the letter *L*.

23

THE LIQUIDATION

"Where were you during the liquidation of Otwock?" I asked Grandma. I couldn't get Poppy's Train to Treblinka Escape Story out of my mind.

"Not today, Noiach. Not today."

"Okay, Grandma," I said, putting away all of the notebooks. "How's everything going?"

"What you want I should say? I'm going on vacation? How should things be? And by you? You gonna get married already? Marissa isn't gonna wait forever." Grandma paused in her sarcasm and reproach before hearing the bell for round two. "You gonna lose her. You don't want to buy a ring? I shouldn't have a wedding?"

"A wedding?" I said, trying to match wits. "What? Are you planning on getting married again?"

Grandma slapped the table. The playing field would not be leveled in her apartment. She was forever married to her dead husband. I rubbed her hand.

"You too cheap to buy a ring, huh?" she said.

"It's only been a few years."

"*Oye broch.* I married in less than a year. A few years? What you need? A hundred years?"

"How many will you give me?" I asked, only partly joking. I could hear in her mourning and remembering—in the way she now feebly *oy, oy, oy*ed—that our time was running out.

"*Gey a vec,*" she said.

Grandma suffered if we talked about the Holocaust, but she found a way to make herself suffer worse if we didn't.

"Noiach, what you ask me before about Otwock?"

"I wanted to know where you were when they sent everyone from Otwock to Treblinka."

"Hiding. My father come to my room before the sun come up and told to me we must leave. I went to go pack. You know what he says? We have no time. We left everything."

Her mood had improved tremendously.

I could picture my father hearing this story as a boy and then running into his room to check on his suitcase the second that Grandma had reminded him there was no time to pack.

"That day, we hid under the train platform. Eight others already inside. I say to myself how the three of us gonna fit?" She tightened her lips and nodded her head. I knew from her expression that the three of them would not fit. "My father went to Sobienie—a nearby town. Me and my mother hide under the platform. He tells to us wait for his friend, a police officer. The police officer would come for us. My mother keeps telling to me, I don't think I locked the door well enough. Everyone tells my mother to be quiet."

I realized that I had probably stood atop same platform, or where that platform had been, when my train had arrived in Otwock.

"Through the holes," Grandma continued, "I saw a shadow standing behind one of the pine trees. She move from one tree to the other. And when she come to the platform, I saw it was a cousin of mine. I wanted to say that we in here. But everyone told to me, there's no more room. My cousin touched the boards." Grandma's eyes sparkled with tears, just as they had when she spoke of the boy at the gates of Warsaw. I knew the end of this story before it even came—Treblinka.

If the years had taught Grandma how to block out the boy from Warsaw, I couldn't see how her cousin, who hung above the light switch in her bedroom, ever left her mind. Grandma's throat tightened with sadness and it became very hard for her to talk.

"I couldn't say nothing. I couldn't let her in."

I squeezed her hand and bit my lip.

"We heard a motor and my cousin had to run back to the forest." She slapped the table, her hand offering the conclusion. "The Nazis took her or the Poles turned her in."

I thought about Teddy's grandmother and the old Jews from the Jewish Center and the women with their pruning shears on Podmiejska Street and the old man who didn't hear me shout the names. Some had been kind.

Some had appeared frightened. But what had they all done on that hot day in August 1942? And Teddy still had not replied to my e-mails.

After Otwock had been liquidated, exactly as her father had promised, the police officer arrived and brought Grandma and her mother to a farmstead.

"He tells to me, 'Get in the stack of hay.'" The thought of having to crawl into the hay still seemed to shock her all these years later.

"There was enough room for you and your mother?"

"What room? I hid in the hay by myself. I shout to him, 'Where are you taking my mother?' You think he *cay-yes*. He wouldn't let her hide with me. I sat in that hay for hours. Days maybe. He tells to me, 'Don't leave until you hear the code.'"

"What was the code?" I asked.

"I didn't know. What should I know from codes? I'm a child then. Then one day, I hear: 'Zylberberg, Zylberberg.' I didn't know if someone was saying my name or something else. I was how you say?"

"Delusional?"

Grandma shot me a stare of reproach—*This is what you think of Grandma?*

"Like I'm hearing things," Grandma corrects. "What you call that?"

"I get what you mean, Grandma." I couldn't come up with a euphemism for *delusional*.

"I think to myself, maybe it's blackmail. But then the voice says, 'You father wants you.' So I crawl out. He takes me to Sobienie. To my parents."

"Where are they hiding?"

"In the barn."

Just as Poppy could have supplanted Lightning Lad in the *Gemara* acrostic, Hadasa Lederman should have stood in for Hawkeye. The woman who sat across from me, who had survived the Nazis and illness and all of her *landsmen*—who had the courage to survive after being thrown from the barn and witnessing her mother's murder—was also unjustly omitted from history.

Grandma and I held hands as she, once more, told her Barn Story. I watched her relive that first murder, the one that began the destruction of her world.

I returned to Grandma's a few days later. There would be no questions about liquidation. It was Yom Kippur, the highest of holy days, the day that Grandma transferred her mourning energies from Poppy to her mother.

I sat at the kitchen table while Grandma buried her face in her hands before the yellow flame of the *yahrzeit* candle. The fire dug a soft grave into the wax. In a tear-choked voice, she recited the prayer for the dead into her palms.

24

GRANDMA'S DETERMINATION

Grandma started to get sick. Every few months, our visits would shift settings from the kitchen table, where the Holocaust was served up like an entrée, to a hospital room, where she underwent rounds of pneumonia and congestive heart failure.

Grandma sat propped up in bed with tubes penetrating her nose and machines connected by wire to her purple, clotted skin. I wondered whether she still had the same determination to join Poppy. Had our time together changed any of that?

"Noiach, they aren't giving me a shower," she said.

"They're giving her a shower." Dad rolled his eyes at this latest allegation, which she was repeating on the hour. He left the room, having lost his patience for this visit in record time.

While our Holocaust conversations at home seemed to lift her spirits, I couldn't initiate a dialogue connected to genocide in this new setting, where we were one long beep away from death.

So I spoke to her about the only other thing that we had in common: cooking Jewish food.

"Grandma, can you teach me how to make kreplach?"

"Noiach, I have no *koyekh*. Poppy's dead." She tilted her head to the side in an attempt to show her lack of strength—her drained *koyekh*.

"That's fine. I'll just look up a recipe online."

"Noiach," she said with offense. "You might get poison."

"From kreplach."

"You got to make sure that when you go to the butcher he grinds a fresh piece of meat for you. Noiach, never get the meat already chopped. They could put in poison." She continued with the rest of the recipe: the spices to flavor the meat and the ways to roll the dough. But nothing was more important, Grandma reiterated, than investing the proper time in worrying about intentionally tainted meat.

Then she looked over at the door, where one of the nurses popped in to check on her condition. When the nurse left, Grandma turned to me. "Noiach, I'm telling you these bastards didn't give me a shower."

"When? Today?"

"No, forget about today," she said, ripping at the oxygen tubes with her purple fingers. "Two weeks ago, when they brought me here. 'You got a shower, you got a shower,' they try to tell me." She poked herself in the chest. "They think I don't know. I know."

"How about the recipe for kishka, Grandma?" I asked.

"You got a shower. You got a shower," she kept insisting, mimicking the staff. "Yeah, I got a shower. They lie about showers like the Nazis."

Food didn't have the same distractibility as Europe, and we fell back into Poland. But I tried, at least, to steer us to the happier times, before the ghettos and camps.

"Do you remember when your grandfather told you that you were the best singer?"

"In the camps?" she asked.

"No, not in the camps. In Otwock."

"We sang in the camps, too."

Despite my efforts to keep us on the prewar streets of Poland, Grandma had slid us into a world of crematories and gas chambers.

"One evening, in Bergen-Belsen, all the women gathered in a circle. Nobody said nothing for a long time." And Grandma didn't say anything for a long while either, reflecting back on those days of disease and death— those same two inhabitants of all the camps now lurked in the corridors of this Brooklyn hospital.

"What were you gathered for?"

"Who knows? This was near the end? Things were very bad then— the night before I slept next to a woman who would not move. You know why this was? She was dead. This is what it was then. But still one of the women, from the circle, she begins to sing the *Hatikvah*. You know the *Hatikvah*, Noiach? *Od lo avdah tikvateinu. Oy, oy, oy.* I can't."

Even the *Hatikvah* was against her.

"It's a very nice song." I touched her swollen arm.

"The next morning, it was raining at lunchtime. We took shelter during the break and there was nowhere to sit. So we sat on dead bodies. And we ate. And then we went back to work."

I could see the barely living rising from the eternally dead like spirits too weak to float, forced to trudge through the purgatory of Bergen-Belsen instead.

"Grandma, we don't have to."

The purple moon-shaped bruise eclipsed the veins in her arm. These might very well be her final stories, I realized. I felt a cry swell in my throat.

"The best singer, Noiach, she was in Auschwitz," Grandma stated, as if the concentration camp were the Juilliard of Europe. "She was a French Jewish girl named Elizabeth. *Oy.* Elizabeth could not work. I remember. They yelled for her to lift the bags and she couldn't lift nothing.

"I remember, she couldn't pull this bag. 'You can do it, Elizabeth,' I said to her. But the Nazi hit her." Grandma's shrug asked why. There was no good answer. "She kept pulling and pulling, but she couldn't move it. Not at all. Then she fall down and I say to her to get up. Elizabeth say to me, 'I cannot move.' I say to her that they gonna kill you if you don't get up. Still she won't get up." Blood clots spanning her appendages, tubes running from her orifices, IV needles puncturing her veins, and still Grandma spoke of Elizabeth as if this girl's survival were her primary responsibility. "So I say to her, maybe you should sing."

Sing? It was as if Grandma had watched too many musicals growing up in Otwock and was convinced that villains could be transformed by song. "Sing?"

"Elizabeth lets the bag fall again and the Nazi, he reach for his gun. Then, very quietly, Elizabeth begin to sing.

"*A yiddishe momme, nisht du kein besser in der welt,*" Grandma sang from her hospital bed. Her voice quivered. The oxygen tubes were attached like lavalieres. "*A yiddishe momme, oy vey tzis bisser ven zie fehlt.*" She stopped to admire the folksy Yiddish song. The swelling in my throat pushed up and forced a painful smile onto my face. "Two more Nazis come and no one do nothing. They let her sing. A beautiful voice. And they let her live. Auschwitz." Grandma shrugged.

Dad came back into the room. "You look strong, Mom."

"I look strong? I look strong? I looked good in the concentration camps, too. The doctors here." She rubbed her fingers together, accusing the medical professionals of being crooks. "What do they do? Nothing."

A few minutes later, one of the accused entered the room with Grandma's test results. "I have some concerns."

My father and I stepped into the hallway with him.

"I think changing her medications could help her, and the procedure we're planning could alleviate her pain, but I have my doubts."

I looked at Dad. The doctor looked at my father, too. Dad studied Grandma, who was inside her room peering at us.

"Doc, don't worry," Dad said. "Hitler couldn't kill her. What's the worst you're going to do?"

By the next visit, the hallucinations had begun.

"Where is he?" Grandma asked me.

I knew she wasn't talking about the doctors. She hated the doctors. I looked around the room. "Who?"

Grandma leaned forward. "Leon."

I gulped. "Poppy's not here." What else from the past was taking shape in her mind?

"She's losing it," Dad said as we left the hospital.

"She'll get better," I said, trying to comfort myself more than him.

"Well, if she doesn't, there's no way they'll be taking her back into the psychiatric ward."

"What do you mean *back*?"

"Back," he repeated. "She's been there. After Poppy died, she forced Anne to check her in. Your aunt didn't want to. Even the psychiatrist said don't lock up a Holocaust survivor. But Grandma persisted, and you know how she gets when something's on her mind. So she went to the psych ward. But after she arrived, she decided that she wanted to go home. But that's not how psychiatric wards operate. You don't just check yourself out. Somehow, and don't ask me how, that lady up there," Dad said, pointing up at the hospital, "put on her hat and coat, walked to reception, and announced that she was ready to leave."

That evening, Aunt Anne received a phone call.

"Sorry to wake you, ma'am," said the police officer. "Your mother has gone missing from the psychiatric ward. We think she might have gone home, and we can't get into her apartment. You need to come down and let us in."

Anne met the cops in front of Grandma's building and took the elevator to the fifteenth floor. Anne used her key, but Grandma's door had been deadbolted. Nobody answered, which forced the police officers to enter the neighbor's apartment, climb over onto Grandma's terrace, and crawl through the living room window.

"The cops brought Grandma back to the ward. The hospital wanted to keep her," Dad said. "But once they realized the potential for lawsuits, they let Grandma return home. So if she does go crazy, again, I'm sure we'll need to find another institution." Dad looked back at the building again and laughed. "The cop told us that no one escapes from that place. No one except for your Grandma."

While Grandma and I were on hiatus from the Holocaust, I wondered whether I had gathered enough of my family's past. I still knew nothing about the mystery camp, and the stories from the Warsaw ghetto felt impossible to retrieve. But how much more could I put Grandma through? And what about me? This didn't feel like the typical life of a twenty-something in New York.

Over the years, as people learned about my conversations with Grandma, they felt the need to dump their Holocaust weight on me. For instance, when one of the English teachers at my school—a daughter of survivors—retired, she left a large box of Holocaust literature and outdated VHS cassettes with a colleague. That colleague passed the box to me, as if I were the receiver of memory. I didn't want most of it, but now that it was in my possession I couldn't throw out testimony trapped in antiquated technology. And when I had considered taking a break from *Night*, I had overheard things from teachers that made Wiesel required reading.

One day, I had been walking behind two teachers outside the building. "Even if we had a football team," one of them shouted, "I wouldn't coach it because of that fucking Jew who runs it. That fucking Jew . . ." He went on and on.

Another time, in the teachers' cafeteria, a few educators who doubled as September 11 conspiracy theorists preached about the inside job and the horrors of the New World Order. They exchanged DVDs on the topics like high school kids trading baseball cards. It wouldn't have been so bad had I not witnessed one of them hand a DVD to a student who showed interest.

I kept gathering facts because denial and delusion were only going to worsen.

The next time I returned to the hospital, I brought Marissa, the woman I would eventually marry. Grandma adored Marissa, and I hoped that her presence would bring something positive to the room.

"Look." Grandma pulled on the curtain that divided the room, revealing a ninety-year-old woman curled up like a fetus.

"Grandma, the nurses already told you to stop pulling on the curtain."

"Look Noiach, she's ninety, that one." Grandma's painkillers had pasted a goofy grin on her face.

"You're only a few years younger," I reminded her.

"And you two? When is the good day?" Grandma asked, remembering some piece of the normal world.

"Every day is a good day, Grandma," I countered.

"You know what I mean. *Oy, oy, oy, oy.*" She winced, pained by my tardy proposal.

Marissa smiled and went to the bathroom.

"So Grandma, how's—"

"So?" Her determination was stronger than the drugs, stronger than the pain. "When you gonna get married? She gonna leave you, Noiach? You too cheap to buy a ring?"

I smiled. We probably would not have to seek out another psychiatric ward. Grandma was back to her normal crazy.

25

GET WELL SOON

"Do you remember something about Grandma and a German shepherd?" I asked Dad, fishing for anything, with Grandma still in the hospital.

"Leave me alone," he said, half joking, half not.

"Try to remember. She mentioned something about a German shepherd the last time I visited, but I didn't want to dig it all up."

"I remember a big German shepherd once jumped on her. She was so freaked out that she started talking to the dog as if it were a person: 'Hello. How are you?'" He laughed. "I think she brought up the weather to the dog, too."

"What about from the camps?" I pressed.

"Seriously, leave me alone," Dad said. "You know who might have stories for you: Morris Pilberg. He survived with them. In fact, you should have started a few years ago. Back then Yadja was alive."

"Thanks. That's helpful." But it was true.

Grandma and Yadja had met in Auschwitz Birkenau.

"Mengele was having selections," Grandma had told me when she had first brought me into Auschwitz at her kitchen table. "We had to run past him, and he sees that I have these little spots on my body." Grandma rolled the heavy flesh of her arm around as if giving herself a soft Indian burn and inspected the skin-colored birthmarks that felt like blisters on her skin.

"Your birthmarks?" I asked.

"No. During the war, I had yellow spots. If Mengele should see them, you know. Well, Yadja starts to laugh and this makes me start to laugh, too. That's when Mengele kicks me." Sixty years later, Grandma jumped.

"You were laughing in front of Mengele?" I shook my head at the uncanniness.

"You shouldn't laugh in front of Mengele," she said, as if this were the advice she had often given to new arrivals at Auschwitz. "But we did, and it was Yadja's fault. Mengele tells to his Slovak assistant something and she writes it down. 'What are these spots on your body?' he shouts to me. Then he pokes me with his stick. I tell him that I was born like this, you know, so not to be sent to the crematoriums. I don't know what the Slovak writes or what he says to her. I think: Am I going there? To the gas chambers? And Yadja. Yadja keeps laughing." Grandma spun her finger around her head. "She was crazy, that one."

Yadja may have been crazy, but worse, now she was dead. Helen was gone. Herman was gone, too. Poppy hung from Grandma's neck like a dead angel. And the list of newly deceased survivors went on and on.

"What about the other women?" I asked Dad after he had reminded me of Morris.

"What other women?"

In Auschwitz-Birkenau, Grandma had befriended eighteen girls from her unit. An identical sisterhood of shaven, bony, fatigued orphans.

But like anything in Birkenau, a group of nineteen is reduced. On a summer day in 1944, as the girls marched to gather apples in a nearby orchard, an SS officer had approached them. "You girls are always together," he noted and left. It seemed inconsequential, the way someone might comment on a drizzle. The girls continued to the field. When the harvest was completed, the same guard saw the nineteen on their return to the camp. "Still together. You five come with me." He selected five from the middle of the group. They were sent to the gas chambers.

The next day, Grandma asked her closest friends, "Why do we always march in the front?"

"Routine," said her friend Esther.

"Routine!? Everything here is routine," screamed Yadja. "I'm sick of routine. No more marching in the front. We're doing things differently today."

When it was time to exit the *Lager* for the fields, the girls who typically marched up front slipped to the middle of the procession.

The same SS officer from the day before selected five more girls for the gas chambers. He pulled from the front of the line. The nine who remained recited the mourner's Kaddish.

"I'm pretty sure that all those women are either dead or *ibberbuttel*," Dad said after I had reminded him of Grandma's Auschwitz family.

"Senile?" I asked, searching for the English synonym.

"Your Yiddish is pretty good."

"Gracias."

I went to the hospital and asked Grandma about her friends from Auschwitz.

"Malka, Sula, Esther. Dead, dead, dead," she said, as if looking at her family portrait that hung above the light switch.

"Rose, too?" I asked.

She shrugged. *What's the difference?*

"Rose," Grandma said. "Rose tried to save me in Auschwitz." Something as simple as a name had transported us to the camps again. "On the three-mile walk to the fields, I step on barbed wire. It goes right through my foot. After the hike, I sit down to pull out the spike and all this blood comes from my foot.

"This big SS, Makros, say to me, 'Why you on the floor?' Makros shoots a girl the week before for much less than sitting on the floor. But I can't move. He put a hand on his pistol and asks again, 'Why you on the floor?'" Grandma smacks the bedsheets. "I'm in pain. So he let me sit there. He don't use the gun. But then, I pass out. He gives me such a *zetz* in the ribs with a foot. I almost . . . *Oy.* No more, Noiach."

"We don't have to talk about this," I reminded her. I had only wanted to know whether the women were still alive, but she had taken us deeper. I looked at the IV bag dripping slowly into a tube, toward the cotton bunched up above her numbers, at the lurid bruise threatening to extinguish the green tattoo. It saddened me that someone who had suffered so much had to continue to feel such pain. But, apparently, there was something familiar and settling in the pain for her.

"Makros wants to know who are my friends," Grandma said, unable to give up on the story. "I have no friends, I tell to him. But there is Rose and Malka and Yadja and Sula and Esther. But I don't want them to have to carry my body back to the camp if he should shoot me. But again he don't shoot me. He gets four Russian girls to carry me to camp. He says, 'Carry this'"—Grandma mouths the word "fucking"—"'Jew back to camp.' Can you believe this? Then they take me to see Mengele and—"

"Wait, you were brought to Mengele a second time?" This was the equivalent of meeting the devil for a second time after he had discovered that you lied to him once already.

"This is not a good thing," she said.

"I know, Grandma, it's just—"

"Yes. This is the second time I see Mengele. Mengele says to me, 'What are you doing here?' Now I say, 'My sciatica.' This is a lie. He pokes me with his baton and says, 'If you're not better tomorrow . . .'" Grandma lifted her hand again and this time pointed to the hospital window. Outside was a bright summer day. "I could see the crematorium," she said. "This is what he points to.

"So that night I use a little mint tea to sterilize my foot and a little piece of blanket for a bandage. The next day I could walk."

"You said Rose saved your life. How?"

"I said Rose *tried* to save my life. She told to me get up when Makros stands over me. Please, you try to stand with barb wire in you foot. This is saving a life? Feh. I save Rose's life," Grandma shouted, bringing in the nurses with her commotion. But she threw a backhand in their direction, which instantly dismissed the hospital staff. She was developing quite a reputation on the floor. "Disgusting, all of them. You know they steal from me."

"How did you save Rose's life?" I asked.

"In Bergen-Belsen, I hear someone say, 'Help me. Help me.'" Grandma mocked the poor soul. "Rose fell from the top bunk, at least six feet to the ground." Grandma shook her head, equating Rose's fall with irresponsibility, though she herself had just fallen from her hospital bed days ago, mapping her skin with more purple contusions than that which remained as continents of her normal sallow hue.

"I helped Rose to her feet. But her ankle was broke. I tell to her, You must walk to roll call. We will be free soon. If you cannot walk they will kill you. You know what? Rose wants to quit. We in Bergen-Belsen. A few weeks from liberation, and Rose wants to quit. Of course we don't know it's a few weeks, but still. *Oy oy oy.*" Grandma grabbed her chest and took a deep breath.

"Maybe we should—" I began, but Grandma could not be stopped.

"Anyway, I get a woman on a bottom bunk to trade beds with Rose for half ration of mine bread, I bring Rose to work with me cleaning the barracks, and I do all of my work and Rose's work. So Rose lives to the end."

I grabbed her hand and smiled.

The nurse arrived with lunch. Grandma stuck her tongue out. "Ech. I'm not eating nothing."

I tried to feed her, snapping off pieces of cracker and carrots, but Grandma had her way.

That evening, I called Morris Pilberg. He remembered for me the family that I had never known: the ones who had perished with the twelve thousand Otwock Jews, the ones incinerated in Treblinka and machine-gunned in the nearby forests, the ones who hung above the light switch on Grandma's wall.

"They used to drink together—your great-grandfather and my father," recalled Morris. But Morris's stories about the Ledermans and Zylberbergs were brief. As expected, he took me down the only path he knew—the murders he had witnessed, the gold necklace he had traded through the bars of the cattle car for a cup of water, the incident when a Nazi had shot at him twice with a pistol that misfired both times. Then his voice rose an octave and it sounded like his lips were quivering. "The Nazis took this baby. I saw them throw the infant from a second-story apartment in Warsaw. That I'll never forget."

Our phone conversation went silent. His sad breathing and my enraged exhalation fused with the static in the receiver.

"I'm sorry. We started talking about your grandparents, but then we started talking about me."

"That's okay, Morris. Your stories interest me, too."

"I do have one story for you. To me, your grandfather was a hero. When we were in camp together, at the end of the war, I did not get my bread."

His words *end of the war* registered in the way that kibbles clanging into an empty bowl would excite a dog in the distant wing of a house.

"I told this to the block leader. He told me, 'Then you will eat tomorrow,' and he stood there laughing at me." Morris sounded hurt by this insult all these years later. "But then your grandfather comes over and shouts, 'You son of a bitch! You give him his bread!' And the block leader, he gives me my bread."

"Morris, what was the name of the camp?" My fingers tingled as I readied the pen on the page. Ink bled out with anticipation. This was the mystery camp.

"It was a small camp. In Germany. I don't recall the name."

"Was it Klein Webber? Ludweissles?"

"I don't recall," he said. "Very small. We weren't there long."

Morris continued and I felt drained. How did he not remember the name of the camp from where he had been liberated? Maybe it was so small that everyone had named it what they wanted. Klein Webber.

"You should have spoken to Ben Markov," Morris said. "He knew about Leo. He was another survivor from Otwock and he had such a memory for this sort of thing. Now, not so much."

I was the clichéd reporter from the comic books in search of the superhero—desperate to reveal the story, the identity, but always too late to the scene.

We hung up. I sat there and remembered all of the survivors who had once surrounded me. All of those green numbers reaching toward my face, grabbing handfuls of cheek. Not once when I was growing up had I ever thought to ask about their versions of the Holocaust. At that age, I was interested in only my grandparents' Holocaust. It pained me to know that the information had once been so readily available, like keys hanging on a wall. Most of those keys to those great fortunes were now melted down. The ones that remained belonged to doors with new locks.

26

THE BRONZE ARM

While Grandma remained in the hospital, I had quickly exhausted the shortlist of living survivors from Otwock. During the weeks that followed, I racked my brain for memories, feeling as though my grandparents' past had to have been interred beneath some fold of my subconscious. I found myself sitting at green lights with honking traffic building up behind me or shivering in the ocean, forgetting to paddle for the waves that passed me by. But I was searching for memories that did not exist.

Then one day, after visiting Grandma in the hospital, I drove south down Ocean Parkway with Marissa toward Grandma's empty apartment in Brighton Beach. Once there, I toured Marissa through the nostalgia of Coney Island: the famed Cyclone, the defunct parachute jump, the notorious Nathan's. But it was a hole-in-the-wall establishment at the opposite end of the boardwalk, in Brighton Beach, that tilled my brain, cultivating one fertile patch of memory.

"Poppy and I would walk this stretch of boardwalk every time I came to visit," I told her. "And he'd always stop right here." I looked down at the rotting boardwalk, the nails and planks rising up against gravity. "His pockets were always huge with quarters. And then I'd go right over there." I pointed to a restaurant that had once been an arcade. "I'd play video games all day."

I watched the memory play out before me as another grandson ran to his grandfather for breadcrumbs to feed to the birds. The grandfather poured the old, crumbled loaf into the boy's hand, just as Poppy had spilled coins into mine. "Play," I remembered him saying, indifferent to the few coins that might have spilled through the cracks of the boardwalk. A phantom whiff of Poppy crept past: Marlboro smoke scented with Drakkar.

"What would he do while you played at the arcade?" Marissa asked.

"He'd sit with his *landsman*." I watched the boy throw his crumbs to the gulls and the grandfather walk away just as Poppy had after the quarters had been transferred. He would always drift toward the benches where the old Jews waxed nostalgic about the old country or cursed the camps in coded Yiddish.

Marissa grabbed my hand and I remembered how my fingers looked against Poppy's, how my hairless arm contrasted with the gray and black hairs that grew through the links and over the face of his gold watch.

"Where did you get that watch?" I had asked him, hoping it had been his Holocaust watch.

"You like it, Noiach? It's yours." He undid the clasp.

"I don't want it. That's not why I'm—"

"*Sheine yingle*," he said, foisting the watch upon me.

He gave me things because he loved me. This I knew. But it was also quite clear that he gave me things because he didn't want to give me the past.

I kissed Marissa's hand. We looked upon the empty benches, the former thrones of survivors. All the riches of that past—the opulence of Yiddish, the grandeur of their histories—were gone. And back then, on that boardwalk, all I had ever concerned myself with were coins for video games.

"They used to all gather on these benches. My grandparents and their friends," I told her. "I bet I missed some impressive stories."

"What would they speak about?"

"The camps, I'm sure. What else? But whenever I returned for more quarters, they shifted gears to complain of the cold—even in summer—and speculate on the forthcoming winter in Miami."

When we visited Grandma and Poppy in their Miami "bungalow," which was their Catskillese way to describe their South Florida condominium, Grandma had managed to bring the scents from her Brooklyn apartment down to the beachfront home. Her welcoming meal consisted of an ocean of gefilte fish, a pool of soup, and a fallen palm trunk of kishka.

"There's a beautiful pool and a very nice beach," Grandma said, giving us the tour of the grounds from inside her air-conditioned unit.

"It's beautiful here," Dad said.

"Ech," she responded. "It's filthy. You should have seen how dirty it was before."

After I finished my compulsory two bowls of soup and three pieces of fish for second breakfast—a shared custom between hobbits and Hadasa—I asked Grandma whether she wanted to join us on the beach.

"Ech," Grandma said. "It's all dirt."

"It's sand," I explained.

"*Ptoy, ptoy, ptoy,*" she spat, as if I had uttered "cancer" or "Hitler" within the walls of her Miami abode. "You see how nice Grandma makes the condominium for you boys. Stay inside and enjoy the air-conditioning."

"Where's Poppy?" I asked.

"Also in the air-conditioning. The card room, playing cards."

I left the apartment and passed the pool, which was crowded with a breed of survivor that I had never known, ones with skin as dark as their numbers—the green lost in their bronze arms. They swam as if life had always been easy, or at least now enjoyable; others stretched out on lounge chairs laughing, having been programmed differently by the Holocaust.

I found the card room. Men and women had gathered around poker, blackjack, and Kalooki tables that were covered in decks, chips, dollars, quarters, and good luck charms that ranged from the secular to the religious. Perhaps it was the only time in history that a photograph of Schneerson would glower beside a pink-haired troll doll.

I kissed Poppy hello and invited him to join us on the beach.

"I need to give them a chance to win it back," Poppy said, indicating the empty spaces before the other players where chips were no longer stacked.

I left him to his cards and found Herman, Helen's husband, in the sand. The man was like a cartoon that had slipped from fiction into reality. All of his features were lovely contrasting parts. His voice scraped like sandpaper but also squeaked with excitement. His nose and ears were great in size, but he was a little man. His newly seventy-year-old body moved with a child's motor. He also had a track record of accomplishing the impossible, like nearly drowning in the overly buoyant Dead Sea or driving the Belt Parkway in reverse.

("Herman, who taught you to drive?" my father once asked him.

"What's to know?" Herman replied. "Green you go, red you stop.")

"Chase me," Herman shouted to my brother and me. Jake took him up on the offer, and the two made circles in the sand, Herman exhaling a laugh that was both a falsetto wheeze and a deep groan. I liked Herman. He always seemed to be making up for a stolen childhood.

Grandma trudged down to the beach in her housedress. She carried a crystal bowl spilling over with fruit.

"Ech. Why do you sit in this dirt? My apartment is much cleaner. We'll eat inside. Come." Grandma held out the bowl, hoping to entice us with plums and grapes that were equal in size. (She always bought strange-sized fruits, from miniature bananas to peaches that had the characteristics of a boulder, both in size and firmness. Any normal-looking fruit she melted down into compote.)

After ingesting my third meal before lunch, I went back to the card room. The opportunity that Poppy had given the men had reduced his pile of chips and quarters and crumpled bills. In the middle of the table sat a pot of cash, and every other arm that extended from the currency was stamped with a five- or six-digit number.

The men spoke in Yiddish. I leaned against Poppy and observed his hand.

Ante, check, fold. Ante, check, fold.

"I thought you always won," I said.

"I tell Grandma I always win." He winked and picked up the two cards dealt to him. "Poppy wins, though. It takes time."

If anyone knew the art of gambling, it had to have been the men and women of this room. They had risked it all.

The dealer gave Poppy two sevens. A third was laid face up for the community to incorporate in their hands. Poppy raised everyone a dollar. The survivors studied him. Poppy bluffed like an expert. But everyone folded.

"Try to keep a straight face, *sheine yingle*," Poppy said and kissed my head. "We don't want them to know what we have."

That night, it took some convincing to get Grandma to accompany us to dinner. She had wanted to cook for her grandsons. But everyone needed to get out of the "bungalow."

"How about Chinese?" Dad suggested.

"It's dreck," she said, holding a grudge based on our last visit to Happy Palace. "No bread," she complained. "No cinnamon for my rice."

We settled on the finest kosher deli south of the Mason-Dixon Line. Grandma, however, was tougher on the deli than Zagat.

"There's dirt," she announced after the hostess brought us to our first table of the evening. Grandma reached above the booth to where the plants sat on a six-foot-high ledge, dragged her finger across the shelf, and showed her dirtied fingertips to the busboy with obstinate victory.

"Un momento," said the busboy, who returned with the hostess.

At the next table, Grandma found crumbs.

"Can we just—" Dad began.

"Shah," Grandma interrupted. "You want to eat dirty, you can go to a less *fency* place."

Sometime between the plate of fried kreplach and tower of pastrami sandwich, Mom announced our next day's itinerary. "Tomorrow, we should all go visit Miami's Holocaust Memorial."

Dad protested. Jake complained. I looked at my grandparents, who had broken into Yiddish. Grandma appeared nervous, Poppy reproachful.

"You don't have to go, Mom," Dad told Grandma.

My nerves tingled. Would the memorial bring about the stories?

The next morning, we arrived at the outdoor memorial.

"I'll wait outside," Poppy said. "Go, go, go."

I stared back at Poppy. Entering into the bulwark that surrounded the memorial without him felt like we were all boarding a train and leaving him in Miami forever.

A forty-foot oxidized bronze arm shot up like a geyser from the center of the space. The sculptor must have imagined the Statue of Liberty losing her torch and being consumed by the earth up to her elbow. But instead of echoing freedom, a scramble of bronze Jews climbed the appendage. Their metal faces wore gasps and panic and final, fixed breaths. It felt like a retractable roof would close, sealing the open-air memorial and transforming the space into a gas chamber.

A dark cloud drifted past.

I exited the space and found Poppy with a young couple. Both the man and woman were hugging him.

I ran over, worried that something had happened. But when I reached Poppy, I heard the woman crying into his ear. "I'm so sorry. Jesus bless you." When she finally released him, she petted the numbers on his arm softly and hesitantly, like she had struck her pet with the family car.

I was shocked and saddened, betrayed and duped. I had to look at some fucking statues, while two gentiles were given a piece of Poppy's Holocaust. And in exchange for what? A few unwanted blessings from Jesus.

He could have given them all of his gold watches. I just wanted the stories.

That evening, we returned to the Miami condominium. But for the second night in a row, Grandma was not cooking; our meal for the evening would be had at Helen's bungalow.

As soon as we arrived, it felt like we were dining in some alternate universe. First, I had never seen Grandma occupy a seat at a dinner table for the majority of a meal except at restaurants. Second, while there were signs of normalcy on Helen's table—bowls of gefilte fish, a pot of chicken soup, and a tub of brisket—Grandma's cousin also served up these little things that resembled doughy cocoons. Jews did not make doughy cocoons.

"What is that?" I asked. "Bite-sized kreplach?"

"Gnocchi," she announced, placing a spoonful of the off-white dumplings onto my plate and slathering them with a sauce.

"The gnocchi is delicious," I told Helen after taking a bite.

Helen beamed. Grandma glared as if I had betrayed the entire family.

But this had always been their relationship. Authoritative love and confused roles. After the war, Poppy had made a living as a butcher in Germany's black markets. But his responsibility extended beyond the woman he had vowed to love; Grandma had made certain that Poppy cared for Helen, too. They lived in the displaced persons camp in a one-room apartment that had once been Nazi barracks. Even though Helen was entitled to her own room, Grandma refused to let her cousin out of sight.

"Too many wild boys run around," Grandma had told her.

Helen met a group of Zionists and fell in love with the idea of living in a Jewish homeland, but Grandma refused.

"You're coming with us to America," she demanded.

When Helen was unable to enter the States on Poppy's HIAS sponsorship, which was for immediate family members only, Grandma registered her cousin as a younger sister.

The camps may have taken away Grandma's family, but they had given her Helen.

Now only Grandma remained. When she returned to her Brighton Beach apartment after three weeks in the hospital, I reminded her of that week in Miami and retold the story of Helen's gnocchi.

"What you think," Grandma began, "Helen was Italian or something? I cooked for Helen, too, don't you worry," she said, wanting, above all things, to set the record straight. "I took care of her."

I knew the story that would follow.

"I was always looking after Helen." Grandma paused to shake her head with eternal disbelief and annoyance. "I tell to her: Helen, you need to keep youself warm." This was her favorite Helen story. "But there was nothing in the camps to keep youself warm with. You know, we slept with sheets, if we were lucky.

"So, I had this friend who was in charge of the clothing from those that go to the gas chambers. I get from her a nice piece of wool for Helen. And I say to Helen wear this under your kerchief, you understand, Noiach? Because if the Nazi gonna see it, he gonna take it. You know what she says:

'It's very pretty.' Pretty! This, in the camps. What does she do? She wears it over her kerchief when I tell her not to. *Oye broch*," Grandma chanted to the lights, a reproach to the heavens for her late cousin. "They took it from her. She never listened to me. Helen never listened to me. *Oy*, Helen."

Grandma had always had one mission: to protect her family. She attempted to do so in Majdanek, but lost her younger brother Shama. From Auschwitz to America, Helen became her responsibility. And forever after, in her Brighton Beach apartment, she tended to her grandchildren. For instance, whenever I slept over, I was never allowed my own room. Grandma had to lay a half-dozen comforters on the floor of her room to form a makeshift bed. And while I tried to sleep there, she popped up every few minutes from her slumber like a groundhog scoping the plains for predators.

"Do you miss her?" I asked Grandma after she stopped scolding the ceiling. I smiled in advance of the answer, knowing full well that the cousins had also been best friends.

"Of course. I miss everyone. I miss her now and I missed her in Bergen-Belsen, when she disappeared."

"What do you mean, 'when she disappeared'?"

27

BERGEN-BELSEN

W e were on the death march from Birkenau," Grandma said, refer- ring to the forced migration from Poland into Germany at the end of January 1945, when the temperatures remained below freezing and the night wind whipped, when the Nazis shot indiscriminantly if the procession slowed. "Helen and me."

"What about your foot? Did it heal from the barbed wire?" I asked.

"I should ask to the Nazis to let me rest? Look, everybody was push- ing. They tell to me, 'Don't slow down or they kill us. If you can't walk let us through.' So I forgot about my foot and I march until we have a break— Poppy marched, too. But I don't know this then. I just have Helen." Grandma looked out her window at the sky that had grown nebular. We had returned so easily to the stories now that we were back at that table.

Grandma continued with the death march: "When we sit down for a rest in the forest, I say something to Helen. I say to her: This is the farthest we've been from Auschwitz in over a year."

The cousins, with wounds and only two rations of bread between them, had completed more than forty miles through the snow, forever diminishing the ancient legend of the Marathon runner.

"And then we come to the next camp. Bergen-Belsen," Grandma said, a sadness lofted in her eyes. "And I look around. I lost Helen. Can you believe it?"

Grandma kept finding ways to shock me.

The first night in Bergen-Belsen, Grandma had been placed in a makeshift tent.

"As soon as the others die, you will be moved into wooden barracks," one of the Kapos reassured her and the other girls.

Death was the purpose of Bergen-Belsen. There was little talk of labor. They had been brought to the camp to see which was faster, the approaching Allied forces or the tenacity of disease, starvation, and frost.

Grandma woke early on that first morning in Bergen-Belsen and crept to the threshold of the tent. She searched the distance for her cousin, but fatigued from the march, she fell asleep on the floor of the tent. When the *Blockaltester* found her there, the Nazi brought her boot heel down onto Grandma's ribs. She writhed in pain, but, accepting the punishment for her error, got to her feet and readied herself for the new camp.

"Noiach, I followed the others to the square to where they were giving out the bread. But before I can even grab a piece, I'm lying on the ground, again. And I'm like this." Grandma scrunched up so that her chin had burrowed into her chest and her hands were cradling her head. "The woman who give me a kick in the ribs, give me a *zetz* on the head. And then I fall asleep there."

"You blacked out," I corrected.

"What's the difference? Noiach, I hadn't eaten in days. She also takes from me my bread. She takes this from me," she said, speaking as if it were her last possession on earth. But in fact, it *was* her last possession on earth.

Two tears formed, and I watched the pair grow heavy and spill, meeting at the bottom of her chin.

I wiped the tears off her chin. Grandma grabbed my hand and kissed it.

"But you know what?" Grandma said. "I hear a voice. 'Hadasa. Hadasa.' This is what the voice says in my ear. It was Helen. She found me. She took care of me." Grandma smiled like a teacher humbled when the student becomes the master.

I smiled, too. "You must have been so happy, Grandma."

"Happy?" Grandma sounded disgusted. She studied me as if I had been listening to the Bambi story and missed the part about the mother doe getting slaughtered. "Happy? I wasn't happy. I tell her to stay with me on the march. And what does she do? She loses me." But then the upwelling of anger was replaced again with a smile. "But I was so hungry. Helen sees this. So you know what she does? She give to me her half-ration of bread. This is what Helen does. This is the importance of family."

28

BETTER AND YOU BETTER

During the spring of 2008, just a few days fresh from the hospital, Grandma had learned that my brother was returning from Korea, where he had been teaching English for a few years. My parents wanted to host a small reunion in Grandma's unused dining room.

"A family reunion," Grandma said to me. "This means a family gets together."

She was making a clever point and not simply proving that she could define such English phrases. I knew that I had better change the subject. But Grandma was quicker.

"So then you invite you cousins," Grandma shouted.

After Poppy's death, Aunt Anne got divorced. And in the way that the conflicts of divorce can extend beyond the couple, my aunt's daughters stopped having a relationship with their mother. For whatever reason, they also stopped speaking to Grandma. Regardless of these cut ties, Grandma never gave up on her granddaughters. While she could hold a grudge against the offspring of the Germans and Poles, if you were family, Grandma had unconditional love that extended even to hated in-laws.

For instance, when Poppy and Grandma had arrived in America, Poppy's uncle's daughter served as the welcoming party. As soon as my grandparents were on US soil, the cousin said to them, "You think you were the only ones who suffered during the war? We, in New York, suffered, too. We couldn't get no meat sometimes. Instead we ate chicken." Even when this cousin mistreated the new immigrants by throwing them into a rat-infested apartment or stealing the first painting they had ever owned right from their wall, Hadasa Lederman wouldn't let her husband cut ties.

Years after Aunt Anne's divorce, my cousins resumed their relationship with their mother and Grandma. Anne forgave them. Grandma forgave them. I had no interest in mending ties. My indifference pained Grandma.

With talk of this family reunion, Grandma began setting the dining room table for the party.

"You know, Grandma, Jake won't be home for another three months."

"Shah," she told me. "I need to get the party ready. All my grandchildren will be here."

I shrugged. I hadn't seen my cousins in five years. There was no way they would show.

Before Poppy died, Grandma's daily phone calls had been as reliable as gravity. His death lifted her of that habit. So I was completely taken aback when, after only thirty minutes of having left her apartment, my cellphone rang and the display screen lit up with an incoming call from *GMA*.

"Noiach, you have a new phone? I had to call you father for the number."

For the first time since Poppy's death, she had initiated a phone call to me.

"I've had it for a few years."

"Noiach, I want you should do one thing for Grandma. Call you cousins."

I cleared my throat. "I don't have a pen. I can't take down their numbers." I couldn't tell her no.

"Noiach, this will make Grandma happy. Call them. I want you should invite them to the party."

I told her that I would. But I think she sensed that I wouldn't. Either way, she was not happy with the speed at which I went about things; her phone calls became part of my life again.

"You call you cousins yet?" she'd ask up to four times each day.

"It was Shabbat," I'd say, running out of excuses and jokes.

"Shabbat," Grandma repeated. "What do you care about Shabbat? You should care about Shabbat. But please, Noiach, call you cousins."

At the very least, the phone calls broke that cycle of transitioning her between health and sickness. Her new task of pestering and family building kept her invigorated and hospital-free.

"Noiach, they you cousins. Please, Noiach. Grandma never asked you to do nothing. Just call them or send them a message. I want they should come to the party too. I love them just like I love you and Jake. Do it for Grandma. Yeah, *tatehla*?"

She got me with the words *Grandma never asked you to do nothing.* She never had. And yet she had lived an underappreciated life doing and doing for her brood. Doing in the camps just to stay alive, to permit all of her children and grandchildren to be a possibility. If Grandma had just stopped doing after her mother was murdered or after her brother was beaten in Majdanek or after her friends were pulled from the work line and sent to the gas chambers or after facing Mengele, twice, I would never have been.

The least I could do for her was make outreach. I sent an e-mail, paying back the woman who allowed me to be a genetic possibility. The message went unanswered.

The next time I visited Grandma, she had a big bowl of fruit on the table.

"You want a fruit, Noiach?"

"No, I'm—"

"When you gonna call up you cousins?" She transitioned from fruit to fury with ease.

"I sent a message."

"I don't do for you?" Grandma asked.

"I just said—"

"Anything you want, I do for you. Try one more time for Grandma. Yeah, *sheine keit?*"

"I'll try one more time. Okay?"

She was elated. I moved over to the window, avoiding possible eye contact, which would be the quickest conduit for returning to the topic of my cousins. I peered down at the snow-covered beach.

"It's really relaxing up here," I told her, changing subjects.

Grandma's square body appeared weak in the chair. Her legs were stretched out and rested on another chair while her sagging arms crossed over her paunch.

"I lived here for nineteen years," she said. "Believe me, I never relaxed."

I needed a stronger segue to move further from her inexorable request. On the beach, a mother dragged her child on a red plastic sled. "Have you ever gone sledding?" The more ludicrous the better.

She looked bewildered. Her eyes said *You think the Nazis gave us time for sledding in Birkenau?*

But then Grandma uncrossed her arms and slammed her hand onto the table. "Noiach," she announced. "If you gonna call you cousins, then I gonna go sledding." She never quit. "Take a pear, *tateh sheine.*"

29

UMSCHLAGPLATZ

As the party approached, I assisted Grandma with taking down all of the hard-to-reach serving trays that had been stowed for nearly a decade in her closet.

"You know that all the food is going to arrive in serving trays," I told her.

"Filthy," she explained. "We use mine. Do you think Mommy gonna order enough to eat for everyone?"

"She'll have enough food, Grandma."

"Mommy gonna bring up *traif*? This is a kosher house."

"The cheeseburgers won't have bacon, Grandma."

"Noiach," she growled.

We both enjoyed setting up for the party. She barked orders about expectations of cleanliness and choreographed the placement of the meal still weeks away; I watched Grandma reanimated, like the woman she had been years ago. But when she brought up my two cousins, I had to change subjects.

"You call the *geels*?" she'd ask after I decrumbed the blue rug with her carpet sweeper.

"The sisters?" I asked, substituting words to change the course of our conversation. "I'm going to. Did you ever know Poppy's sisters?"

"I knew, I knew, but what did I know?"

I had no idea what she meant.

"This is a great carpet sweeper." Sweep, sweep, sweep away the crumbs of cousin conversation.

"Sisters," she repeated. Her mind had shifted from this future party in Brooklyn to some place of memory.

"In Bergen-Belsen there were sisters." From Brighton Beach to Bergen-Belsen once more. Years ago I had to beg for the stories; now they could be conjured by introducing one non sequitur into the conversation. "Two sisters in our bunk with a disease. One day when we out in the field, they start to shout, 'We are free. We are free.' But it was nonsense. Hallucinations. I, with Helen, we grab the two girls around the mouth because the Kapos looking to find these two girls for making the noise."

"What happened?"

"The Kapo hits another girl in the mouth 'cause he can't find who make the noise. But then he goes away."

"So you saved the two sisters then."

She was like a comic book hero growing more powerful with the passing of each issue.

"Saved . . ." Grandma's defeated tone insisted that I had been wrong to describe it like that. "Who knows what we did?"

The following week, my cousins replied to my e-mail. They would attend the party. I visited Grandma the next day to deliver the news. I was nervous that she wouldn't be able to handle such excitement.

"Noiach, I can't cook." She looked terrified. "How my gonna cook for all these people? For the *geels*?"

"My parents are ordering food. You just have to have fun."

"Fun? *Oy*. Noiach, I'm so happy what you did for Grandma," she said, touching my arm where the Nazis would have tattooed a number on me if I had been born in a different time. She stood and paced the kitchen as if to whip up something for the party, still two weeks away. But when she tried to bend down for a pot or pan, she couldn't. She returned to the table looking feeble.

"There's so much *schmutz* on the rug," Grandma said, assessing her clean apartment. "Maybe mommy gonna use my good china . . . Who gonna make sure they don't use the wrong forks? I'm kosher. Ah, kosher, who *cay-yes* anymore."

"You want me to go out and pick up some shrimp then?"

"Noiach, please. We don't eat this. My father would always bring home the most delicious kosher fish after he sold to the fishmongers in Otwock. He would never think to bring home a shrimp."

I realized that in all of the stories, she never really spoke of her father. It was always her mother. In the few stories where he appeared, he was always hiding the family and moving on, or shuttling them from place to place.

"What was your father like?"

"He was a strong man," she said, describing every girl's memory of a father. "Still, he cried. I saw him cry three times: Once when Froyim Richner come to tell us that he helped to make gas chambers."

"The gas chambers in Treblinka?"

"Yes, in Treblinka. He cried again when he find me in Karczew because he thought that I was dead. And then in Warsaw when we were pulled from our bunker on Ostrowska Street and were marched down to the Umschlagplatz."

There was that word. The site in Warsaw almost overlooked during my travels that had brought Grandma and me so close. This site of destruction that had resurrected her spirit decades later. But I still didn't know what had happened at the Umschlagplatz. And there were two prizes still out there for me: the mystery camp from which Poppy had been liberated and the stories of the Warsaw ghetto, culminating with the battle that would lead the survivors to the Umschlagplatz.

"You know," she continued, "I remember a time before that, looking out the window of my apartment in the ghetto and I watch something like three thousand Jews led to the Umschlagplatz. I say to myself: 'Why don't they do something? Why don't they fight back?' They knew they were going to Treblinka. You know how many SS there were? Only three. Why didn't they do something? What can you do? We did nothing also. And we ended up in the Umschlagplatz, a big square. Jews are everywhere. The Nazis go through the crowd, shooting children. So to hide my brother Shama, I sit on him." Grandma showed me how she did this in the form of a charade. Grandma puffed herself up like a mother hen protecting her eggs. When she released the pose, it sapped her of her strength. "Oy."

We were inside the Umschlagplatz. I panicked that she would shuttle us back out, so I stammered out a question. "Th . . . th . . . they didn't see Shama?"

"All I know is that the Ukraines came to me and one of them reaches out." She stopped. I waited. This was the Umschlagplatz.

"My friend, Yentel," she finally said. "Yentel was the daughter of the *moyle* from Otwock. Such a beautiful girl. They didn't grab Shama. They grabbed her. And they pulled her through the Umschlagplatz. Pulled her into a bathroom or something." Grandma looked down at the tablecloth and picked at something that wasn't there. "When they brought her back, Yentel was white like a ghost. I say to her, 'What did they do to you, Yentel? What did they do?' But she doesn't say nothing. Eyes, empty. I comb her hair with my fingers." Grandma brushed her shaking hands through her own thin, gray hair. "But there's so much blood coming from down her legs. Do you understand?"

I nodded, but asked no follow-up questions. I just wanted to go back to setting up the party, to forgetting for a moment all of these things that were so terrible. I feared that the Nazis would grab her next.

"You know what Yentel asks me a few months later in Birkenau? She says, 'Maybe I'm pregnant?' I come back from the field later that day and Yentel was gone. Do you understand this?"

I nodded again and clenched my fist around the pen.

With her thick, shaky fingers, Grandma reached for her pillbox and opened the compartment labeled "AM." She tilted the entire morning section filled with eight tablets into her mouth and swallowed all the pills at once. She picked up her water, and the straw bounced around before she was able to grab it between her lips.

"You know on the train from the Umschlagplatz I see a man eat a dead man's ear. Can you believe?" And then with hardly a pause. "Noiach, I got so much to do to prepare for the party."

Grandma shuffled away from the table and away from the memories. It was baggage that could never be lost, but now the contents were shared, as much as anything like this could be shared. The mystery of the Umschlagplatz was revealed, and my heart hurt for Grandma quite a bit more.

30

THE MYSTERY CAMP

I thought often of Poppy's mystery camp. I had been able to track him from Majdanek to Buna, where he had spent most of his concentration-camp tenure. And I could follow his path after the death march to Dora and then over to Ravensbrück. But then a week before liberation, he vanished, as if he had crafted a magic ring of invincibility instead of working on the V-2 rockets that the Germans made the Jews construct in the underground lairs at Dora. Poppy had said to both my father and the Shoah Foundation interviewer that he had wound up in Ludveissles at the camp Klein Webber. But Ludveissles and Klein Webber—or any variations in spelling—did not exist in any book or Internet page or Yad Vashem database. Ludveissles and Klein Webber were a pair of ghosts. And Poppy had somehow vanished from the Holocaust, only to reappear after liberation in the displaced persons camps in Fallingbostel and then Bergen-Belsen.

I was baffled. Where had he spent that final week of the Holocaust? Who wouldn't remember the details of liberation? How could he have gotten all the names associated with that place wrong?

The questions and absence of closure gnawed at me. His liberation felt like the only unrecorded event in a war where the villains kept meticulous records.

I returned to the now-tattered page on which my father had written the names of the camps that Poppy had survived—*Majdanek, Auschwitz-Buna (IG Farben), Dora-Mittelbau, Ravensbrück*, and *Ludveissles*. Next to that vanished location, my father wrote *Poppy liberated*.

Had Ludveissles ever existed? Klein Webber sounded like a law firm that might have been around before the Nuremberg Laws were enacted.

The only information I had on the camp was that it was near Berlin, if it existed at all. I studied prewar, wartime, and postwar maps of Germany and Berlin. I played Poppy's Shoah Foundation interview again and again, forcing family members to weigh in on his pronunciation.

"It sounds like he's saying 'Klein Webber,'" was everyone's verdict.

I listened as he spoke about the American army that had freed them on the second day of May. What an incredible day to have lost.

"Why are you driving yourself crazy over this detail?" Dad asked.

Maybe it was because my family was made incomplete by these events. My grandparents' story didn't need to stay incomplete also. Or maybe it was because we lived in a world that still fostered anti-Semitism and disbelief, and I felt it my responsibility to possess something seamless.

Klein Webber on Google brought up Facebook profiles.

When I traveled to Berlin, I had spent an entire day walking the city, asking locals whether they had heard of Ludveissles and Klein Webber.

"I don't see it anywhere on any map," the curator of the newly opened Jewish Museum in Berlin replied as he flipped through documents.

Were these code names, mispronunciations, or misspellings? Was Poppy confused? Was he lying? Was there something he did not want anyone to know? Maybe he really had a fucking magic ring. Or perhaps it was that gold watch from the boardwalk.

Grandma was never any help when it came to locating this final camp. "Who can remember?" was her preferred response. And on the days she chose to cooperate, she only corroborated with the confounding evidence. "Ludveissles. He was liberated from there, you Poppy."

I confronted my father again and again about Klein Webber, repeating questions about the camp in the way that a forty-niner might relentlessly pan at one place in the river he was certain contained gold. After a few dozen queries, I uncovered something that gleamed.

"Actually I do remember Poppy telling me that in the last camp—I guess Ludveissles," he said, not sure how to pronounce it anymore, "there was this Nazi who told him, 'You think you'll make it through this war?' I think the man had a dark scar on his cheek. Poppy didn't respond, of course, and the Nazi told him, 'You won't live till the end of this day.' But then, during the liberation, Poppy found that Nazi. Dead. And Poppy knelt down next to him and said, 'Look who saw the end.'" Dad nodded. "That's it. That's all I know."

Ludveissles and Klein Webber were jigsaw puzzle pieces with the pictures completely torn away, reduced to the brown cardboard underneath.

Each night, I pored through my notes, certain I had missed something.

I followed the death march from Auschwitz Buna to Dora-Mittelbau, where the crematoriums operated relentlessly, where twenty to thirty were hanged each day. I reread Poppy's stories from the camps just before he would arrive at the mystery camp. There were so few details, yet the stories that had escaped places like Dora were invaluable.

"They are only choosing Jews to be sent to Bergen-Belsen," Poppy's group leader in Dora told him. "It's not a place you want to go." The *Gruppenführer*, a gentile, slid off his armband and gave it to Poppy. "They won't select me anyway. And I like you. You're a good man."

Poppy had asked the group leader whether four other Jews could work under his command. The group leader allowed this and turned to the gentiles to issue a warning: "You will follow this man's command. Otherwise you will answer to me."

Only five Jews avoided that selection.

Maybe it was the armband that had made him disappear. Maybe the four Jews Poppy had helped save were named Lud, Veissel, Klein, and Webber. Maybe he had been liberated from Dora with those four Jews and we were all just mishearing his story.

But of course not, because two months later, in April 1945, he was transported to Ravensbrück, a camp designed to hold 15,000, though the Nazis made accommodations for eight times that number. Ravensbrück didn't have cement gas chambers; it had mobile freight compartments to conduct the gassings. Poppy cleared the corpses from the square. He was still quite present in that hell.

I rewatched the Shoah Foundation tapes and set the scene of Ludveissles with Poppy's words: No beds. Mountains of bodies. No time to incinerate the corpses. And then, without any sense of finality, on May 2, 1945, American soldiers marched in, liberating Poppy and the rest of the Jews of this mystery camp. They told them not to eat because they had heard what had happened in Bergen-Belsen.

Poppy sat down in the middle of the camp and cried. His entire family had died, but he had survived. His voice on the tapes narrated what happened next:

An American soldier from Chicago approached Leon Lederman. The young man spoke in Yiddish.

America had given a Jew a gun, Leon thought in satisfied disbelief.

Two more soldiers joined them. One, an Italian American, carried a gun that could have inspired the Rambo films. He had it trained on two Nazis, who held up their hands in surrender.

"These are your bullets and my pulling," the Italian said, and squeezed the trigger.

The cloud of gunfire cleared, revealing two dead Nazis and men with vengeful smiles. Leon wore his lion's grin.

I allowed the video to play and followed Poppy into postliberation Germany, looking for clues about the mystery camp.

He left for Fallingbostel's Russian sector. He wanted nothing to do with the British, not after the drafting of the White Paper and the Balfour Declaration, which retracted the promise of a home to the Jewish people in what would eventually become Israel.

But Poppy never digressed to return to Ludveissles and Klein Webber, a place that existed only on the lips of my dead grandfather. History felt lost.

The winter of 2010 arrived, and I spent one late-January afternoon in the surf, riding frigid swells until dusk made the temperatures unbearable. Exhausted by the waves and loopy from the cold, I returned to my apartment and heated up some water for tea. I sat down with a book on the Dora concentration camp and wondered how many years the authors had invested in researching Dora—five? Ten? But they had a substantial record to show for their time; I had spent just as long contemplating Ludveissles and didn't have even a sentence beyond hearsay. The possibilities that could point to some truth felt endless.

I sipped my tea and read. Focusing on the text, however, was difficult. The surf had made my mind fuzzy and disconnected. But I did not want to waste a night away from the books. I plunged into the dull text and found that the only way to maintain focus was to read with some flippancy. I pronounced the names of camps and towns in Poppy's thick Yiddish accent. "Ravensbrück. Ravens-brook. Ravens-broke," I read, testing out the words, rediscovering how his Yiddish accent had flavored speech. "Mittelbau, Metal-bow, Middle-bo."

But one word stopped me.

Ludwigslust.

Poppy's copied accent had transformed *Ludvigslust*'s *W* into a *V*. I said it again. His borrowed inflection blended the *G* and *T* into the tough sounding *S* of Yiddish.

And then I had it. There it was. Always and forever on the page. *Ludveissles.*

Ludveissles had always been Ludwigslust. And four miles from the town was a concentration camp that had never been called Webber. It was Wöbbelin.

"You've got to be fucking kidding me," I said, abandoning this game of intonation. I grabbed the phone. "Grandma, I found the camp. Where Poppy had been liberated. It was called Wöbbelin."

"This is what I always told you—Wöbbelin and Ludwigslust," she said, pronouncing them like the more familiar Webber and Ludveissles, two made-up places that I had come to know most intimately.

"You did always tell me, Grandma."

We said goodnight, and I spent the rest of the evening collecting the shards of information scattered in this explosion of discovery. I smiled each time a new fact about Wöbbelin or Ludwigslust appeared. And then laughed uncontrollably whenever I stopped to think about the years I had spent befuddled because of something as simple as two misheard words.

The camp and town had been there all along; I just needed the correct accent to access it.

Just as Poppy had said, the Americans liberated the camp on May 2. Over the next few weeks I dug up what I could on this concentration camp established in the final months of the war. After the 82nd Airborne Division and the 8th Infantry liberated Poppy and 3,500 other survivors from Wöbbelin, the army forced the Ludwigslusters to act as pallbearers. German women, bedecked in feathered hats and fur-lined coats, and German men, suited in Sunday's best and topped with fedoras, carried two hundred narrow, open caskets down the cobblestone avenues of Ludwigslust for a proper burial. For the first time, the citizens of Ludwigslust could examine what they had ignored.

That was all that I had. But it was something. It was the one fact that I had hunted longest; the missing piece of the puzzle. It gave me a more complete way to preserve my grandparents' Holocaust. And preservation was the only way that I had ever known to make sense of this impossible past. I had gotten to the stories that I was never supposed to have.

After the discovery, life seemed to go back to a time when the Holocaust wasn't everything I read and researched, a time when the camps weren't standing in my mind.

And the reunion was celebrated. All of Grandma's grandchildren had reunited under her roof to eat, drink, and "be married already," she begged.

But then Grandma got sick. And with the same insistence of her congestive heart failure, the Holocaust reared its head again.

31

A RETURN TO THE CAMPS

I'm going to Majdanek," I told Grandma as she lay in her hospital bed. I would be traveling to Poland and Prague as part of the Jewish Enrichment Center's Holocaust Mini Master's Program. It was the summer of 2010. While I had already completed my grandparents' timelines from those two awful decades, the JEC was offering an opportunity that I could not turn down—to travel to the camps with a survivor.

"Haven't you been to Majdanek?" She could hardly lift her purpled arms.

"Just the Warsaw ghetto, Auschwitz, and Terezin."

"I wasn't in Terezin," she reproached.

"I know, but I—"

"I wanted to run from Majdanek and you run to go see it." She shook her head. "That was the worst camp. More worse than Auschwitz. Ask you Poppy, if he was alive (Oy, Leo," She dedicated a moment for lamentations, finding the strength to place her pudgy hand over her sick heart, smothering Poppy's golden face that lay atop her gown. "With a stick, they give you a *zetz* on the feet in the morning and another *zetz* on the head after work. That's how they greeted you in Majdanek.

"I remember when we get to the camp, they take my brother Shama away from me. They put him on the men's side and then they give us uniforms and make us stand in the . . ." She drew a square in the air.

"A courtyard."

"Yes, a courtyard, that's right." Grandma abandoned her pain for a brief moment to offer up a smile. She patted my hand, as if I had done something much more remarkable than recall a common English word. "And then this Nazi, Brigida, she screams at us to give up our jewelry. I have all mine mother's jewelry, the last things she give to me in the barn. I think maybe to not give it in."

I grew excited. All through my childhood I had been studying Poppy's wrists and fingers as if the gaudy jewelry that he had worn had been artifacts from the war. But maybe it had always been Grandma's collection that had been heirlooms from the Holocaust, proving once again that I had been an idiot child and a terrible sleuth.

"But they tell us if we don't give it in, they gonna kill us," Grandma continued. "So I go up and place it in the box."

My heart sank.

"Then the Nazi sees my boots and she says for me to give them to her, too. What can I do? I give them to Brigida. Then we just stood at roll call like this every morning."

"What was roll call like?" I asked.

"What can I tell you? They loved us so much that they wanted to make sure we weren't missing. If someone go missing, it was like a . . . a diamond got lost. What can I tell you about this?" Her sarcasm had teeth. "It was roll call, Noiach, isn't it obvious what they did at roll call?"

The day before I left for Poland, I visited Grandma again in the hospital from which she had once escaped. Her health had worsened. Her pain had filled her countenance. It grew wings and flew the gap between us, burrowing into my heart. I knew this would be the end. How long could one survivor fight a perpetual illness?

"I'm heading to Poland tomorrow," I told her.

She sighed. Grandma had the ability to shrug and nod at the same time. To voice indifference and concern, confusion and understanding. Her arms were a lurid purple. If she were healthier, she would have told me to be careful, to watch out for the Poles, to eat well, but she could only shrug and nod.

"I'm going with thirty-five other Jews and a survivor," I said to reassure her or to fill the quiet room with life.

Shrug and nod.

The survivor on our trip was a barrel-chested, eighty-year-old man named Leo Zisman. Leo had grown up in Kovno, Lithuania, and had been a prisoner of four concentration camps. He had white hair and a faded orange triangular patch set like a goatee in his white beard.

Of the participants, only a few had grandparents who had survived. I noticed one difference between the regular Jews on the trip and those with survivors in their families. The former group engaged in Jewish geography, where one Jew states where he is from and which high school he attended and the other Jew asks whether the first Jew knows Doug Rosenberg or Sarah Applebaum.

The latter group played concentration camp archaeology.

Did you lose any family in Majdanek? Mine were killed on Aktion Erntefest. Buried among the eighteen thousand. . . . Auschwitz? My family survived there. . . . The rest? Scattered ashes in the fields near Treblinka.

In all my years, I had never actually thought to discuss the Holocaust with other grandchildren of survivors. In fact, that first conversation I had with another grandchild only took place a year or so prior to this trip, when a Dutch writer interviewed me for a book she was researching about the Holocaust's effect on the grandchildren of survivors. She asked me how the Holocaust had impacted my life.

"It's been a part of my identity," I told her. "It's part of my people's history and my family's history. It always made me proud of my grandparents."

"But emotionally?" she asked.

"Emotionally?" I had never really thought about it that way. Part of me felt, as I considered the question, that the events weren't mine to be emotional about. My grandparents had to suffer the past as they moved into the future. I was simply there in case they ever wanted to unburden themselves of the stories. Or maybe all the fact-finding that I had invested a life in was my catharsis. "It made me want to know the stories, I guess."

"What I mean is," she said, "were you scared that something like this would happen again to your family? Did you have anxiety? Things like this."

"Scared? Maybe a little, but mostly just prepared." In the same way that my father had been prepared with that suitcase beneath his bed, I had in mind my bank, a prescription vial filled with the contents of a survival kit, and I always considered my escape route.

She put down her pen. "For example, I was anorexic when I was younger. I had food issues, which I believe stem from my grandparents' experience in the Holocaust."

"I didn't realize that the third generation could be affected this way." It seemed, at most, a second-generation problem.

"They are," she told me. "Everyone else that I interviewed has told me how they were affected by their grandparents' stories. You are the only one who seems to not have the same emotional attachment."

I thought about some of my friends whose grandparents had been survivors, too, and suddenly I recalled their youthful tribulations. Their troubles ran the gamut from depression to self-injurious behavior. Could it all have linked back to a time they had never known?

"My father and aunt were affected," I offered. "She's always on edge, and he grew up jealous of those who had grandparents. He kept a suitcase under his bed in case the Nazis ever returned. But I can only remember feeling pride in the fact that my grandparents had done the unthinkable. That they had survived. Imagine that there was a group set on murdering you for more than half of a decade. And in the end you won. I could only think that's something to be proud of."

I felt that same pride when we landed in Warsaw. *We're back, assholes.* I was shocked to find that this was the majority sentiment of the group. We boarded a bus and drove straight to the last remaining section of the ghetto wall. Above us, Poles kept their blinds closed and hung laundry from their balconies.

"Why didn't we resist? Why didn't we communicate with the other ghettos?" Leo Zisman screamed. On the plane, the old survivor had been all smiles and engaged himself in pleasant conversations, but standing before this wall, in this Polish courtyard, he was enraged. For the next week he burned with a passion, as if that faint red triangle in his beard was the fire manifest in him. He hollered his stories for the Poles to overhear and screamed rhetorical questions about man's morality.

As we moved from gravesite to gravesite—for the whole city was one big unmarked grave—I felt nothing but disgust for man and what he was capable of.

The stories Grandma had told me, and the ones Poppy had revealed on the tapes, were information I had not known during that first visit six years earlier. Now I could see the boy at the gates beg for his life. I could imagine Klaustermeyer and Blosche riding circles around Poppy and chasing Grandma and her family into hiding. *Was that the manhole cover that led to the tomb of Grandma's fallen comrade?* I walked the old Muranowska Square on Nalewki Street, where Poppy had smuggled wood for a baker named Kagan in order to receive a few extra rations of bread. Kagan had always been as faceless as the rest of the victims and perpetrators in my grandparents' stories, but in Warsaw, he was vivid and complete.

"Why didn't they have the opportunity to have names and to have children?" Leo asked as we stood in a Jewish cemetery along a pathway that had been suspended over forty thousand Jewish bodies buried in a mass grave. The grave, after the bodies had decomposed, was now a large depression in the earth, like a bomb crater. Leo's face reddened. His eyes fogged with tears. No one had an answer, of course. He sang the Kaddish.

Leo moved among the dead. I couldn't imagine Grandma coming back here, traveling these grounds, and having patience for thirty-something young people armed with questions about her past. But Leo did, and he entertained all curiosities.

"How do you feel being here?" I asked Leo as the group wandered ahead among the dead Jews.

His eyes narrowed, and he adjusted the *kippah* on his head. "If I had a machine gun, I could kill all of them, the Germans. But when I see blood I faint. I can't explain it. I hate all of them. Those sons of bitches." He stopped to gaze upon the headstones, most so withered that the Hebrew writing looked like runny paint. Then he turned to me again and spoke with a voice desperate to hold back tears. "I saw a German take a baby, maybe a month old, and rip it up like a chicken."

It was the first time anyone had ever haunted me with their words. For some reason, of all the terrible events that had been revealed to me, this one I couldn't erase from my mind. Warsaw and Leo and the murdered newborn had made this atrocity more real than I had ever fathomed. And years later, when I would become a father, on the day that Marissa and I took our first daughter home—when I realized that I was responsible for this fragile baby and had to raise her in this world capable of such cruelties—it was the image of the murdered newborn that supplanted that first week of joy. For the first time, the Holocaust filled me with despair.

In the cemetery, after Leo had told me that awful story, he said something else: "Why didn't we fight back? We'd have more than six million more."

Grandma had asked me that very question when she had recalled watching three Nazis lead three thousand of her people to the Umschlagplatz of Warsaw. In the cemetery, we were just a few blocks from that horrid site. Warsaw was a place that still inspired rebellion in the hearts of these ancient survivors.

I wondered what would have happened if Leo and Poppy had met in Auschwitz, where Leo had had the gall to do the unthinkable. He had slugged a Nazi in the groin. He had organized a mini-coup that saved him and other boys from being led into the gas chambers. In Auschwitz, Leo had smuggled his *tefillin* from a pile of contraband. What would have happened if he had met Poppy—the man who had run a pitchfork through a Nazi's throat in a barn near Otwock, who had jumped from the cattle cars and escaped certain death in Treblinka, who had fought in the uprising—here in the Warsaw ghetto? I would like to think that Molotov cocktails would have fallen from rooftops for a few more days.

Poppy's Hebrew name had been Aryah Yehudah Lieb. All three monikers meant or were symbolic of a "lion." In the comic-book panels of my mind, he had always been the king of the ghetto. In Warsaw, I felt as if I were now standing with the Leo of the camps. Leo and Leon, the lions of Auschwitz.

But they hadn't met. And they were only cubs back then, when two-thirds of European Jewry had been wiped out. And here we were, walking through a cemetery where the Nazis had filled another mass grave.

Despite his impression on me, I avoided Leo on that return trip to the camps. He made me feel guilty. While he bounded through these scenes of tragedy, Grandma deteriorated back in Brooklyn. I had abandoned her in the present to return to her past.

The next day we drove to Lublin.

Within ten minutes of walking the city's main road to welcome in Shabbat at a *yeshiva*, I found a swastika in the main square. The anti-Semitic symbol didn't bother me as much as I would have imagined. In a way, it just reminded me that half a century was not that long ago and that people don't change all that much. I thought about the Poles whom I had met in Otwock six years earlier. Had any of them truly wanted to help? Or were they just secret artists of that Nazi emblem?

When we arrived at the *yeshiva*, the façade resembled a ransacked tenement. The walls were graffitied and the fence full of holes. Despite the neglected exterior, the inside was immaculate. Newly installed wooden pews were set between beautiful jade-colored columns.

Our leader, Rabbi Lawrence, was a balding young Brit with a big nose, a big *kippah*, and an interminable five o'clock shadow. If some in the group were scared to look Jewish in Poland, Rabbi Lawrence was not the man they wanted to walk with in the streets.

"Anytime a group like ours arrives in Lublin," he said, "the city's Jewish population doubles or even triples. Come. Let's go downstairs and celebrate Shabbat."

The synagogue served cholent.

"This is amazing," said my neighbor.

"You should have tasted my Grandma's," I told her.

"When did she pass away?" she asked.

"She didn't. She just doesn't cook anymore." But the question left me wondering. In the past few hours, while I marched past swastikas and sites of tragedy, while I ate someone else's cholent, Grandma could have died in her hospital bed. The cholent stopped tasting amazing.

On our walk back to the city center, Poles at a biker bar and Polish drivers shouted invectives at us.

"What did they say?" I asked our Polish security guard.

"Not nice things."

The next morning, we returned to the *yeshiva*.

"Let's say one morning you awoke and found a red button on your chest," Rabbi Lawrence suggested, always with passion and pauses injected into every hypothetical. He stroked his beard as we contemplated. "Now you have the opportunity to press this red button, but by doing so, you would forever change your religion . . . meaning you would never be Jewish again. Would you press the button?"

We went around the room, answering his question.

"My story is a little different," Adrianna, a Colombian Jew, told us. "I was baptized Catholic and only discovered my Jewish roots a few years ago. I finally understood why my grandmother always said to never use the pot for sancocho, which is a pork dish, to boil milk for the coffee." She wouldn't press the button.

Two participants had immigrated to New York from the Ukraine when they were teenagers. On account of anti-Semitism rife in the Ukraine, the button had glowed on their chests with the same luminosity zits radiate on teenage foreheads. They wouldn't press the button.

"I couldn't understand why my first cousins celebrated Christmas," a girl named Remy admitted, "while my family was Jewish." They celebrated Christ's birthday, Remy revealed, because her grandparents had pressed the red button while living in Nazi-occupied France. "I wouldn't press it," she added.

In the end, nobody would have pressed it. Even though many of us were secular or atheists, we were all Jews. Observant or not, that was our identity. But even if we had wanted to press the button, it wouldn't have worked. To the world, to the Poles of the 1940s, to the Poles of this millennium, to everyone, we would always be Jews. Anyway, pressing red buttons to get rid of Jews was what Hitler and the Nazis had been doing, so why would I?

"Helloooo," Leo Zisman hollered when we all entered the dining room, unintentionally mimicking his namesake, the Uncle Leo from *Seinfeld*, with his overdramatic, heavily accented greeting. "Let me tell you why I didn't push the red button. I wanted to carry on the Jewish people." Then excitedly, Leo singled out Adrianna. "Here's what she's gonna do: she's gonna marry a Jewish guy, and I'm gonna give you my address, and you're gonna invite me, and I'm gonna come. . . . This is what it's all about. By the end of this trip we'll need half the number of rooms." The rabbis blushed. Leo's wife glared. Somebody poured the alcohol.

"Get Marissa a ring already," Grandma had shouted at me during each visit for the past few years. "I don't deserve a wedding?"

"Soon, Grandma, soon," was always my response. I knew she didn't have "soon" any longer.

32

MAJDANEK

Will there be signs that say 'Goodbye, Jews'?" Igor, one of the Ukrainians in my group, half-joked as we drove out of Lublin. A few blocks later, our bus stopped at a red light, and a man waiting for the public bus turned to the lady beside him. He pointed at our bus with his chin, and the two compatriots laughed.

"What do you think they're laughing about?" I asked.

"Majdanek," said Igor. "Where else would a tour bus around here be heading? They laugh about it still."

From Lublin to concentration camp Majdanek was a fifteen-minute drive. The guard towers and barracks were visible from the main road. Unlike the other camps, which were tucked away in forests, easier for those culpable to at least deny, Majdanek sat in plain sight. An award on a shelf. It had been built to be seen, to remind the Jews that no one cared. The gas chamber stood a few hundred feet from rush-hour traffic.

Silence filled the bus. I watched as a mother pushed her baby in a stroller along the perimeter of the camp. What a place to rear the future.

In the near distance lived her neighbors. Hundreds of apartment buildings were painted in colors that felt as bright as Miami Beach pastels. Their terraces faced the black barracks, the gas chambers, and the crematorium. Every morning was breakfast at Majdanek.

I couldn't believe that homes had been built outside the camp. But then again, the Poles had to live somewhere. In a country with so many killing grounds, if the parliament had restricted new construction to land that had never been the site of genocide, the Poles would only be allowed to build in other countries.

We went inside the visitor's center. The gift shop—yes, the gift shop—at Majdanek sold concentration-camp posters, coffee mugs praising

Lublin—*Beautiful Lublin*—and stickers that warned other drivers to have some regard for a traveling baby. Regard for babies. That one hurt the most.

We watched a film about the camp, and as it played, I searched for images of Poppy and Grandma. After all, my father had once spotted Yadja and Grandma getting pulled onto a British tank on a *60 Minutes* episode about the liberation of Bergen-Belsen. But the only image that struck me as familial was when two corpses were photographed at the bottom of one long pit. An adult and a child. Perhaps it was Uncle Shama and my great-grandfather David Zylberberg, two of the few dozen that hung above the light switch. *Dead, dead,* and many more *dead* to come, said the empty hole in the earth before it left the screen.

The film ended, and we entered the camp, crossing through an entryway where the barbed wire was stitched through cement columns. We marched straight into the gas chamber. The cement walls were stained blue. The rabbi spoke of the macabre, but the words that were most piercing were those that minimized Majdanek—he described the room as *relatively small* since it was used to *kill only* eighty thousand people. It could hold about three hundred at once, and in the space between the people and the ceiling, the Germans would add a *few infants*.

We stepped out into the light. I stared across the field toward the crematorium. The story that Grandma had told me about the women using the toilets, which were nothing more than large holes in the ground, was made most awful by the horrid tangibility of the camp. She had said that the Nazis atop the lookout towers used these women as target practice, knocking them into the shit and piss. By interlacing Grandma's stories with setting, it was easier to imagine the demented games the Nazis had developed, the ones in which the loser was executed. I could see the Polish Kapos issuing their futile work orders, forcing Jews to unearth boulders from the frozen ground and move them across the field, only to have them shuttle the rocks back to their original location the day after. Past the wire was the forest, where Grandma had harvested poison ivy for the evening soup.

I entered the barn-sized barracks, where photographs of Majdanek's victims lined the walls. The few possessions scattered about were meant to symbolize the thousands murdered here. Brushes, keys, worn suitcases, cracked mirrors, shoehorns, toothbrushes, prayer shawls, shofars, and dolls. A case of dolls. And tangled human hair.

One room housed only shoes. Thousands of shoes were piled up in head-high cages. The path between them was like a parted sea, and the pressure of the shoes against the metal cages threatened to snap the welding. In the endless browned leather one little red shoe sat atop the pile, as if this were the place that had given birth to Spielberg's red-coated child in *Schindler's List*.

Leo was outside the barracks, shouting.

"They are not showing the real picture. Why do they say eighteen thousand? Maybe it was eighteen thousand and three. Why can't we count those three? Why can't we remember them, too?

"Did you see the little girl from the film?" Leo asked again and again, as more members of the group gathered outside. "Why did she die? When we go back, what should we do?"

Educate. Speak up. Never again. Over the week, the group had given all of the trite answers that felt neutered by repetition and inaction.

We walked toward the crematorium. A chorus of chirping crickets sat in the high grass. Our guide pointed out bone fragments in the dirt.

After the Jews had led uprisings in concentration camps Sobibor and Treblinka, the Nazis made certain that revolt died like a people. In Majdanek, they selected a few hundred prisoners to dig a pit as long as a football field and as deep as a swimming pool behind the crematorium. The Jews dug for three days.

On November 3, 1943, loudspeakers inside the camp blared German waltzes. They lined up eighteen thousand Jews on the edge of the pit and machine-gunned them into the mass grave. The picture of the small corpse and the larger corpse from the film we saw earlier could have been the start to that mass murder.

I touched the earth above the death pits where Shama and David had been killed. I wondered who had been murdered first. I hoped that it was David.

A tour bus started honking.

I sat by myself and thought of the forty-two thousand Jews murdered in Majdanek and the neighboring camps on that day in November, a mass killing completed in eleven hours. They called it Aktion Erntefest, a German euphemism meaning "Harvest Festival."

Those killed during the Aktion were no longer below ground. They had been exhumed and incinerated, sweeping their way across Poland as ashes. Some of the ashes, however, had been collected and mixed with earth to sit like a giant anthill beneath a UFO-like mausoleum with a message chiseled into the frieze. Translated, it read, "Let our fate be a warning."

It was another fucked-up and impotent way to say "Never again."

We recited the Kaddish.

I stayed a bit longer with the ashes and watched my group return to the bus. While Majdanek made Grandma's horrific accounts all the more devastating, it made the hero's stories more powerful.

Poppy had once told my father he knew that if he could just get out of Majdanek, he believed he would survive the war. Such an odd thought with Auschwitz ahead. But he had always known—known!?—that he could survive Auschwitz because he could work. Majdanek, he said, was a death camp for even the strongest.

I stared at where the bus idled, ready to depart. Had that been the place where the cattle cars departed for Auschwitz? If so, it would have been where Leon Lederman had saved Mandela Mandelbaum. When Poppy had been selected by the Nazi officer to go to Auschwitz, either he was given some mark on his jacket that signaled he was suitable for transport or some identifying number on his coat had been copied down. Regardless, instead of just boarding the train, he took his friend Mandela's jacket and put it on. Mandela was too weak for Auschwitz. He would never have been chosen. Leon Lederman approached the same Nazi with the clipboard. The Nazi studied him in Mandela's coat and selected him for Auschwitz, too.

As we left Majdanek, an iPod clicked on, and the Orthodox reggae artist Matisyahu sang a modern-day version of the *Hatikvah*.

> It's not about
> Win or lose
> Because we all lose
> When they feed on the souls of the innocent
> Blood-drenched pavement
> Keep on moving though the waters stay raging.

Later that night, we heard that song again, this time performed live by the artist in a synagogue in Kraków. Matisyahu appeared onstage in a gray sweater, jeans, and neon-green shoes. He had tied back his sidelocks and beatboxed songs about Israel and HaShem. It felt like he was haunting the city like some golem with his song about Jerusalem. But then Matisyahu paused his show to thank the Poles for being gracious hosts.

Did he really feel that he was accepted here? Or was I being too obdurate to think that I wasn't?

The day after the concert, that second question bothered me. It was one swastika, I tried to rationalize. We couldn't expect the elimination of anti-Semitism completely. Maybe the fact that there hadn't been fifty swastikas was a step in the right direction. I thought about the German whom I had met in Nicaragua. He had been so genuine about his compunction; he had shed tears for the things he had never done. Maybe the Poles were like him and I just hadn't given them that chance. Maybe Matisyahu had been right to preach respect from the stage.

That afternoon, we arrived at a conference room to hear from Jews living in Poland. Polish Jews. The term, post-Holocaust, felt like an oxymoron. An Orthodox girl spoke first. "You know how the word 'Jew' is used in Poland," she said. "It's like 'gay' where you are from. When a teacher gives a test, something the students hate, they'll call the teacher a Jew . . . or they might refer to a corrupt politician as a Jew."

"Never again," someone from my group said as we exited the conference room. "Never again will I come to Poland."

Nobody played Matisyahu's music on the bus anymore.

33

BIRKENAU

Leo stood in the middle of Auschwitz-Birkenau and began to holler. His baritone voice cracked with anger or disbelief.

"I prayed and wrapped my *tefillin* here. In Birkenau. And when they found out, they whipped me so many times that for months I had to sleep on my belly." He just kept on remembering and remembering as we pushed deeper into the camp. He shouted so we wouldn't forget. He yelled about digging up potatoes from the frozen ground. He roared about hiding in the hay, abdicating his responsibilities, risking death in this place of death.

But he challenged Birkenau now. He kicked the ground. "And I kicked that Nazi right in the groin. He put the gun to my head and I screamed, 'Shoot. Shoot, why don't you?' He didn't shoot me. And I'm here."

The only time that I had ever felt more proximate to Birkenau than walking its grounds was when Grandma told me the story about the girl in the blue dress.

"She wore a blue dress." Grandma's eyes had gone vacant, staring through me. "Oh, how she was so pretty. A beautiful girl. She was in my work unit and they shot her in the head because she couldn't lift the wheelbarrow."

Her knuckles slammed down on the glass table.

"She was so pretty and they shot her in the head. Why?" Grandma paused, allowing the question to hang like a fog between us. "We had to drag her body back to the camp that night so they could put her in the crematory. She looked so nice in her blue dress and they shot her."

Once more I thought of Spielberg's girl in the red coat—an innocent, a life magnified by a stroke of color on black-and-white film. But

Grandma's girl in the blue dress wasn't carted off cinematically and with haste; she was left to loom in place and in memory.

I wondered why that story came to mind. Why had she selected this one story to represent all of her memories of Birkenau when I had asked her to tell me about the camp? I scraped my nails across her tablecloth. The tablecloth was blue. So was the bowl in the middle of the table, as was my shirt and Grandma's velour jumpsuit. The tiles beneath my feet were blue, and they gave way to an ocean of blue carpet that stretched across her entire living room. I looked into Poppy's eyes where they seemed to forever hang, as if he had only existed in this form on the gold pallet dangling from Grandma's neck. His eyes were blue as well.

As I stood in Birkenau with Leo, I wondered what stories Grandma would have recalled had we been surrounded by green or red or the gray skies of the camp. I wondered how often the Holocaust returned to her through colors.

Leo walked us down a path that traveled between the remnants of hundreds of barracks, all of which had been torn apart by Polish peasants after the war. They had used the barrack walls and beds as firewood. Only brick chimneys stood in those footprints of genocide. They lined up like the ribs of a giant elephant carcass. Auschwitz-Birkenau was enormous. One million people could have easily fit into only a section of the camp.

We stopped beside a destroyed crematorium to light candles for the dead. The wind kept blowing them out. Then we moved on to a building where the Nazis had kept all of the possessions they had stolen from the Jews.

"Why is this door locked?" Leo demanded. He kicked the door with all of his strength.

Everyone looked around uneasily. *You can't kick down doors in Auschwitz.* But then again, it was Leo, a survivor of Birkenau, and he could kick down every fucking door to this place.

"This door's open," someone with the good sense to check a second entrance announced, saving Auschwitz-Birkenau from Leo.

We gathered in front of all the flattened crematories that had been reduced to roofs atop rubble and listened to Leo's stories of rebellion.

But Leo was an aberration. This was not a place for revolt to prosper. Birkenau was where rebellion got ushered into the gas chambers. I walked over to a gray pond. It was the one thing that I had remembered most vividly from my first visit to this place, six years earlier. The edges of the rectangular pool were still coated with green algae, and the water itself was dark gray, as if the ashes could never be separated from the two parts hydrogen and one part oxygen they had fused to. These melted-down corpses were now elemental, a symbol on the periodic table. I couldn't stop staring at the pool. I couldn't stop thinking: How could people still deny the Holocaust?

In 2004, on my first visit to Birkenau, I had entered the women's barracks and wondered whether I had accidentally stumbled upon Grandma's bunk. I had searched for her presence. I wanted to find HADASA ZYLBERBERG WAS HERE chiseled into the bed frame. But, of course, there were no carvings. In 2010, however, I had returned to Birkenau with her barrack number.

Grandma's barrack number had always been one of those unanswerable questions. Yet I could not accept that Grandma didn't know. She had remembered everything else in such detail. So, now and again, I would ask the same question hoping for a different result: "What barrack were you in at Birkenau?"

"Noiach, how many times I should tell you This I don't know. Who should remember? Leave me alone "

But on one particular visit, Grandma was adamant about telling Birkenau stories.

She told me about how they had been forced to strip down upon arrival, how the women were forced to take pills to stop their ovulation. She told me about the dream she had the night before the death march. Her dead mother had come to her in sleep and predicted her survival, but refused to tell her about her brother Shmuel, who, she would later learn, was murdered by a Pole just before the end of the war.

My throat twisted with each detail until it felt as if my trachea had been torqued to its limit.

But eventually the sadness and grimness led to Grandma's happy story, which was also set in Birkenau.

"One night, Helen wandered into the wrong barrack," Grandma said, reproach lining her words. "And that's how we found each other in Birkenau. They called out her name, we both step forward, and I get hit. But I saw her. How someone could forget their barrack number, I don't know. It was all you had to remember."

I had nearly missed it—the quick chastising of her dead cousin for forgetting something that had been so simple to remember (and yet so simple to forget).

"Grandma." I paused. "What number was your barrack?"

"Eighteen. Who could forget this?"

It was another fact. Another victory over the diminishing past. An additional truth against denial.

In Birkenau, armed with that detail, I sat on the thin boards of a bunk inside barrack 18. All that remained was moldering wood and neglect. But to me, sitting inside the barrack felt like visiting some long-lost cousin. It was a piece of the family tree thought snapped, but reclaimed. She survived this. Here. I could feel my skin prickle with goose bumps.

But when I left barrack 18, I found a sign informing me that the barrack numbers had been reassigned later in the war. So there was a second barrack 18, where the doors were locked. I struggled against the lock and for a moment felt as if I had some right to kick down the doors of Birkenau, too. But I paused and breathed. I knew it was time to accept the inevitable: I wouldn't know it all, and eventually Grandma would be gone, leaving me behind with loss and questions.

I stood in the rain and peered through the windows. Then we left for Auschwitz.

34

AUSCHWITZ

When Grandma was in Majdanek, she stood in the soup line and bowed her head. She held out her bowl but received none of the thin broth. When she looked up, she saw a boy holding a ladle.

"I have a message from your father," he whispered.

She suddenly recognized him from Otwock.

"He says, if you can, you must leave this place immediately."

Somehow, she had gotten herself onto a transport to Auschwitz. Aktion Erntefest happened soon after.

I entered the tourist cafeteria outside the gates of Auschwitz. The camp was now serving chicken and pork. It felt wrong to eat lunch in a place like Auschwitz. But I ordered like the rest.

The lunch lady piled potatoes onto my plate. Five little potatoes. One sitting atop four.

I finished the chicken but couldn't touch the potatoes.

"You're not going to eat those?" Igor asked me, pointing at the spuds with his fork.

One afternoon in Majdanek, Grandma's job had been to push the wheelbarrow while the other prisoners piled on potatoes. Suddenly, the handle slipped, the cart wobbled, and five potatoes fell from the pyramid of tubers. Grandma raced to gather them. But the Polish Kapo cracked her whip and ordered the others to grab her. Lower her pants, the Kapo had instructed. The other Jews held my grandmother down as the Kapo split her flesh with the riding crop. Blood, then unconsciousness.

"You can have them," I said, stepping away from the potatoes and into Auschwitz.

The infamous black letters hung above the entranceway—ARBEIT MACHT FREI. The steel banner clung like a silhouette against the ashen sky.

"Work sets you free," I translated to myself. I still found it strange that Poppy, on that train to Auschwitz, the camp responsible for more than one million deaths, knew he would survive the war. Still, I couldn't comprehend the idea that he *knew* this. But after surviving Majdanek, the torture camp, where being the strongest was of little value, where making no mistakes guaranteed you nothing, where the Nazis tortured prisoners for fun, Poppy knew that he would survive Auschwitz.

I looked around at the guard towers, the wires once hot with electricity, the skulls and bones on the placards.

Entering with a survivor was much more harrowing than my first visit in 2004. Back then—maybe it had just been the day—it felt too much like a museum drained of its emotional impact. Perhaps it was because some tourists had treated Auschwitz as if it were a theme park. I watched as they had walked to the next attraction while chatting on cellphones. I saw people giggling as they sought out the gift shop, where they probably hoped to leave with an *I Survived Auschwitz* T-shirt or coffee mug.

But on this visit with Leo, the camp was empty.

I couldn't tear myself away from the tangled web of spectacles that sat behind glass like a creature at the zoo. That twist in my throat had traveled like a clot into my heart, forcing it to beat irregularly. Eventually, I moved on to stockpiles of prosthetic limbs and metal bowls and mountains of hair and shoes lumped together like corpses.

I couldn't stop thinking about how my mother had bronzed my baby shoe. All of these shoes sat limp, and the plans of one million mothers had been erased.

Poring through the past in tomes and having Grandma's stories contrasted with her noodging had always made the Holocaust seem less threatening. But standing in this room, I felt small and alone and sad.

These rooms were only so large. They held only a small sample of the atrocity. They were a microcosm of the horrid. I imagined that the hair, shoes, and brushes of six million Jews, of eleven million people, could have buried Poland.

35

THE BUNA

Our bus departed from the Auschwitz parking lot. I asked our Polish guide, Tomasz, about Buna Monowitz, the third camp in the Auschwitz complex.

"There's not much left of the Buna. We never take tours there."

"Can we drive past it?"

Tomasz nodded and instructed the driver to take a detour.

Abandoned factories stood behind a line of forest and fence. It was hard to differentiate between new construction and that which dated back to the Holocaust. Not much of the Buna had survived.

The bus driver parked and turned on his hazards. Outside, through the static of rain, was a memorial. I got off the bus and stood before the structure built on a roadway median. To avoid the rain, most of the group stayed on the bus. But to me, this land mattered. It was here that Poppy—cheekbones sharpened, skin loosened, eyes sunken by hunger— had lifted hundred-pound bags of concrete for IG Farben. It was here that he had pushed his cart over the wreckage after the Allied forces bombed the camp. It was here that he survived.

Primo Levi had written in *Survival in Auschwitz* that of the prisoners with a tattoo number lower than 150000, "only a few hundred had survived; not one was an ordinary *Haftling*." These particular prisoners were called the "old Jews," and the old Jews survived "through their astuteness and energy in successfully organizing, gaining in this way . . . the indulgence and esteem of the powerful people in the camp."

Poppy, in his teenage years, had worn the badge of the old Jew inked to his arm. 128142.

As I stood in the place that had made him an old Jew, I felt there was no way that I could get any closer to that past. A half-decade—a lifetime, in fact—of pursuing the answers was satisfied here. From the facts that I had compiled, I was able to see their pasts complete in my mind. Or as complete as they ever would be. I had done what I could to piece together what was lost. I now knew of the time when they had endured, overcome, outthought, and survived to live as more than just stories.

I got back on the bus.

36

LIBERATION

It was an April morning in Bergen-Belsen when Hadasa Zylberberg woke to distant cannon fire. It had been days since anyone had received work details. The Nazis, it seemed, had handed the prisoners over to starvation and typhus.

She walked from the bunk as if strength were a thing of the past. She could hardly differentiate between the still-living and the already-dead. They were all bodies dwarfed by protruding knees, bulging ribs, and massive skulls.

And even as the ninth hour of April 15, 1945, brought forth a jeep carrying four British military police with loudspeakers blaring, "You are free," most of sixty thousand survivors of Bergen-Belsen could not move. (Eleven thousand would die in the coming days. Their withered bodies could not digest the foods that the British fed them.)

Hadasa and Yadja ran to the long procession of troops. Helen ran in the opposite direction.

"Helen, where are you going?" Hadasa yelled.

"To get souvenirs."

"Are you crazy?" Hadasa screamed to her cousin. "This is the last minute of the war. The Nazis are still out there. And you want souvenirs?"

"You're always so afraid," Helen hollered back.

"What do we do now?" Helen asked Hadasa as they watched the Nazis bury the dead Jews, of course, with British guns trained at them. A bulldozer rumbled forward and plowed hundreds more into the depths of the ten-foot pit.

They sat down and cried.

"Do you know where any of your family is located?" asked a man, a British rabbi.

Hadasa gave the name of a distant cousin in Haifa, Shmuel Weinberg. She inquired about her grandfather, who had left Europe before the war. A response came from Weinberg. Even her grandfather was dead.

The concentration camp in Belsen was burned to the ground to prevent the spread of typhus. Hadasa and Helen, like the rest of the survivors, moved into the Nazi barracks in Bergen. They slept in the beds of killers and dreamed of Palestine, though the dreams would always succumb to the nightmares of the camps.

Life slogged on, and Hadasa looked out at the world beyond Bergen, hoping to find someone or something of the past.

On a cool summer morning, she sat on her front patio fashioning a skirt from an old army blanket. That was when she noticed the most puzzling thing.

"No. Is it? It can't be," she thought, but stood as he approached.

37

IN SEARCH OF NEW BEGINNINGS

Leon Lederman, after being liberated from Wöbbelin, arrived at a displaced persons camp in the Russian-occupied zone of Germany. He pulled out a wad of tobacco and laid it across a sheet of paper, rolling and marrying the two together.

"Give me that," an officer demanded.

Leon struck a match.

"You are in the Soviet zone," the officer warned him, "and your tobacco now belongs to the Union."

Leon inhaled the cigarette. Next to him, another Jew refused to give up his valise. The officer barking orders to the man with the suitcase had had enough. He wrestled the luggage from the man's hands and threw its owner to the ground.

"Give me your tobacco," Leon's officer demanded again.

Leon handed over his smokes and turned to his friend. "I didn't survive Hitler to be abused by the Communists. I'm leaving."

"We can't leave, Leo," the friend told him. "We're part of the Union now."

Inside the barracks, the bunk leader barked orders to the new arrivals. One of the commands was to wear no jackets in the courtyard; it gave the impression that a man would want to escape Mother Russia.

Leon removed his coat and pulled off his shirt. Then he buttoned the jacket back onto his bare chest, fitted the shirt over the jacket, and tucked the hems into his waistline. He walked outside, kicked a few stones about the courtyard toward an imaginary goal set against the metal gate. When he was far enough, Leon sprinted back to Fallingbostel.

For the next few days, he wandered the German countryside. He felt like the last of the Jews. He spent cold nights in abandoned banks, fueling his campfires in these abdicated halls of finance with once more inflated marks.

He traveled for days in search of hope. Maybe one of his sisters had also worn a wire around her waist as the train left for Treblinka. Maybe she survived the fall and the Polish countryside and the ghettos and the camps. On his journey past the rubble of the German countryside, he stumbled upon a small displaced persons camp a few hours outside Berlin. A man there told him about another camp, a place called Bergen-Belsen, where thousands of Jewish women had survived.

"Thousands? That many survived?" Leon asked.

The man nodded.

Leon found a bicycle and pedaled for two hours, wondering, *Had Treblinka been so kind?*

Bergen was an oasis, removed, it seemed, from the chaos of Hitler's earth. Jewish women hung linen on drying lines, and men formed *minyans*, staying congregated after the prayers for debate and stories, and then more Kaddish. Even a few Jewish children played on the grounds. Jewish children.

"Is this Bergen-Belsen?" Leon asked men gathered before a game of dominos.

"Where are you from?" was the question. All were suddenly matchmakers born of Hitler's failed extermination, his murderous Diaspora.

"Otwock. In Poland."

"My wife, Rose, has a friend from Otwock. You want to meet her?"

Leon dropped the bicycle.

Which sister?

The man led him to the girl.

"There. That one," he said, pointing to a twenty-two-year-old, cherub-faced girl fashioning a skirt out of an old army blanket. "She is from your Otwock."

Hadasa looked up and paused in disbelief. Why was Rose's husband pointing at her? It couldn't be, she thought. She dropped the army blanket and ran to the new arrival.

"Shama!" she cried, sprinting to the twenty-year-old whom she thought was her little brother. "Shama!" She threw herself upon him, arms grappling his neck, lips wet against his cheek.

"Lady, I'm not this Shama," Leon said, chuckling and touching the site of the very first kiss.

Hadasa pushed him away. He looked so familiar to her.

"You're not my brother," she said, recognizing her mistake.

"Now I'm your brother," Poppy joked, and he smiled at Grandma, pointing to that planted kiss that would seal them in matrimony.

EPILOGUE

I returned from that second visit to Poland and found Grandma, this time in hospice. Her eyes opened once, a shrug, an attempt to move the oxygen mask. I kissed her cold, clammy forehead.

I had wanted to tell her about barrack 18 in Auschwitz Birkenau, the factories that Poppy had worked in at Buna-Monowitz, the Kaddish I had said for her brother and father at Majdanek. I wondered whether mentioning these places and events could pull her back into life the way the Umschlagplatz had tugged her out of her depression.

But I felt that Grandma was, for the first time, too weak for the Holocaust.

I listened to her moan in her sleep, through dreams or nightmares, trapped certainly in the painful prison of her dying. I took her swollen arm in my hands and rubbed the purple skin and green numbers. There wasn't much more that I could do, and anything that I tried to do would never be enough. She shrugged as if to say there wasn't more that she could do, either. I wanted to lift her up and give her one more hug. To thank her for everything: for her love and the stories, for her life and survival.

She developed a fever before I left that evening.

As the sun rose the next morning, my father called.

"Grandma passed away."

Her old wish to join her husband had come true. We placed her in the earth beside Poppy. I picked up a shovel and buried the woman who had asked only two favors of me—to call my cousins and to have a wedding before she died. Her constant wish had been to rebuild and preserve her family, to replace all who had been destroyed. The *dead, dead, dead* above the light switch.

221

I handed the shovel to my cousin, who handed it off to Morris Pilberg, another survivor from Otwock. Morris had been friends with Grandma's brothers, the boys she had outlived by more than sixty-five years. He carried earth to her place of rest. Like so many young boys who had survived Otwock, he was now, if he hadn't been before, a Karczew gravedigger—one of the boys who had been kept alive to bury the four thousand Jews shot in the woods. It would be the last time one Otwock Jew would bury another.

Morris handed the shovel to my future wife and then kneeled before Poppy's grave. With a branch that clutched the last of its yellow flowers, Morris brushed the dirt covering Poppy's footstone.

When he was finished, I stood in the space before the two graves. I smiled because their bodies were once again, unknowingly, beside each other in New York, in the same way as they had moved through the war from Otwock to Karczew, Warsaw, Majdanek, and Auschwitz. And then I stopped smiling and felt the lump from my heart swell up and buoy in my throat.

There would be no more questions, no one to tell me *Not now*, no numbers on forearms to drag my fingers across. But I guess I was left with the stories—the ones that had been hidden, the ones that offered catharsis, the ones that gave me a second hero, the ones that resurrected a family, the ones that would survive even death. The nearly lost stories from my grandparents' Holocaust.

ACKNOWLEDGMENTS

First and foremost, thank you to my wife, Marissa. Besides encouraging me through the writing process, Marissa sat at the table with Grandma and me during many of the difficult talks. And she was present bedside for the sad hospital visits. She was always there to take Grandma's hand when the tears came and, with a warmth and sensitivity that I (and most others) lack, could elicit stories from Grandma that would have otherwise gone untold.

This memoir, having taken the better part of a decade to write and research, owes any success to a number of readers whose feedback was integral in reshaping and improving the book. Those early readers include Frances Northcutt-Green, David Rothman, Phyllis T. Smith, Henya Drescher, Marcy Ross, Robert Ross, Kristen Elde, Bernard Rittersporn, Andie Davis, Mike Radice, Eric Egana, Davina Rosenberg, Alice Jurish, and Jake Lederman.

Thank you to my wonderful agent and trusted advocate, Amy Tannenbaum. This book would not have been possible without her belief in the project and her guidance. Susan McEachern and the team at Rowman & Littlefield, including Audra Figgins and Janice Braunstein, gave life to this book, and I cannot thank them enough. From the very beginning, I knew that my grandparents' story and my journey had settled into competent hands.

Thanking my parents in a book feels insufficient; they deserve much more. Nevertheless, thank you. Beyond offering love and encouragement, Mom served as my first editor, poring over many early, contrived writings with warmth, patience, and an astute eye, while Dad was the ever-present cheerleader, the kind who finds no fault in a team with a losing record.

And of course, without my father's stories this would be a much weaker memoir.

I'm also indebted to Aunt Anne, Morris Pilberg, and Dorothy Greenstein, all of whom taxed their emotions by conjuring up memories important to this book.

Obviously, *A World Erased* would have been impossible had my grandparents opted to stay completely silent. I owe everything to them: they who survived, who loved, who protected, and who shared, eventually. Thank you and I love you.

Finally, thank you to my daughters, who have allowed me to better realize all who were lost.

SOURCES

This memoir would have been impossible to write without the USC Shoah Foundation's hours of interviews, which captured many of my grandparents' stories. Additionally, documents that the Red Cross and the Holocaust and War Victims Tracing Center uncovered, and the Yad Vashem Archives held, helped to bring lost and important nuances to the book. Dozens of books allowed me to make better sense of a time and place that was sometimes delivered to me in pieces or as video testimony that I was unable to question. The works that gave me the best sense of the towns, ghettos, and camps were *Am I a Murderer?* by Calel Perechodnik, *At the Mercy of Strangers* by Gitel Hopfeld, *Cyanide of Potassium* by Roman Grunspan, *Notes from the Warsaw Ghetto* by Emanuel Ringelblum, *The Bravest Battle* by Dan Kurzman, *Memoirs of a Warsaw Ghetto Fighter* by Simha Rotem, *Smoke over Birkenau* by Liana Millu, *The Crime and Punishment of I. G. Farben* by Joseph Borkin, *Eyewitness Auschwitz* by Filip Müller, *Night* by Elie Wiesel, *Survival in Auschwitz* by Primo Levi, *Belzec, Sobibor, Treblinka: The Operation Reinhard Death Camps* by Yitzhak Arad, *Between Two Streams* by Abel J. Herzberg, and the *Auschwitz Chronicle*. I also discovered important facts from the website JewishGen.org and various Holocaust museums around the world, like the United States Holocaust Memorial Museum in Washington, DC, and others listed in this book. However, the greatest source was Grandma, who relentlessly shared her stories during the last years of her life.

ABOUT THE AUTHOR

Noah Lederman's writing has been featured in the *Economist*, the *Boston Globe*, the *Miami Herald*, the *Washington Post*, the *Philadelphia Inquirer*, the *Chicago Sun-Times*, *New Republic*, *Slate*, *Salon*, the *Jerusalem Post Magazine*, and elsewhere. He writes the travel blog *Somewhere Or Bust*. He lives with his wife and daughters in New York.